D0966365

No
Castles
American Authors and Their Homes
on Main
Street

No
Castles
American Authors and Their Homes
on Main
Street

by Stephanie Kraft

Rand McNally & Company
Chicago · New York · San Francisco

Picture Credits

Special acknowledgment is made to the following individuals, groups, and institutions for permitting the author and her husband to take and publish pictures of their private property, including interiors:

The University of Maryland School of Social Work: H. L. Mencken House
The Trustees of Reservations of Massachusetts: The Old Manse
The Ernest Hemingway Home and Museum
The Thomas Wolfe Memorial
The Willa Cather Pioneer Memorial: Willa Cather at 63, Cather home, Pavelka farm
The Mark Twain Memorial
David Emerson and the Museum of the Concord Antiquarian Society: Emerson's study
Bronx County Historical Society: The Poe Cottage
The Center at Foxhollow: The Mount, home of Edith Wharton
The University of Mississippi: Rowan Oak, home of William Faulkner
The Laura Ingalls Wilder–Rose Wilder Lane Home and Museum
Walt Whitman House
Mr. and Mrs. William J. Dunigan: Home of Sherwood Anderson, Clyde, Ohio
Mrs. Edward F. O'Connor: Flannery O'Connor's Milledgeville home and Andalusia Farm
Ohio Historical Society: Paul Laurence Dunbar House
Riley Old Home Society
Mrs. Charles Reily: Home of George Washington Cable, New Orleans
Mrs. M. C. Cavanagh: Home of George Washington Cable, Northampton
Mrs. Ethel D. Cline: Home of F. Scott Fitzgerald, St. Paul
California Department of Parks and Recreation: Ruins of Jack London's Wolf House
Jack London Estate: Jack London's study
Mr. and Mrs. Donnan Jeffers: Tor House, home of Robinson Jeffers

Library of Congress Cataloging in Publication Data

Kraft, Stephanie.
  No castles on Main Street.
  Includes bibliographical references.
  1. Authors, American—Homes and haunts. 2. Literary
landmarks—United States. 3. Authors, American—
Biography. 4. Historic buildings—United States.
I. Title.
PS141.K7   810'.9   79-9816
ISBN 0-528-81828-7

Photograph on page 2:   *Main Street, Sauk Centre, Minnesota*

Acknowledgments

All pictures not otherwise attributed were taken by my husband, David Kraft. For his companionship in this project, for the energy and enthusiasm he showed in meeting every situation we encountered as we traveled around the country, covering 300 to 700 miles a day, I owe him even more than for taking the photographs. I also wish to thank Ms. Priscilla Whitaker of Amherst for her sympathetic but discriminating reading of the manuscript.

Grateful acknowledgment is made to the following authors, publishers, and authors' representatives for permission to quote from the following copyrighted works:

Sherwood Anderson: *Tar: A Midwestern Childhood*. © 1926 by Boni and Liveright, © 1954 by Eleanor Anderson. Reprinted by permission of Harold Ober Associates. *A Story-Teller's Story*. © 1924 by B. W. Huebsch, © 1951 by Eleanor Copenhaver Anderson. Reprinted by permission of Harold Ober Associates. *Sherwood Anderson's Memoirs*. © 1942 by Eleanor Anderson. Reprinted by permission of the U. of North Carolina Press. *Winesburg, Ohio*. © 1919 by B. W. Huebsch, © 1947 by Eleanor Copenhaver Anderson. Reprinted by permission of Viking Penguin.

Carlos Baker, *Ernest Hemingway: A Life Story*. © 1969 by Carlos Baker and Mary Hemingway. Information extracted by permission of Charles Scribner's Sons.

Mildred R. Bennett, *The World of Willa Cather*. © 1961 by the U. of Nebraska Press. Information extracted by permission of the U. of Nebraska Press.

Martha Dickinson Bianchi, *Emily Dickinson Face to Face*. © 1932 by Martha Dickinson Bianchi. Reprinted by permission of Houghton Mifflin.

Gordon Bigelow, *Frontier Eden: The Literary Career of Marjorie Kinnan Rawlings*. © 1966 by the Board of Commissioners of State Institutions of Florida. Information extracted by permission of the U. of Florida Press.

Joseph Blotner, *Faulkner: A Biography*. © 1974 by Joseph Blotner. Information extracted by permission of Random House.

Charles Breasted, "The 'Sauk-centricities' of Sinclair Lewis," *Saturday Review*, August 14, 1954. Reprinted by permission of *Saturday Review*.

Willa Cather: *O Pioneers!* © 1913, 1941 by Willa Siebert Cather. Reprinted by permission of Houghton Mifflin. *My Antonia*. © 1918, 1946 by Willa Siebert Cather. Reprinted by permission of Houghton Mifflin. *Song of the Lark*. © 1915, 1943 by Willa Siebert Cather. Reprinted by permission of Houghton Mifflin. "Old Mrs. Harris," from *Obscure Destinies*. © 1930, 1932 by Willa Cather. Reprinted by permission of Alfred A. Knopf. "The Best Years," from *The Old Beauty and Others*. © 1948 by Alfred A. Knopf.

Clara Clemens, *My Father Mark Twain*. © 1931 by Clara Clemens Gabrilowitsch. Reprinted by permission of Harper and Row.

Emily Dickinson: *The Letters of Emily Dickinson*, ed. by Thomas H. Johnson. Cambridge, Mass.: The Belknap Press of Harvard U. Press. © 1958 by the President and Fellows of Harvard College. Reprinted by permission of the publishers. *The Poems of Emily Dickinson*, ed. by Thomas H. Johnson. Cambridge, Mass.: The Belknap Press of Harvard U. Press. © 1951, 1955 by the President and Fellows of Harvard College. Reprinted by permission of the publishers.

Ralph Waldo Emerson, *The Heart of Emerson's Journals*, ed. by Bliss Perry. © 1926 by Houghton Mifflin. Reprinted by permission of Houghton Mifflin.

William Faulkner, *Selected Letters of William Faulkner*, ed. by Joseph Blotner. © 1977 by Joseph Blotner. Reprinted by permission of Random House.

F. Scott Fitzgerald: *The Letters of F. Scott Fitzgerald*, ed. by Andrew Turnbull. © 1963 by Frances Scott Fitzgerald Lanahan. Reprinted by permission of Charles Scribner's Sons. *The Crack-Up*. © 1945 by New Directions Publishing Corp. Reprinted by permission of New Directions. *The Great Gatsby*. © 1925 by Charles Scribner's Sons, © 1953 by Frances Scott Fitzgerald Lanahan. Reprinted by permission of Charles Scribner's Sons.

Ellen Glasgow: *A Certain Measure: An Interpretation of Prose Fiction*. © 1938, 1943 by Ellen Glasgow. Reprinted by permission of Harcourt Brace Jovanovich. *The Woman Within*. © 1954 by Harcourt, Brace. Reprinted by permission of Harcourt Brace Jovanovich.

Contents

Foreword

When I was a youngster in Florida, my mother, who shared the enthusiasm of her generation for "Papa," took me to see Hemingway's home on Key West. I always remembered the white house with its tall green shutters, set in its jungle-like yard full of tropical trees. Living now in Amherst, Massachusetts, a dozen times a week I pass the square brick house, nearly concealed behind a high hemlock hedge, that was the home of Emily Dickinson. To this house visitors of all sorts, including people of note, come to spend quiet moments in contact with their sense of the poet's life and art, and with their own thoughts. But I had never thought about authors' homes in general until 1976, when I was commissioned to write an article on them for the quarterly magazine published by the National Trust for Historic Preservation. As brochures and letters arrived in the mail from historical societies and state agencies in charge of historic sites, it became clear that the subject involved a wealth of human interest and aesthetic variety.

I read about Carl Sandburg's birthplace by the tracks in Galesburg, and the other house that his father had to pay for twice out of his railroad worker's wage of fourteen cents an hour; the board-and-batten bungalow at Cross Creek where Marjorie Kinnan Rawlings slept for years with a snake snugly quartered under her bedroom; the stone house on the cliff above Carmel that Robinson Jeffers built largely with his own hands; the plain frame house on a very ordinary street where

Willa Cather grew up; the mansion, lavish with gables and polychromatic brick, that Mark Twain built with one of the first fortunes ever amassed by an American author from literary earnings; the sparsely furnished cottage at Fordham where Virginia Poe lay in the last stages of tuberculosis with a cat on her chest to keep her warm.

A year and a half later my husband, our six-year-old daughter, and I drove across the country to see them for ourselves. On a trip to visit family in Florida at Christmastime, 1977, we stopped by Thomas Wolfe's house in Asheville, North Carolina. Traveling down into Florida, we left I-75 for a foray into the grove and cattle country below Gainesville and found Marjorie Kinnan Rawlings's bungalow at Cross Creek. This was the Florida that I knew from childhood, palmetto-studded hammock country where white egrets feed beside lakes hidden among the orange groves, and many tourists visiting the coastal resorts never see it. Twelve hours later we were off through the mangrove swamps and across the long bridges of U.S. 1 to Key West.

Home again after eleven days of almost incessant driving, we sized up the odds and decided that our chances of remaining sane on a three-week trip to California in a Rabbit were unacceptably low. In February we decided to join the RV crowd and bought a red and white VW camper van with a pop top. The van was four years old, but road tests suggested that the engine had been rebuilt, and the interior, with its brown and gold plaid curtains and upholstery, was homey and immaculate. We worried about wind, we worried about the engine dying on the Sierras, but it all proved unnecessary. Its age notwithstanding, the van was probably the most roadworthy vehicle we've ever driven, and at night we had plenty of leg room as our daughter lay above us, snug as a sardine in a sandwich.

The trip west was scheduled for the end of May. In March we took the van down to Atlanta and turned right for New Orleans and Austin. The fields of Alabama were spring green spangled with redbud; New Orleans was peeling paint but the jazz bands of the Quarter were their unsinkable selves. In the farmlands on the way to Faulkner's house daffodils were in bloom, and at every bend in the road a cooperative cotton gin and a sprinkling of sharecroppers' houses suggested that the ancient bases of the economy only change to stay the same.

On May 26 we hit the long road that led to Steinbeck's Salinas. Unintentionally I had made an appointment to visit the homes of James Whitcomb Riley on the day of the Indianapolis 500. The big race caused us no inconvenience except that on the bare streets of Indianapolis there was no one to clear up our confusion when our directions to Lockerbie Street proved inadequate, and we felt like hoisting a black and white checked flag ourselves as we circled the same neighborhood five times before someone pointed us up Michigan Street to Lockerbie Square. The next day we were in Lincoln country—Petersburg, Illinois, next to historic New Salem—then across Spoon River to Galesburg, down along the Mississippi bluffs to Hannibal and St. Louis, and west to Nebraska by way of Laura Ingalls Wilder's house. In Missouri I realized that I had never really seen grass, not like the long, rich, bluish grass of the Ozarks, or the windblown grass of Willa Cather's prairie, from which the sound of an approaching car will start up a pheasant or a covey of smaller birds.

To live on the eastern seaboard is to forget that there are towns in the interior of the country that have had no population growth in the last eighty or one hundred years. This is true of Red Cloud, Nebraska, and, incidentally, of Sauk Centre, Minnesota, the birthplace of Sinclair Lewis. Whatever the implications for the culture and economy of Red Cloud, this lack of expansion allows visitors to see the surrounding countryside very much as Willa Cather must have seen it. The homes of people who figured in her novels still stand on the Divide and are marked along routes mapped out by the Willa Cather Pioneer Memorial. A few miles outside of town we saw the farm of Anna Pavelka, who was "My Ántonia," with the fruit cave described in the novel. The sight was moving, not only because of the struggles and rewards of Anna, but for the same reason that it is affecting to see one of W. O. Wolfe's angels standing on a grave in the Oakdale Cemetery at Hendersonville, North Carolina. It has to do with a reassurance that there is more to art than the success of the artist in seducing my imagination with the products of his, no matter how beautifully executed.

I was reminded as well that the achievement of Willa Cather should have rid American letters of the habit of using the term "regional" condescendingly, as if the sense of place were a drawback rather than an aspect of richness in a story. True, much of what we call "local color" is facile and obvious. But the fact that an author like Marjorie Kinnan Rawlings could be frightened away from writing her Florida stories because of the fear of being labeled a "regionalist" shows how entrenched the derogatory connotation of the word has become. I know of no one who has been able to put this matter in perspective better than Flannery O'Connor did in *Mystery and Manners*. She wrote, "The best American fiction has always been regional. The ascendancy passed roughly from New England to the Midwest to the South; it has passed to and stayed longest wherever there has been a shared past, a sense of alikeness, and the possibility of reading a small history in a universal light."

After our day on the Divide, we headed west to see Owen Wister's cabin at Medicine Bow, Wyoming. On Route 30 above Cheyenne and Laramie our eyes learned to travel along the fences and watch for the gates and cattle gaps that sometimes signaled a ranch house in the distance. Here and there an oil rig working on a hill reminded us that the region is rich in energy sources, including uranium. On the austere-looking sagebrush flats we saw deer and even a few antelope; tiny wild flowers of vivid yellow, orange, and purple were visible even from the moving camper. Touring the Virginian Hotel at Medicine Bow, we were shown an antique dresser with a bullet hole in it. Our daughter, to whom time frames are still a little vague, wrote postcards to friends in Amherst and told them, in six-year-old epistolary style, that there was a lot of fighting going on in Wyoming. When we reached home I assured one or two recipients of these puzzling messages that indeed nobody had shot at us.

The road through southwestern Wyoming took us past nude bluffs and scattered enclaves of mobile homes. Morning in Utah was a glare on the salt flats that stretched for mile after monotonous mile. Our eyes bounced helplessly across the ashy whiteness except when there was a blue mountain in the distance to anchor our vision. But all these sensations built up to a magnificent climax of refreshment when we had crossed Nevada and entered the deep green Sierras in the vicinity of Lake Tahoe, and in a couple of hours we were racing along I-80 beside parkways full of pink and scarlet oleanders, sure of reaching Salinas that night.

We knew the season of lupine and poppies would be over in Steinbeck's valley, but the bronze hills with their dark green oak trees in fantastic shapes were utterly satisfying. The next day we toured the Steinbeck house and investigated the neighborhood that we devoutly hoped had been the old red-light district described in *East of Eden*. That night we sat happily in a good Mexican restaurant in the middle of Salinas, eating refried beans and thinking of other beans: spicy pinto beans and beef in a café in Nevada; red beans in their own thick, ham-flavored gravy over rice in New Orleans; dry beans with chopped onion in a country diner in Mississippi on the way to Faulkner's house; exquisite black beans and yellow rice hobnobbing with turtle steak and fried plantains in the incomparable El Cacique on Key West. We had made it. We had got from here to there.

I not only admit, I want to emphasize, that this book omits many houses that are of no less interest than those included. Washington Irving's home near Tarrytown, New York, the Hamlin Garland homestead in West Salem, Wisconsin, and Arrowhead, the home of Herman Melville, in Pittsfield, Massachusetts, are among those that come to mind instantly. The first consideration in deciding which houses to include here was to make the geographical distribution as nearly equal as possible; hence the omission of several important houses in the East. I also tried for a certain balance, though the factors would not allow for mathematical equality, between men and women, and between fiction writers and writers in other genres. In general the quality of the sites—that is, the condition of the houses and their surroundings and the amount of original furniture or personal property they contained— was a major consideration, though it became a problematic one in regions such as the West, where there were fewer sites to choose from. There were also cases in which the importance of an author and his or her use of a setting simply overrode the lack of original material at the site, as with the home of Sherwood Anderson in Clyde, Ohio. As the selection process went on, choices made helped to determine other choices, since it became clear that the book would be strengthened internally if associations were made between authors who were related to each other by friendship or influence.

A final criterion, and one that didn't present itself until I had gained some acquaintance with the sites and the literature about them, was the importance, as best I could judge it, of an author's home to the community in which it was located. The question of whose house is preserved seems to have even more to do with writers' relationships to their localities than with the long-range consensus as to the quality of what they achieved. Otherwise why would the homes of James Whitcomb Riley be house museums and not the childhood home of T. S. Eliot? These chapters are rooted in towns and regions where people remember that somebody who lived around the corner or down the road from them wrote good books.

1

H. L. Mencken and the Hollins Street House

Mencken at forty-nine. National Archives

It looks so discreet and respectable, even modestly elegant, the narrow brick town house with its white fanlight door and marble steps. Who would guess that on a warm summer's day during Prohibition its owner nearly blew it up over the heads of his family and guests when several dozen bottles of his home brew exploded in the tiny back garden?

That hospitable bootlegger was H. L. Mencken, whose home still stands at 1524 Hollins Street in Baltimore, across the street from Union Square. His father and mother moved into the decorous row house in 1883, when their eldest son was a pudgy, precocious toddler of three. Mencken's literary voice as a newspaperman and critic was notoriously impudent and iconoclastic; he dealt in such maxims as "No one in this world, so far as I know,—and I have searched the records for years, and employed agents to help me—has ever lost money by underestimating the intelligence of the great masses of the plain people." Yet he lived in an utterly conventional, close association with his family. Except for the five years between his marriage and his wife's death, he spent all the epochs of his long life in the Hollins Street house.

Today the Mencken home serves as a housing facility for the University of Maryland. Visitors are admitted one afternoon each week to the first floor of the house, which contains Mencken family furniture, and to the backyard, whose brick walls were erected and decorated with exotic tiles by Mencken. His memoirs weave pastorals around

> the backyard in Hollins street, which had the unusual length, for a yard in a city block, of a hundred feet. Along with my brother Charlie, who followed me into this vale when I was but twenty months old, I spent most of my pre-school leisure in it, and found it a strange, wild land of endless discoveries and enchantments. Even in the dead of Winter we were pastured in it almost daily, bundled up in the thick, scratchy coats, overcoats, mittens, leggings, caps, shirts, over-shirts and underdrawers that the young then wore. We wallowed in the snow whenever there was any to wallow in, and piled it up into crude houses, forts and snowmen, and inscribed it with wavering scrolls and devices by the method followed by infant males since the Würm Glaciation. In Spring we dug worms and watched for robins, in Summer we chased butterflies and stoned sparrows, and in Autumn we made bonfires of the falling leaves.

At day's end the family retreated to the front rooms facing Union Square: "I recall my mother reading to me, on a dark Winter afternoon, out of a book describing the adventures of the Simple Simon who went to a fair, the while she sipped a cup of tea that smelled very cheerful, and I glued my nose to the frosty window pane, watching a lamplighter

The Mencken home at 1524 Hollins Street, Baltimore. Mencken boasted that the town house was the ideal form of domestic architecture.

light the lamps in Union Square across the street and wondering what a fair might be."

In time the world expanded to include the square, Hollins Street, and its adjacent alleys. There was always something to see or to hear: dogfights that tore up the turf of the square, the clucking of chickens, the clattering of cabs whose horses sometimes dropped dead in their very tracks, the shouts of children playing in the cobblestone street. As school days came on, afternoons were spent at the neighborhood livery stables, where boys and grooms swapped tall stories, tips on the care of horses, and notes on the facts of life.

A few years farther into time and prosperity, there appeared at the Menckens' a brand-new piano with "a shiny black case, a music rack that was a delirium of jigsaw whorls, and legs and ankles of the sort that survive today only on lady politicians." Mencken's father, an indefatigable provider, furnished a mustachioed German to give his son lessons on the instrument. The lessons did not produce a great musician, but they did accomplish two things. They gave the father a means

of shortening conversations with unwelcome visitors, who could endure the boy's pounding away for just so long. They also turned young
Mencken into an enthusiastic amateur musician, an interest that
lasted for decades.

It was another gift from his father that stimulated the youthful
Mencken's first venture into print. After wandering into the office of a
small newspaper in the summer of 1888, the boy, then eight years old,
became enthusiastic about printing and demanded a printing press of
his own. Mencken senior, never a man to shirk the demands of father-
hood, bought him a Baltimore No. 10 Self-Inker and a font of type. On
Christmas morning he rolled out the press with a flourish and proceeded to try to show his son how to operate it.

This demonstration became a disaster. Before long the press was
covered with ink and the living room floor with smashed type. The
gauge pins and the ink roller broke. Mencken recalled, "It was a sad
caricature of a printing-press that went to the cellar at mid-day, when
my mother ordered a halt and a cleanup."

By the new year the boy had taught himself to work the press. His
first successful product was a set of business cards on which he
printed, in three incongruous type faces,

𝕳. 𝕷. 𝕸𝖊𝖓𝖈𝖐𝖊𝖓
Card Printer
124 HOLLINS STREET
BALTIMORE, MD.

He explained this unpremeditated debut of the famous name in its famous form: "Up to this time I had always written my name Henry L.,
or Harry. . . . My change to H. L. was not due to any feeling
that the form better became the dignity of a businessman, but
simply to the fact that my father, in the course of his Christmas
morning gaucheries, had smashed all my Black Letter lower-case
r's, and I had to cut my coat to fit my cloth."

For the rest of his life Mencken attributed his enthusiasm for journalism to this momentous gift. "If it had been a stethoscope or a copy
of Dr. Ayers' Almanac I might have gone in for medicine; if it had been
a Greek New Testament or a set of baptismal grappling irons I
might have pursued divinity. As it was, I got the smell of printer's ink
up my nose at the tender age of eight, and it has been swirling
through my sinuses ever since." It was one thing for the elder

Mencken to humor the wish of an eight-year-old boy for a printing press to play with; to take seriously the enduring obsession that grew out of the adventure was something else. August Mencken was a second-generation German-American of unassailable bourgeois values. With the money that he and a brother had gained from their self-made cigar business, he had placed his family in a situation that was stable, decent, gracious. An eldest son himself, he fulfilled his family obligations and assumed that his own cherished eldest son would fulfill his. The mother waited to see what would come from the boy himself.

After Mencken's graduation from the Baltimore Polytechnic Institute, the issue moved into the foreground. Unable to fly in the face of his father's wishes, Mencken went to work to learn the ropes of the cigar business. At night he composed sketches for a correspondence course in writing. When he began to receive commendations for his accounts of night fights in Hollins Street and its alleys, his conflict intensified.

Before he could figure out how to untie this Gordian knot, it was cut with shocking abruptness when his father developed a kidney ailment and died in 1899, at the age of forty-four. Almost overnight Mencken, then eighteen, found himself head of a household that included his mother, his sister Gertrude, and his brothers Charlie and August. The loss left him responsible for keeping them solvent, but free to do it his way. He worked at the cigar business by day but legged it around the suburbs as a stringer for the *Herald* in the evenings until an opening appeared on the staff. In 1906, after the demise of the *Herald,* he began his long relationship with the *Baltimore Evening Sun.*

After hours Mencken set up his base of literary operations in a room on the third floor of the Hollins Street house. Amid a perennially growing welter of books and papers he rooted, expostulated, and stormed away on his typewriter. Through the writing of *The American Language,* through his collaboration with George Jean Nathan on the *Smart Set* and the founding of the *American Mercury,* through his ups and downs with Theodore Dreiser and his drinking bouts with "Red" (Sinclair) Lewis, through World War I and the crash of 1929, the third-floor room was his kingdom. Though it was barely navigable by strangers uninitiated into the mysteries of its rich, diversified clutter, Mencken insisted that it was "the most orderly room in the house."

From 1900 to 1920 Mencken, then in his prime as a commentator on the literary and political scenes, discharged his artillery at whatever features of American culture struck him as absurd. In the pages of the *Sun,* the *Smart Set,* and the *American Mercury* his epigrams exploded into the public consciousness like landmines.

The moment everyone begins to believe a thing, it ceases to be true. For example, the notion that the homeliest girl in the party is the safest.

A great nation is any mob of people which produces at least one honest man a century.

All government, in its essence, is a conspiracy against the superior man; its one permanent object is to oppress him and cripple him.

What ails the beautiful letters of the Republic, I repeat, is what ails the general culture of the Republic—the lack of a body of sophisticated and civilized public opinion, independent of plutocratic control and superior to the infantile philosophies of the mob—a body of opinion showing the eager curiosity, the educated skepticism and the hospitality to ideas of a true aristocracy. This lack is felt by the American author, imagining him to have anything new to say, every day of his life.

Broad as is the contrast between the images of Mencken the Bad Boy and the aristocratic Edith Wharton, Mencken's latter statement expresses the same frustration that once drove Mrs. Wharton to snap, "The American landscape has no foreground and the American mind no background!"

Meanwhile Mencken became more entrenched in his family life and in his house, which underwent major evolutions in the '20s. The floors and heating system were replaced, the kitchen was enlarged, all the new labor-saving devices were installed. Into his third-floor office Mencken introduced a private secretary to help with his voluminous correspondence, since he was temperamentally incapable of letting any kind of communication go unanswered.

The backyard was always a favored setting for leisurely meditation. In 1920 Mencken decided to wall it in, and laid the bricks with his own unpracticed hands. He studded the walls with exotic tiles, added a fountain, and when his dog died in 1921 decorated one wall with a bronze plaque to "Tessie."

In 1925 Mencken lost the mother with whose partnership he had organized his life since his father's death twenty-six years before. He wrote to Theodore Dreiser: *"I begin to realize how inextricably my life was interwoven with my mother's. A hundred times a day I find myself planning to tell her something, or ask her for this or that. It is a curious thing: the human incapacity to imagine finality. The house seems strange, as if the people in it were deaf and dumb. But all life, I begin to believe, resolves itself into a doing without."*

The years in which Mencken grieved the loss of his mother were carrying him toward other major rearrangements. His energy, acumen, and humor, which had fed on the expansiveness of the '20s, simply could not find their medium in the conditions of the next decade. His work of introducing and championing Dreiser, Lewis, and others of their generation had largely been done. He lost many readers because he was optimistic to the point of flippancy about the hardships of the Depression and the Nazi menace that followed it.

But his development was proceeding along other lines, astonishing lines to a public who had spent decades reading his cracks about love and marriage. In the late '20s he developed a serious relationship with a young writer, Sara Haardt, whom he had met during one of his lectures on "How to Catch a Husband" at Goucher College. In 1930 they were married. Mencken was nearly fifty, Sara thirty-two.

The marriage was an exceptional combination of hilarity, pathos, and tenderness right from the start. Hilarity, because no less a term than shock can describe the feelings of the nation on learning that Mencken had defected from the cult of bachelorhood. Even close friends were uncertain about whether to take seriously such announcements as this:

> *If any scandal-mongers call you up and try to make you believe that Sara and I are to be joined in connubial bonds on August 27, don't deny it, for it's a fact. The solemn announcement will issue from Confederate GHQ in about a week. Your congratulations I take for granted, for you know Sara, and you know what a lovely gal she is. If you write her please say nothing of my heavy drinking, or about the trouble with that girl from Red Lion, Pa., in 1917. I still maintain I was innocent of any unlawful or immoral purpose.*

But Sara, charming, brilliant, described by the novelist Ellen Glasgow as "a lovely, loyal, and gallant spirit," was also ill. She had tuberculosis, and its draining effect made her susceptible to other ailments.

The bride and groom set up housekeeping in a large flat at 704 Cathedral Street, and furnished, decorated, debated, compromised, wrote, and socialized in the best newlywed style. By all accounts they were deeply happy—for five years. Sara died of meningitis in the late spring of 1935. "When I married Sara," Mencken told a friend soon afterward, "the doctors said she could not live more than three years. Actually she lived five, so that I had two more years of happiness than I had any right to expect."

Mencken planned to remain in the Cathedral Street apartment, but when his misery at being alone there did not abate after several months, he moved back to Hollins Street. His sister Gertrude moved to another part of the city, and he and his brother August took up a companionable bachelor existence under the ministrations of the maid and cook who came with him from Cathedral Street.

Once a pattern of home life and work reestablished itself, Mencken's vitality began to return. For a study he commandeered his mother's old bedroom on the second floor, which overlooked Union Square and a nearby convent, the House of the Good Shepherd. He recharged his batteries by working at the fourth edition of *The American Language*, whipping off notes to assure friends that *"the Holy Ghost stands beside me, guiding me to the truth."*

For the next twelve years he filled the role of elder statesman at the *Sun* and produced three volumes of memoirs. The warm welcome his memoirs received suggested that his prose, still vigorous as broncs in

Mencken's backyard: under the mulberry tree, a death mask of Beethoven.

a rodeo, would regain popularity with the post–World War II audience. But in November, 1948, just a few months after he made a hilarious adventure of covering the Democratic convention, he was stricken with a coronary thrombosis, and he never regained the ability to write.

Until his death in 1956 he spent his days good-humoredly, for the most part, in his home on Hollins Street, with August as his constant companion. Years before he had written to Dreiser that *"all life . . . resolves itself into a doing without,"* and now he was destitute even of the ability to verbalize and compose that had made his other losses bearable. But his wit could never be annihilated; as he neared seventy he remarked on the fact that God had favored his piety with long life. And he was in possession of another blessing that many people in a more mobile society will never know.

Watched over by a brother with whom he had been close, he must have seen his life come full circle as he looked out the front windows at Union Square, where stood the same cast-iron Greek temple, fishpond, and tiny squarekeeper's house that he had seen from childhood. Often he sat in the back garden, pointing out to visitors the death mask of Beethoven that he had installed there along with the memorial to Tessie and other unique features of his famous brick wall. At such moments he was also surrounded by what they could not see: the earliest scenes of his life, a chain of family relationships unbroken except by death, all the accumulated garnishes on the richly weathered walls of his memory.

2

Hawthorne and the Old Manse

The Old Manse, Concord, Hawthorne's "antique house," family home of the Emersons from 1770 to 1939.

The old house—in Hawthorne's day weathered, now painted, a shad-owy gray—sits at the end of its long avenue as if the avenue were time. Morning and evening it fills with light and then with mellow gloom as though with aged wines, while the seasons frame it in snows, in reju-venating greens, in spilt cornucopias of orange and yellow leaves and ripe apples.

Built around 1770, the house was already venerable by American standards when Hawthorne first saw its frame exterior, the gambrel roof fitting down closely over its shuttered windows, the attic dormer with its gable of Gothic steepness. Entering, he had crossed the inter-val that separated the everyday realities of Concord in 1842—Emerson and his audiences, the free-spirited Thoreau, the strenuous Margaret Fuller, the necessities of splitting kindling and answering fire call with leather buckets leakproof and at the ready—from the atmosphere of pre-Revolutionary days, when the line between fact and legend was seductively blurred.

Hawthorne was the first to call the house the Old Manse. It had been built by the Reverend William Emerson, grandfather of Ralph Waldo Emerson. All its occupants had been clergymen until Haw-thorne, not even a churchgoer himself, rented it from the heirs of Dr. Ezra Ripley, who had lived in it after his marriage to the Reverend Emerson's widow until he died in 1841.

"It was worthy to have been one of the time-honored parsonages of England in which, through many generations, a succession of holy oc-cupants pass from youth to age, and bequeath each an inheritance of sanctity to pervade the house and hover over it as with an atmo-sphere," runs Hawthorne's description of his home in *Mosses from an Old Manse*. "It was awful," he added, "to reflect how many sermons must have been written there."

The mention of England and the use of words connoting antiquity—"time-honored," "many generations"—are crucial. Since 1820 Amer-ican literati had fretted about Sydney Smith's question in the *Edin-burgh Review:* "Who reads an American book?" Fed from childhood on the lore of his Puritan ancestors—one had been a judge in the Salem witch trials and, according to a family legend, cursed by the husband of a condemned witch—Hawthorne in the 1840s was incubating the body of fiction that would culminate in America's first formally exqui-site, psychologically sophisticated novel, *The Scarlet Letter*. But his temperament required an environment with some aesthetic or historic richness. Unlike his friend Emerson, the prophet of an America with "no castles, no cathedrals, and no kings," Hawthorne gasped like a fish out of water amid the crass makeshift newness of a country in the

Upstairs hall, the Manse: by the window, the desk at which Dr. Ripley stood to write his sermons. The free-standing bookshelves could be thrown out in case of fire.

making. He put it politely in his preface to *The Marble Faun:* "No author, without a trial, can conceive of the difficulty of writing a romance about a country where there is no shadow, no antiquity, no mystery, no picturesque and gloomy wrong, nor anything but a commonplace prosperity, in broad and simple daylight, as is happily the case with my dear native land. . . . Romance and poetry, ivy, lichens, and wall-flowers, need ruin to make them grow." Ruin was drama in retrospect. Yet among the historic remains and art treasures of Italy, which furnished background for *The Marble Faun,* Hawthorne seems to have been overwhelmed by an embarrassment of riches, for the novel reads in parts like a museum catalog. The atmosphere of the Manse nurtured without dwarfing him. No place was ever so congenial to Hawthorne as the "antique house" where he and his bride, Sophia Peabody, made their peaceful *ménage à trois* with the Muse.

The place didn't have everything. As Hawthorne complained in his *Note-book,* ". . . it is one of the drawbacks upon our Paradise, that it contains no water fit either to drink or to bathe in. . . ." But it had spacious grounds, stately trees, and views of the winding Concord River. It had already acquired a certain literary fame. Emerson had written "Nature" there, to say nothing of the three thousand sermons that Dr. Ripley was supposed to have composed at the high desk still to be seen in the upstairs hall, standing all the while so the pain in his legs would tell him when each homily was long enough. The Manse also boasted a lively live-in ghost or two: "Our ghost used to heave deep sighs in a particular corner of the parlor, and sometimes rustled paper, as if he were turning over a sermon in the long upper entry. . . . Once, while Hillard and other friends sat talking with us in the twilight, there came a rustling noise as of a minister's silk gown, sweeping through the very midst of the company so closely as almost to brush against the chairs."

The house and its grounds were situated near the Old North Bridge, where at the beginning of the Revolution the ancestors of Hawthorne's fellow townsmen had "fired the shot heard 'round the world." The setting of that battle was visible from the north window of the Manse's second-floor study.

> It was at this window that the clergyman [*William Emerson*] who then dwelt in the Manse stood watching the outbreak of a long and deadly struggle between two nations; he saw the irregular array of his parishioners on the farther side of the river and the glittering line of the British on the hither bank. He awaited in an agony of suspense the rattle of the musketry. It came, and there needed but a gentle wind to sweep the battle smoke around this quiet house.

The Revolutionary battleground wasn't the only part of the setting that gave Hawthorne's imagination a frame for its interweaving of present reality with a mythical past. The field between the house and the approach to the bridge was full of Indian remains—spear tips, arrowheads, chisels. These were first called to his attention by Thoreau, who, said Hawthorne, had "a strange faculty of finding what the Indians have left behind them. . . ." Stooping to pick up a stone tool or arrowhead, Hawthorne envisioned the Indians and their village, "the painted chiefs and warriors, the squaws at their household toil, and the children sporting among the wigwams, while the little wind-rocked pappoose swings from the branch of the tree. It can hardly be told whether it is a joy or a pain, after such a momentary vision, to gaze around in the broad daylight of reality and see stone fences, white houses, potato fields, and men doggedly hoeing in their shirtsleeves and homespun pantaloons."

In his three years at the Manse Hawthorne was living out, and turning into literature, a Yankee pastoral that would do for New England what Irving's "Legend of Sleepy Hollow" and "Rip Van Winkle" had done for New York. "The Old Manse" is a blending of the overflow of feeling from an exceptionally happy marriage with images collected from his surroundings: the Revolutionary lore, the Indian relics, the pantalooned potato-hoeing neighbors, the benign ghost of Dr. Ripley.

The business of Eden was gardening. Hawthorne, as proprietor of Paradise and a recent alumnus of Brook Farm, logged for posterity his summer hours of communion with peas, beans, and squash. He raided Spenser for images to describe "autumn, with his immense burden of apples, dropping them continually from his overladen shoulders as he trudged along."

The Hawthornes had reason to be thankful for Dr. Ripley's apples, currants, and peaches, for while life in the Manse was rich in affection and poetic fancy, money was scarce. A letter written by Sophia to her mother late in December, 1843, cheerfully describes what was in reality a rather skimpy Christmas dinner of *"preserved quince and apple, dates, and bread and cheese, and milk."* The next fall Sophia wrote to a friend, *"I break my fast upon fruit, and we lunch upon fruit, and in the evening, also, partake of that paradisaical food."* Hawthorne loved the apple trees for their character as well as their fruit: ". . . they stretch out their crooked branches, and take such hold of the imagination that we remember them as humorists and odd-fellows."

Always at the center of this New England idyll was the house. It gathered like a basket the harvests of fruit, flowers, vegetables from the garden, fish from the river, and news, ideas, and images from outside. Hawthorne did his writing on the second floor, in "the most delightful little nook of a study that ever afforded its snug seclusion to a scholar." Out of its west windows he could see, between the fringes of a willow and the branches of apple trees, the small round mirror of polished pewter that was the river. Eventually he built a fold-down desk on the opposite wall to avoid being distracted by the view.

In Hawthorne's study, his portrait (right) and fold-down desk (left).

The study and the desk can be seen today, together with another feature of the room that gives a startling sense of the Hawthorne's lingering presence in the Manse. On a west window the couple cut notes to each other with Sophia's diamond ring. Still perfectly legible, the inscriptions read:

> Man's accidents are GOD'S purposes.
>   Sophia A. Hawthorne 1843

> Nath Hawthorne
>   This is his study
>   1843
>   The smallest twig leans clear against the sky.

> Inscribed by my husband at
> sunset April 3d 1843
> In the gold light   S. A. H.

More than a century later, the words still stand out in each day's late afternoon light.

The same sense of intimacy also pervades the dining room, where the two-hundred-year-old grandfather clock keeps perfect time. The clock sits across the room from a massive secretary built by a local craftsman, Joseph Hosmer. When the British occupied Concord on April 19, 1775, and began seizing and setting fire to military equipment, it was Hosmer's exclamation, "Will you let them burn the town?" that brought down the order for the Minutemen to advance on the British at the Old North Bridge. On the north window of the dining room is an inscription made by Sophia months after the Hawthornes' first child, Una, was born in the bedroom upstairs:

> Una Hawthorne stood on this window sill January
> 22, 1845, while the trees were all glass chandeliers,
> a goodly show which she liked much tho' only ten
> months old.

Preoccupied as they were with their private life, the Hawthornes mingled to some extent in the intellectual circles of the village. Emerson and Thoreau were the Concord friends Hawthorne cherished most, though his sympathy for their Transcendentalist enthusiasms had its limits. In his *Note-book* Hawthorne described his early impressions of Thoreau, who had not yet written his manifestos, *Walden* and "Civil Disobedience": "He is ugly as sin, long-nosed, queer-mouthed, and with uncouth and somewhat rustic, though courteous manners. . . . Mr.

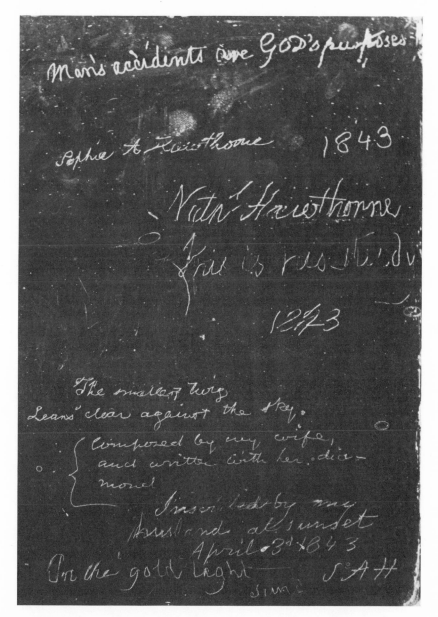

"The smallest twig leans clear against the sky." Notes cut with Sophia's diamond ring on the windowpane in Hawthorne's study at the Manse. Trustees of Reservations

Thorow is a keen and delicate observer of nature—a genuine observer, which, I suspect, is almost as rare a character as even an original poet; and Nature, in return for his love, seems to adopt him as her especial child, and shows him secrets which few others are allowed to witness.''

Hawthorne reveled in his trips on the river with Thoreau. He was full of admiration for his new friend's adroit handling of his skiff *Musketaquid,* which he had built himself and sailed during his famous excursion on the Concord and Merrimac rivers. Thoreau, in need of cash, sold Hawthorne the boat for seven dollars. "I wish," lamented Hawthorne, "I could acquire the skill of its owner for so reasonable a rate.''

Hawthorne and Emerson were never easygoing intimates, but their high regard for each other lasted the rest of their lives. The atmosphere created by the followers of Emerson and Alcott got on Hawthorne's nerves; he described some of them as "bores of a very intense water.'' He couldn't agree with Emerson that Margaret Fuller, editor of the Transcendentalist journal the *Dial,* was one of history's greatest women. Hawthorne found her intriguing, worthy of respect, but a too strenuously self-made person, with a forced rather than natural set of gifts. As he put it, she had "stuck herself full of borrowed qualities.'' But apart from such differences of opinion Hawthorne was deeply fond of Emerson, with his "pure intellectual gleam diffused about his presence like the garment of a shining one; and he so quiet, so simple, so without pretension, encountering each man alive as if expecting to receive more than he could impart.'' Emerson sought Hawthorne out, as Sophia humorously reported in a letter to her mother: *"Mr. Emerson delights in him: he talks to him all the time, and Mr. Hawthorne looks answers. He seems to fascinate Mr. Emerson. Whenever he [Emerson] comes to see him, he takes him away, so that no one may interrupt him in his close and dead-set attack upon his ear.''* Meanwhile Emerson confided to his journal his low opinion of his friend's art: "Nathaniel Hawthorne's reputation as a writer is a very pleasing fact, because his writing is not good for anything, and this is a tribute to the man.''

Thanks to Sophia, an accomplished artist with an eye for the picturesque, we have a sketch of Hawthorne and friends in a skating party on the Concord River.

One afternoon, Mr. Emerson and Mr. Thoreau went with him down the river. Henry Thoreau is an experienced skater, and was figuring dithyrambic dances and Bacchic leaps on the ice. . . . Next him followed Mr. Hawthorne who, wrapped in his cloak, moved like a self-impelled Greek statue, stately and grave. Mr. Emerson closed the

*line, evidently too weary to hold himself erect, pitching headfore-
most, half lying on the air. He came in to rest himself, and said to me
that Hawthorne was a tiger, a bear, a lion, —in short, a satyr, and
there was no tiring him out; and he might be the death of a man like
himself.*

The Hawthornes' life at the Manse lasted from July, 1842, to October, 1845. It ended because their landlords, the Ripleys, wanted to
take up residence in the house again. It ended too because financial
and developmental imperatives were closing in on Hawthorne. During
this period he wrote a number of the stories that were later gathered in
Mosses from an Old Manse and the second edition of *Twice-Told
Tales* and sold them to magazines. The pay was not only low, it was
notoriously slow in coming. The Hawthornes at this period were poor,
there was no getting around it, and things that were jokes to a couple
became anxieties for a family. Sophia wrote in May, 1845, *"The other
day, when my husband saw me contemplating an appalling vacuum in
his dressing-gown, he said he was 'a man of the largest rents in the
country, and it was strange he had not more ready money.' Our rents
are certainly not to be computed; for everything seems now to be wearing out all at once, and I expect the dogs will begin to bark soon,
according to the inspired dictum of Mother Goose. But, somehow or
other, I do not care much, because we are so happy."*

In years to come—after Salem and *The Scarlet Letter*, after Lenox
and *The House of the Seven Gables*, after Europe and a consulate—
the Hawthornes would return to Concord. They would buy the "Hill-
side" that was the setting for *Little Women*, rechristen it "Wayside,"
and enjoy being homeowners for the first time. But a couple of thousand dollars and Sophia's best decorating efforts would never rid the
house of a certain cramped feeling.

Meanwhile financial worries, tensions from the Civil War, and anxiety over Una's recurrent illness aged Hawthorne irreparably in the
1860s. He seemed to be unable to collect the parts of himself that had
been left in various homes. Settled in Concord, he wanted to be by the
sea, in Salem. At home in the United States, he wanted to be in England, enjoying again the life of London. In the Manse years a stately
foundation had been laid for his art and his personal life. Afterward,
though his best work was still before him, happiness would never again
wear such a bloom.

3 🏠

Carl Sandburg and the Railroad Town

Carl Sandburg's birthplace, in 1878 an unheated three-room cottage. The unplastered walls were lined with newspaper to keep out drafts.

As soon as the shooting stopped, the hammering started. Four years after the Civil War ended, a golden spike was driven at Ogden, Utah, to celebrate the building of the transcontinental railroad. In the same year, 1869, the Union Stockyards opened in Chicago and the nation's pigs went to market by rail, along with the cattle, the wheat, and the oil. In the twenty years between 1870 and 1890, a hundred thousand miles of track were laid by Irish, Chinese, Scandinavian, and Italian immigrants and Civil War veterans, many of them working for ten cents an hour. Red and yellow, black and white, they were just good cheap labor in the sight of capitalists like Jim Hill, who was quoted as saying "Give me enough Swedes and snuff and I'll build a railroad to hell."

The railroads fed the young prairie towns like Galesburg, Illinois, a division point on the route of the Chicago, Burlington and Quincy. At seven in the morning the hammering started down by the tracks in the C.B. & Q. shops, which employed most of the town's blue-collar workers in the 1870s. Many of them were Scandinavian; others were Germans, Irish, blacks, a few Italians. Many lived in cottages near the railroad yards where they put in their ten hours as blacksmiths, section hands, brakemen, or firemen for a dollar to a dollar and a half a day. Such a one was August Sandburg, who in 1878 lived two houses east of the tracks at 331 East Third Street. His home was a three-room frame cottage sided with rough-cut lumber. Newspapers were pasted over the unplastered walls inside to keep out the winter wind.

In the Third Street cottage on January 6, 1878, Carl Sandburg, like the Lincoln whose biographer he would become, was born on a corn-husk mattress. A Swedish midwife announced, "Det ar en pojke" ("It's a boy") and tucked him into the cradle just vacated by his sister Mary. He was succeeded in his turn by five more brothers and sisters. His memoirs express vividly his early impressions of his mother, who was the daughter of a woman who had been a gooseherd in Sweden. After her mother's death Clara Sandburg had come to America to escape an uncongenial stepmother.

> She had fair hair between blond and brown—the color of oat straw just before the sun tans it—eyes light-blue, the skin white as fresh linen by candlelight, the mouth for smiling. She had ten smiles for us to one from our father. . . . Her full and rich white breasts—how can I forget them, having seen the babies one by one, year on year, nursing at them, having seen her leave the washtub to take up a crying child and feed it and go back to the washtub? . . . The father always called her "Clara," spoken in Swedish as "Klawrah."

Clara and August Sandburg, Carl Sandburg's mother and father. Illinois State Historical Library

His account of his father's routine is much more than just a personal reminiscence; it is a page from the history of nineteenth-century industrialized America.

> My father was a "black Swede," his hair straight and black, his eyes black with a hint of brown, eyes rather deep-set in the bone, and the skin crinkled with his smile or laugh. . . . He was at the C.B. & Q. blacksmith shop, rated as a "helper," the year round, with no vacation, leaving home at six forty-five in the morning, walking to arrive at the Q. shop at seven, never late, mauling away at engine and car parts till twelve noon. He walked home, ate the noon "dinner," walked back to the shop to begin work at one and go on till the six o'clock whistle. Then he stood sledge alongside anvil and walked home.
>
> In late spring, summer, and early fall, he would often work in the garden till after dark, more than one night in October picking tomatoes and digging potatoes by the light of a moon.

The growing boy stored up details from the day-to-day saga of a family of nine living on a laborer's wages, pondering about what that life meant to his parents and what their relationship was like.

They were mates. I am sure they had sweet and wild nights together as bedfellows. They had strengths from clean living, hard work, and tough peasant ancestors. They were a couple and their coupling was both earthy and sacramental to them. Across the many passing years they slept in the same bed, even when the babies came. When the midwife had left after her two or three days of attendance, the husband was the night nurse performing the needful for his wife. There were at times smiles exchanged between them that at the moment I didn't understand but later read as having the secret meanings of lovers who had pleasured each other last night.

Differences between the "Old Man" and the mother came out once in a while, like the time she spent a hard-earned dollar and a half on a book called *A History of the World and Its Great Events* because Carl—christened Charles and known in-house as Sholly—wanted to read about big shots like Napoleon and Nelson and their battles. When August came home, the war was on in the house.

I won't go into the scene the Old Man made when he saw the book and heard the price paid. He stormed and hurled reproaches and cried aloud we were heading for the Knoxville poorhouse. *"I hela min tid"* —in all my time. *"Gud bevara"* —God help us. It was a sorrow and a shame. If it ever happened again he didn't know what he would do. It was a real grief with him. It ended mother's listening to book agents.

The mother had visions and hopes. She could say with a lighted face, "We will hope for the best," as I bent my head over *A History of the World and Its Great Events*. The Old Man would stand over me saying, "Wat good iss dat book, Sholly?" And I had no answer. I didn't like his saying such a thing. But I had some dim realization too that he had in his mind mortgages on which payments must be made. In his way he was as good as any of the Greeks at Thermopylae or any of the Swedes fighting with Gustavus Adolphus in the Thirty Years' War—but at the time I didn't know that, and I was a long time learning it.

Right in his home the boy had a little microcosm of Galesburg. For seventeen years, from 1882 to 1899, the Sandburgs owned a two-family house at 622–624 Berrien Street. They divided it into four apartments, lived in one, and added to their income by renting the other three. From one tenant, "Uncle Joe" Elser, Carl and a brother imbibed the lore of the Civil War. The boy who was destined to write the definitive account of Lincoln in the war years watched as the old veteran shoved piles of kindling around the floor to show the shifting positions of the armies. These sessions were recalled long afterward when Carl wrote "House," a poem in *Cornhuskers:*

> Two Swede families live downstairs and an Irish
>   policeman upstairs, and an old soldier, Uncle
>   Joe.
>
> . . . .
>
> Joe tells the Swede boys all about Chickamauga and
>   Chattanooga, how the Union soldiers crept in
>   rain somewhere a dark night and ran forward
>   and killed many Rebels, took flags, held a hill,
>   and won a victory told about in the histories in
>   school.
>
> . . . .
>
> The two Swede boys go downstairs with a big blur
>   of guns, men, and hills in their heads. They
>   eat herring and potatoes and tell the family war is a
>   wonder and soldiers are a wonder.

These were the staples of the long winter evenings of boyhood: a howling wind, war stories, *sill och potatis* (herring and potatoes), the faces of his brothers and sisters around the table—two younger brothers died of diphtheria on the same day in 1892, and the grief was long remembered—the mother with her accents becoming more Americanized each year, the father still saying "Sholly" for Charlie, "iss" for is, "Gilsburg" for Galesburg. Sandburg, like Mencken, who was also close to his Old World heritage, developed a preoccupation with the American vernacular. He did so partly because in his family the process of Americanization was still self-conscious, the family conversation rooted in a foreign language. Having to depend on a new language for survival gives one a speedy grasp of the essentials, like the Marine in Sandburg's poem "Threes," who learned in every port how to say three things: "gimme a plate of ham and eggs—how much?—and—do you love me, kid?" Sandburg said that, though his father's accent was faulty, "he had his syllables perfectly correct in most of the important words he spoke, such as house, pump, water, money, tariff, politics, C.B. & Q., Republican, Democrat, America, Blaine, McKinley, sick, hammer, lamp, kerosene, good morning."

Right in his own home the boy learned how working people could be financially set back if not wiped out by illness, accidents, or quirks in the system. By 1883 August, who could make one cigar last a month and a pint of liquor all winter, had nursed his spare nickels and dimes into a hoard big enough to buy as an investment a house and lot on South Street. For five years he spoke of it with satisfaction as "a nice piece uh proputty." Then he got a letter summoning him to court, hinting that the property might not legally be his. Puzzled, he went to trial and was confronted with a nineteen-year-old sleeping mortgage that the previous owner probably hadn't even known about. He could keep the property but would have to pay for it all over again—another $800 to be squeezed out of his fourteen cents an hour.

After one brief day of stony depression, he took it in stride and paid. But his son recalled that "a certain warmth of kindliness, an ease, a laughter and merriment that formerly came not often came now less often." It gave the boy a lifelong sympathy for those who had to make their way with scant resources under a system where the law itself could get turned around and take the fairness out of things.

Almost like parents to the Sandburg youngsters were another immigrant couple, Clara's cousins John and Lena Krans. On Sunday mornings the Sandburgs would hitch their mare to the wagon and ride out to the Krans farm near the little crossroads of Soperville. Lena told how, as a young woman in Sweden, all her news of America had come from Soperville. "In her mind Soperville became the liveliest and most wonderful place in America. So when she got off the sailing ship in New York and saw the crowded streets and tall buildings, she said, 'If this is New York, then what will Soperville be like?' "

John Krans, who dandled Carl on his knee and called him *"min ille gosse"* ("my little boy"), became to the child the prototype of the Illinois farmer. A lifetime later an aged Carl Sandburg borrowed the imagery of this poem from *Cornhuskers* to describe Krans's passing:

> The wind he listened to in the cornsilk and the tassels,
>   the wind that combed his red beard zero morn-
>   ings when the snow lay white on the yellow ears
>   in the bushel basket at the corncrib,
> The same wind will now blow over the place here
>   where his hands must dream of Illinois corn.

Hands dreaming of corn, hands dreaming of steel. Carl's father would stroke the small hammer he had brought from Sweden and exclaim with a light in his eyes, "Ah! Dat iss Svedish steel!" The boy's imagination, like that of the whole country, was fired by the imagery of the Steel Age that moved in with the large-scale development of the

Bessemer and open-hearth processes. Day and night in cities like Pittsburgh iron poured into converters, sparks flashing as air was forced through the white-hot mass. Steel could challenge the wind and sky, it could leap over rivers. Bridges fascinated Carl. In the vest-pocket biographies that his friends saved for him from cigarette boxes, he read about James B. Eads, who built the bridge over the Mississippi at St. Louis. Years later, riding the boxcars, he saw the bridge between Omaha and Council Bluffs that enabled the immigrants to carry their households west by train or wagon without having to be ferried across the river. That bridge appears in "Omaha," a poem from *Smoke and Steel:* "A span of steel ties up the kin of Iowa and Nebraska across the yellow, big-hoofed Missouri River."

Sandburg's childhood in Galesburg taught him about the expansiveness and exhilaration of the post–Civil War era, and it taught him about hardship, exploitation, confusion. Work was the pride of men like his father, unemployment their dread, poverty and accidental maiming their plagues. The boy saw the railroad from a hundred points of view: the luxury of dining cars and first-class coaches, the men who toiled for next to nothing to keep the tracks smooth enough so water couldn't spill from the flower vases on the dining tables, the men who died coupling moving cars until the Westinghouse automatic coupler came along, the service of the railroad in moving people and freight, the crowds of people given employment by the railroad, the crowds of people kept at subsistence wages by the railroad.

Galesburg had plenty of people who remembered Lincoln, for in 1858 Knox College had been the scene of a famous debate between Lincoln and Douglas. Under the shadow of the plaque that marked the site, Sandburg saw work and sickness and jokes and festivals make brothers out of people from different races, and he saw bigotry too. In the 1890s, when immigration in the United States was heading up toward its peak and Galesburg had given a wave of Italians its rough-and-ready welcome, the streets of the prairie town were full of sights like those the boy might have seen in the Old World: fleets of Italian fruit vendors, a strolling German band.

When there was good fellowship between the various nationalities, it was robust. Ethnic jokes laced with the humor of hard times could be simultaneously brutal and sidesplitting, like the story of Nigger Duke, the black man who spoke Swedish. He was a cripple, having had both legs amputated after spending a freezing night in a boxcar. He was the pride of the Swedes in the Q. yards because he had learned to speak Swedish as well as they could.

We were told in our school days that Nigger Duke happened to be at the Q. depot once when a train loaded with green Swedes fresh from Sweden came in, headed for Nebraska. Nigger Duke lifted himself to a car platform and walked along the aisles of the cars talking Swedish and telling the newcomers, "After a while when you have been in this country as long as I have you'll turn black like I am." His Swedish was perfect and his white teeth glistened and his laugh rippled as he told this to Swedes who had never heard a black man speaking Swedish. . . . I believe most of the Swedes on the train took it as a good joke.

To Sandburg and his gang of friends, the "Dirty Dozen," racial epithets in themselves weren't dirty words. But they knew hostility when they heard it.

A Jew was a "sheeny." The Irish were "micks." A Swede was a "snorky." A Yankee was a "skinflint." The Germans were "Dutch." The Italians were "dagoes." A Negro was a "nigger" or a "smoke." I heard Irish boys say of themselves, "Us micks" and Negroes speak of themselves as "Us niggers," and one Swede boy to another, "Hello, snork." When you hated and wanted to be mean you said, "goddam mick" or "goddam nigger." We believed that the "sheenies" on the quiet might be calling us "snorkies" and calling the Irish "micks" and that would be all right with us because that's what we were. But if they called us "goddam snorkies" or "goddam micks" then we would look for bricks to heave.

One night a mulatto ex-prizefighter knocked a man through a saloon window. Broken glass cut an artery and killed him. The mulatto was jailed, and a few nights later the town that had been an active station on the Underground Railroad heard a mob shouting, "Kill the nigger!" An excited young Sandburg watched as the sheriff palavered with the mob outside the jail while a car whisked the defendant away from the back door to a prison in Peoria. Galesburg, which had never had a lynching, kept its slate clean.

The financial disaster of 1893, which bit so deeply into the closing years of Mark Twain's life, made it rough going for Sandburg as a boy. After the eighth grade he had to quit school and work because his father's time at the shop had been cut back to four hours a day and his wages to about sixteen dollars a month. By the time he was nineteen he had worked at every job in the book. He was a paperboy, milkman, drugstore janitor, potter's apprentice, ice harvester, farmhand, barber's porter. For three days he was apprenticed to a drunken tinsmith, for two weeks he washed bottles in a pop bottling works. What counted in the end was that the jobs gave him a chance to see work and people from so many points of view. Delivering milk and papers he saw homes rich and poor, their front and back entrances, their yards, their privies, their luxuries or privations. At the Union Hotel as a barber's porter he drew water for customers to bathe in, scrubbed their backs, knew the town's leading citizens and famous visitors through their whiskers.

From the time he was knee-high he learned how people—immigrants and pioneers—had to work for their living, contrive to live on what they made, and somehow find the time to understand the system and get a voice in improving things. He saw people searching for solutions to their problems by becoming Republicans, Populists, advocates of free silver, of temperance. He knew, or knew people that knew, old-line Abolitionists, like Elizur Wright, father of his friend Professor Philip Green Wright of Lombard College. With all the hardship of the postwar days, there was optimism too. The people had licked the slaveholders; they had no intention of being bought and sold by robber barons. In 1888 the C.B. & Q. strike made an impression on the boy, and he was a sympathetic though not very partisan observer of the growth of the railroad workers' unions.

He saw the people make mistakes, place their trust in unworthy leaders like James G. Blaine. He never forgot the hanging of the anarchists after seven policemen were killed in Chicago's Haymarket Riot in 1886, or his father and mother shaking their heads and exclaiming, "Dose arnashists! Dose arnashists!" In time it grew clear that the case against those convicted was shoddy, that the jury had been packed, that a man unconnected with the defendants had thrown the bomb. Then the jubilation people in Galesburg had felt about the convictions seemed as wrongheaded and sinister as the New England witch hunts. Sandburg knew what he was talking about when he wrote in *The People, Yes* in 1936,

> The people will live on.
> The learning and blundering people will live on.
> They will be tricked and sold and again sold
> And go back to the nourishing earth for rootholds,
> The people so peculiar in renewal and comeback,
> You can't laugh off their capacity to take it.

He could speak for people caught in the Depression in lines like

> Once I built a railroad
> . . . now . . .
> brother, can you spare a dime?

because he learned the whole grammar and vocabulary of struggle in Galesburg, on Berrien Street and by the tracks.

By 1896 Galesburg wasn't big enough anymore. Carl pestered his father for a pass on the Q. and saw Chicago for three days. He walked the streets, listened to the noises of drays, trolleys, and wagons, saw Lake Michigan for the first time, then headed for home when his dollar and a half savings ran out. In June, 1897, he took to the boxcars, bound for Kansas and the wheat harvest. He saw the Mississippi River, Iowa, Nebraska. He met other hoboes and learned the codes of the road. He got a bloody mouth from a brakeman who couldn't get him off a coal car headed west from Kansas City. After a stay in Kansas he left for Denver and spent a harrowing night trying to stay awake so as not to tumble off the bumper of a train crossing the Rockies.

In Denver he took a dishwashing vacation and pondered about whether to make for the West Coast or go back to Galesburg. It was the end of a long sorting-out process; the last two years had been a long quiet crisis of bewilderment about his needs and talents, frustration with what seemed to be his choices. He decided to go home, and took the freights for Omaha, a town he'd always wanted to see. On October 15 he pulled into Galesburg. "I walked along Berrien Street until I came to the only house in the United States where I could open a door without knocking and walk in for a kiss from the woman of the house." Lombard College, service in the Spanish-American War, a career with the *Chicago Daily News,* all were part of a future that had yet to unfold. Sandburg didn't know what the next step would be, but readiness was what counted. He was ready.

In 1948 Carl Sandburg, then seventy and living at Flat Rock, North Carolina, visited his restored birthplace on Third Street in Galesburg. Seeing a modern bathroom, he remarked, "This is an anachronism." A bronze plate bearing the words "The Anachronism" was promptly nailed to the door. Other changes have been made in the house since the Sandburgs lived there (1873–1879). In 1889 the house was purchased by a carpenter who clapboarded the outside and plastered the interior. A heating system has also been added; when the Sandburgs lived there all the heat came from the kitchen stove. Today the cottage, owned by the Illinois State Historical Society, contains Sandburg family photographs, kitchen utensils, and chairs; Mrs. Sandburg's sewing machine; a dresser from the room Carl slept in when he visited the Krans farm; the Remington typewriter on which he wrote part of *The Prairie Years* and some of the *Rootabaga Stories*; and photocopies of a deed and tax title to the South Street house that the father paid for twice. To one of these documents August Sandburg, who never learned to write his name, affixed his mark. The Sandburgs' Swedish family Bible used to be on display at the house, but it has been transferred to the Illinois State Historical Library in Springfield for safekeeping.

Nobody would agree more than Carl Sandburg with the idea that the history of a nation should be the history of its working people. The Third Street house is preserved not only as a landmark connected with Sandburg but also as a nineteenth-century working-class home, an illustration of the conditions under which pioneers and immigrants labored to develop this country. Sandburg's ashes are buried in the park behind this cottage, now four doors down from the C.B. & Q. tracks.

4 🏠

Emily Dickinson and the Homestead

The Dickinson Homestead, 280 Main Street, Amherst, Massachusetts.
Lionel Delevingne photo courtesy of Amherst College

A small white cotton dress hangs in Emily Dickinson's bedroom closet upstairs in her father's house in Amherst, Massachusetts. The dress is ornamented only with rows of tiny tucks and narrow white lace. Its skirt falls almost straight from the slightly fitted waistline to the floor. Nothing could stand in more dramatic contrast to the dashing, elaborately styled, voluminously skirted ensembles that were fashionable in the 1870s and '80s.

Suggestions, enigmas cling to this survivor from the poet's wardrobe. Did her habit of dressing in white symbolize bridal devotion to someone, and if so, to whom? For all the speculation that has been advanced on the subject, no one knows conclusively. But it is certain that the white gowns were part of the style of a life fashioned with extreme selectiveness. At the age of thirty-eight she wrote to a friend, *"I do not cross my Father's ground to any house or town."* Her motives for thus circumscribing her territory form a biographer's mystery; her writings never explain them in so many words. But they seem to have included a need for economy, a drive to define boundaries and then perfect her functions within them. By severely limiting the scope of her everyday existence—by no means a painless sacrifice—she avoided wasting motion and dissipating psychic energy, freeing herself to broaden the scope of her imaginative life.

Just as surely as Hemingway on safari or Sandburg sleeping sheetless in a boxcar, she traveled—she soared, she encompassed. How much she did achieve, how far she ranged and what rare things she brought back, no one knew until she died in that same bedroom in May, 1886, when she was fifty-five. On a day full of apple blossoms she was carried across the fields to lie beside her father and mother in the West Cemetery. Only then did her sister Lavinia, sorting through her drawers and boxes, discover the poems. Hundreds of poems, in little bunches tied with twine; 1,775 of them, enough to account for a whole working life.

She died in the house where she had been born, the "Homestead," on Main Street in Amherst. Now the property of Amherst College, the brick structure with its white pillared portico and square cupola retires behind a high hedge of evergreen. Next to it is the Italian villa-style home Emily Dickinson's father built for her brother Austin. In the same neighborhood are the First Congregational Church, which Austin helped to design; a Queen Anne frame house once occupied by Mabel Loomis Todd, through whose efforts Emily's poems were posthumously published; and the stately homes of the Hills family, Amherst industrialists with whom the Dickinsons lived in close touch. On the other side of Amherst College is a childhood home of the novelist and

*Behind Emily Dickinson's small white gown, a daguerreotype
(copy) of her at seventeen.* Lionel Delevingne photo
courtesy of Amherst Historical Society

Indian advocate Helen Hunt Jackson, a schoolmate and in later life a cherished correspondent of Emily's, who recognized the importance of Emily's poetry and urged her to publish.

Emily Dickinson was born on December 10, 1830; born, like Hawthorne, into a family long enough rooted in Puritan New England to be part of the history of that region, and to be deeply involved in living out its own myth. Hers was the eighth generation of Dickinsons in the Connecticut Valley. Emily's grandfather, Samuel Fowler Dickinson, was one of the founders of Amherst College. Her father, Edward Dickinson, was a lawyer, for over thirty years treasurer of Amherst College, a Massachusetts state legislator, and for one term a representative in Congress. His responsibilities, his inflexible dignity, his beaver hat and gold-headed cane, drew from Amherst people the epithet "Squire" Dickinson. It's doubtful that the class-consciousness latent in the title would have disturbed him, for where his conception of authority intersected with his self-image, he seems to have been utterly humorless.

As a young woman, then, Emily Dickinson was part of what amounted to a village gentry, though never a very affluent one. But at the time of her birth her father was still struggling to become established. His father, Samuel, had built the Homestead in 1813 but was compelled to sell it when his fortune dwindled. In 1830 Edward Dickinson took out a mortgage to buy back the house, and moved in with his wife and their son Austin, together with the Samuel Fowler Dickinsons and their still numerous family. So Emily was born in a household where thirteen people lived in close quarters, sharing four bedrooms.

When Emily was in her third year the mortgage on the Homestead was foreclosed and her grandparents moved to Ohio, but the Edward Dickinsons stayed as tenants of the new owner, still crammed into their few rooms. By 1840 Mr. Dickinson was able to purchase a white frame house on North Pleasant Street, and for fifteen years his family of five (Lavinia had been born in 1833) lived in that attractive home, which now exists only in pictures.

Some of the stress and strain involved in Edward Dickinson's efforts to strengthen his financial underpinnings was evidently felt by his children. As a girl of sixteen Emily wrote to Austin from South Hadley, where she was attending Mount Holyoke Seminary, *"Well, I dreamed a dream & Lo!! Father had failed & mother said that 'our rye field which she & I planted, was mortgaged to Seth Nims.' I hope it is not true but do write soon & tell me for you know 'I should expire with mortification' to have our rye field mortgaged. . . ."* This is a playful letter, running on to ask, *"Has the Mexican war terminated yet? Are we beat? Do you know of any nation about to besiege South Hadley?"* But the idea of Father's failing couldn't have been seized on even in jest if the danger it suggested hadn't been present at some level in the family consciousness.

Though it grieved Emily to leave North Pleasant Street, it was a milestone for the family when in 1855 Edward was able to buy back the Homestead and spend an additional $5,000 to make it a showplace. Austere as he was, he indulged a real love of beauty in the furbishing of his house. He put in the charming Italian marble fireplaces, sculptured with clusters of grapes, that can be seen in the house today. He built the square cupola on top, with its superb view of the village rooftops amid a rolling landscape ringed in the distance by blue hills.

About the same time he took Austin as a law partner, and built the "Evergreens" for Austin and his bride, Susan Gilbert, right next door to the Homestead. With the installation of Emily and Lavinia in the old home, and Austin in the neighboring house, Edward had established the scenario for the futures of all three of his children. By 1856 the setting was complete and all the *dramatis personae* were in their places. After Emily Dickinson was twenty-five the conditions of her life never underwent any material change. All that adult development encompasses had in her case to be accomplished internally, with very little outward change or variety to reinforce the psyche's motions toward self-renewal. Life at the Homestead was a drama that juxtaposed several intense personalities, notably Emily's and her father's, within a compact space.

Emily's earliest surviving letters, written when she was eleven, are as chatty and artless as one would expect of a child. But even as a little girl she showed an unself-conscious wit, and a faculty for turning the events of household life into winsome mock epics that matured into a major poetic technique. These are excerpts from two of those early letters, written to Austin when he was at boarding school:

> *We miss you very much indeed you cannot think how odd it seems without you there was always such a Hurrah wherever you was . . . the hens lay finely . . . Cousin Zebina had a fit the other day and bit his tongue into* [sic] *. . . .*
>
> *. . . the other day Francis brought your Rooster home and the other 2 went to fighting him while I was gone to School—mother happened to look out of the window and she saw him laying on the ground—he was most dead—but she and Aunt Elisabeth went right out and took him up and put him in a Coop and he is nearly well now—while he is*

shut up the other Roosters—will come around and insult him in Every possible way by Crowing right in his ears . . . Aunt Elisabeth said she wished their throats would split and then they could insult him no longer. . . .

This letter to a beloved girl friend, Abiah Root, was written during the fifth of Emily's seven years at Amherst Academy: *"Viny and I both go to school this term. We have a very fine school. There are 63 scholars. I have four studies. They are Mental Philosophy, Geology, Latin, and Botany. How large they sound, don't they? I don't believe you have such big studies. . . . I am growing handsome very fast indeed! I expect I shall be the belle of Amherst when I reach my 17th year. I don't doubt that I shall have perfect crowds of admirers at that age."*

For a fourteen-year-old, the normal yearnings, the normal poses. But the script wasn't written that way. She attended Mount Holyoke Seminary for the term 1847–1848, battled homesickness, picked up some intellectual stimulation, and settled—negatively—two crucial issues. The first was religious. The atmosphere of Mount Holyoke was devoutly evangelical, and the students were repeatedly urged to accept Christ as personal Savior. Emily found herself permanently unable to make that commitment, and was too reverent as well as too honest to feign capitulation for social reasons. The second issue was that of separation from home. The year at Mount Holyoke represented her only attempt to live away from "her Father's ground." Her going home seems to have amounted to a tacit admission that it didn't work.

Not that, at her age, it seemed as final as all that. *"Amherst is alive with fun this winter,"* she wrote an uncle early in 1850. *"Sleigh rides are as plenty as people."* There were parties, balls, flirtations, valentines, long visits from friends and cousins, outdoor frolics in the summer. Youth, gregariousness, dreams—she didn't give it all up in a day. Indeed her life expanded when she met Ben Newton, a young law student in her father's office. Newton introduced her to the writings of the Brontë sisters and of Emerson, whose influence gave her a way of reconciling her Puritan heritage with a philosophy of self-realization.

The artist in Emily was just beginning to draw strength from this friendship when Newton died in 1853. He became the first of a succession of men whom Emily Dickinson loved and revered as "mentors": Samuel Bowles, the brilliant editor of the *Springfield Republican;* the Reverend Charles Wadsworth, after whose move to California in 1862 she took to dressing in white; and Judge Otis Lord, to whom she wrote intimate, ardent letters in the '70s and '80s.

By 1855, when she and her family settled permanently at the Homestead, Emily had a threefold developmental task. She had to clarify and carry out her vocation as a poet; she had to continue to work through the loss of Newton, which was the prototype of the cycles of love, nurturing, and grief that she would experience with so many loved ones in years to come; and she had to do all this while making her contribution to the life of her family. She had long since sized up the problems of domestic coexistence, as this letter to Austin in 1851 suggests: *"We don't have many jokes tho'* now, *it is pretty much all sobriety, and we do not have much poetry, father having made up his mind that its pretty much all* real life. *Fathers real life and* mine *sometimes come into collision, but as yet, escape unhurt!"*

In her home Emily Dickinson didn't lead a life of ornamental leisure. Totally apart from her writing, she had a great deal to do. The Dickinson household, like many of its time and place, produced a large proportion of its own food compared to modern homes. The work and general ups and downs connected with that are reflected in her letters from girlhood on. There are, for instance, the chickens. In a letter to Austin at Harvard Law School in 1853, Emily laments that he didn't get home for a hoped-for visit, though the family expected him until the last minute. *"And we had a new custard pie, too, which is a rarity in these days when hens don't lay. . . ."* In 1860 she wrote her cousin Louise Norcross, *"We have at present one cat and twenty-four hens, who do nothing so vulgar as lay an egg."* On their land the Dickinsons raised hay for their horse, garden vegetables, cherries, pears, plums, and apples. *"We have no Fruit this year,"* Emily wrote a friend in 1884, *"the Frost having barreled that in the Bud—except the 'Fruits of the Spirit,' but Vinnie prefers Baldwins."*

One servant outdoors and one in wasn't a great deal of help in a day when food had to be processed from scratch and cleaning done without laborsaving devices. What Mrs. Dickinson, Emily, and Lavinia didn't have to do, they had to supervise. Besides a large number of relatives, the Dickinsons had, during Edward's lifetime, the social responsibilities of a prominent family. Emily's letters describe a fairly steady stream of visitors and house guests, climaxed by the commencement season at the college, when a large tea was given annually at the Homestead. If anyone fell ill in the home, the others had to nurse. In 1875, a year after her husband's death, Mrs. Dickinson was paralyzed and remained bedridden until her death in 1882. In 1880 Emily wrote her cousins and confidantes, Fanny and Louise Norcross, *"I have only a moment . . . Mother's dear little wants so engross the time,—to read to her, to fan her, to tell her health will come tomorrow . . . this is so ensuing, I hardly have said, 'Good-morning, mother,' when I hear myself saying 'Mother, good-night.' "*

Housekeeping frustrated but balanced and strengthened Emily. She called it "a prickly art." She compared the kitchen fires to the fires of Smithfield, where Queen Mary burned the Protestants, and herself to the martyrs. *"'House' is being 'cleaned,' "* she wrote a friend in 1866. *"I prefer pestilence."*

Yet as years went by she coped with sickness, death, quarrels, and other calamities by baking, gardening, dispensing small luxuries and necessities to family and friends. Her gingerbread was peerless. When Austin's children played in their grandfather's garden, she would lower cakes of it to them from her bedroom windows. To her niece and nephews the mysterious richness of the gingerbread was a symbol for all that was unique and magical in the world to which they were admitted in the hours they spent with her. Her niece Martha Dickinson Bianchi remembered ending a childhood argument by squelching her opponent with: "Anyway, you don't have an Aunt Emily! Your aunts are just common ant-heap ants!"

Flowers were among Emily's greatest enjoyments. *"If we love Flowers, are we not 'born again' every day, without the distractions of Nicodemus?"* Her father added a conservatory to the house so she could garden indoors the year around. The more she retreated from the world, the stronger grew her habit of sending flowers—her own tenderly bred blossoms, personal as the marks of a signet ring—with the short notes she wrote constantly to friends.

Her poems were made of images gathered from the house and housekeeping, and from the village and its life. Many used imagery from weather and the seasons:

> The Sky is low—the Clouds are mean.
> A Travelling Flake of Snow
> Across a Barn or through a Rut
> Debates if it will go—
>
> A Narrow Wind complains all day
> How some one treated him
> Nature, like Us is sometimes caught
> Without her Diadem.

Her poem 585 about the railroad gives a picturesque turn to the coming of the iron horse, represented locally by the Amherst and Belchertown Railway, which Edward Dickinson helped to establish.

I like to see it lap the Miles—
And lick the Valleys up—
And stop to feed itself at Tanks—
And then—prodigious step

Around a Pile of Mountains—
And supercilious peer
In Shanties—by the sides of Roads—
And then a Quarry pare

To fit its sides
And crawl between
Complaining all the while
In horrid—hooting stanza
Then chase itself down Hill—

And neigh like Boanerges—
Then—prompter than a Star
Stop—docile and omnipotent
At its own stable door—

The poem conveys a graphic sense of the landscape associated with the railroad—the hills that broke up the view and made the route circuitous, the trackside shanties, and the quarries so typical of western Massachusetts—all of which the author very seldom saw by the time this piece was written (around 1862).

The 1860s were, artistically, Emily's most productive years. The mastery of style and rhythm that she achieved in her thirties never deteriorated, but in no other period did she write so many poems. "I find ecstasy in living," she said in 1870 to Thomas Wentworth Higginson, a reformer and literary critic who was also a trusted friend both to Emily and to Helen Hunt Jackson.

But griefs, which had walked in slow though steady single file through her early and middle years, assaulted her on a new scale after her father's death in 1874. In 1878 Samuel Bowles died, and in 1880 George Eliot, whom Emily never met in person but passionately revered. Asked once what she thought of *Middlemarch,* she replied, "What do I think of glory?" In 1880 one of her "mentors," Charles Wadsworth, came to see her unexpectedly. When she asked him how long his journey had taken, he answered, "Twenty years," the length of the interval since their last visit. Two years later he was dead. In the same year her mother died, and her friend Otis Lord fell ill.

What was no doubt the unkindest cut of all came in 1883. Emily doted on her nephew Gilbert, eight years old and full of health, vivacity, and charm. He died that year after a sudden, short illness. Early in

1884 Judge Lord died, and in the summer Emily collapsed. She wrote to the Norcross cousins, *"The Dyings have been too deep for me, and before I could raise my Heart from one, another has come—."* In 1885 Helen Hunt Jackson died in California. The beginning of 1886 found Emily gravely ill, the sickness diagnosed as Bright's disease. By the time the fields between the Homestead and the cemetery were in bloom, she was gone.

But something was unfinished. Her sister Lavinia knew, when it was too late to ask, that Emily had wished for her poems to have a destiny. Lavinia was helpless; she had no knowledge of the literary profession or ways of dealing with publishers. Left to her own resources, she didn't even have any way of assessing the merit of the poems. She only knew they were Emily's.

The obvious solution was to deposit the problem at the Evergreens with her sister-in-law, who had been congenial with Emily in years gone by. Sue was literary, and more accomplished than the Dickinson women at dealing with the world. But Austin and Sue's marriage had long since deteriorated, and with it relations with the family at the Homestead. Little Gilbert's death had removed the last cherished link between the houses. So long, in fact, had Austin's marriage been bleak that he had been romantically involved for some years with the young, vivid, and talented wife of his colleague David Todd, a professor at Amherst College.

It was to Mabel Todd that Lavinia finally turned when Sue's equivocal attitude about editing the poems turned into a passive refusal. Mabel debated; Lavinia's request put her in a sensitive position, to say the least, and the task of editing the hundreds of handwritten manuscripts was formidable. Even Austin, whose deepest lifelong attachment was probably to Emily, warned her against undertaking it. But she was convinced of the stature of Emily's achievement, and went ahead. She enlisted the help of Thomas Wentworth Higginson, who had described Emily at her funeral as "our friend who has just now put on Immortality, and who seemed scarce ever to have taken it off. . . ." The rest is history.

5 Hemingway and the Island in the Sun

Ernest Hemingway's Spanish colonial house, 907 Whitehead Street, Key West: a compromise with repatriation.

Ninety miles north of Havana the ocean turns from blue to bright green. A heap of low light-colored buildings rises above the sea: Key West. In April the water is docile and shimmering above the wrecks of ships broken on the reefs or lashed to splinters by hurricanes. The lore of the Keys includes dark legends to the effect that when times got hard enough the natives used to turn out the lights in the lighthouses so boats would founder and the community—or some quarters of it— would use the plunder to get the pot boiling again. Fishing, fighting, smuggling, drinking, making love; through it all the rhythm of wind and water ties day to night and winter to summer at a seductive average temperature of seventy-six degrees.

Cruising in from Havana, Ernest Hemingway and his second wife Pauline came in view of Key West in April, 1928. Their journey had begun in Paris, at the end of Hemingway's expatriate years, after the break-up of his first marriage to Hadley Richardson. In Europe Hemingway had been interested in the stories John Dos Passos told of visiting the island town in 1924; of crossing the Keys by train, the railroad viaduct spanning immensities of green water between palm-and-pine-tufted islands until it reached its terminus at Key West. For Hemingway, already acclaimed as the author of *The Sun Also Rises* and full of the new story that would grow into *A Farewell to Arms,* the island had several advantages. The fishing was superb, the pace relaxed, the flavor exotic, and it was only a day and a half by train to New York and Scribner's.

On this first visit the Hemingways moved into quarters at the Trevor and Morris Apartments on Simonton Street. In their day that site, later the Old Island Inn and now gutted by fire, was one of the hotels most favored by visiting dignitaries, including Cuban officials. Pauline Hemingway was expecting their first child. Her husband worked mornings on his new novel, then sauntered barefoot around the town where every street ended at a beach, talking with the native "Conchs," Cubans, fishermen, sailors, bootleggers. In the late afternoons he fished with Charles Thompson, owner of a number of waterside businesses: a fish house, a ship's chandlery, a tackle shop. Thompson's wife Lorine also became a staunch friend of the Hemingway family, and the Thompsons' cook introduced them to such delicacies of Key cuisine as turtle steak, black beans and yellow rice, raw conch salad.

They met Joe Russell, a little man full of staunch loyalties and dry witticisms that Hemingway found quotable, like "People dying this year that never died before." Russell made a good part of his living in liquor, first illegally, by rum running during Prohibition, then on the right side of the law as the proprietor of Sloppy Joe's Bar. Hemingway also got to know Captain "Bra" Saunders, an old Bahamian fishing guide, who told an intriguing tale of finding a sunken Spanish liner, the *Val Banera,* off Key West after a hurricane in 1919. Saunders dived again and again but couldn't break the portholes. Through the glass he could see the body of a woman wearing a fortune in rings. This incident Hemingway eventually turned into a story called "After the Storm."

The Hemingways' first stay at Key West lasted only six weeks. While they were there they were visited unexpectedly by Hemingway's parents, who had made their way south from Oak Park, Illinois, where three of his boyhood homes still stand. Hemingway noticed that his father, a doctor, looked gray and drawn and complained of diabetes and heart trouble. But his impressions faded into the background as he and Pauline drove west to visit Pauline's family in Piggott, Arkansas, to await their baby's birth. That November the Hemingways had just returned to Key West and settled into a rented house on South Street when Dr. Hemingway shot himself with an old .32 that had belonged to his father, a Civil War veteran.

This stunning event, which was to reproduce itself in Ernest Hemingway's own self-imposed death thirty-three years later, he seemed at the time to meet with relative equanimity. He saw to the readjustment of the family's financial affairs and prepared to contribute to its support by finishing *A Farewell to Arms,* which he called "my long tale of transalpine fornication." His editor from Scribner's, Maxwell Perkins—who was also superintending the careers of Scott Fitzgerald and Thomas Wolfe—made a trip down from New York to pick up the manuscript. Out in a fishing boat with Hemingway for ten hours a day, a suntanned Perkins read the book in a week and called it a success.

It was in 1931 that the Hemingways bought their Key West home, a dignified but decrepit Spanish colonial mansion at 907 Whitehead Street. Built in 1851 by a shipping tycoon named Asa Tifton who later founded Tifton, Georgia, the house was made of blocks of stone with wrought-iron railings around its balconies and tall green shutters covering its round-topped French windows. It was set far back from the street in a large jungle-like yard full of palm and banyan. After a few years Hemingway had his handyman Toby Bruce build a brick wall around the grounds to discourage sightseers. In the side yard was a carriage house that became a workroom for Hemingway. Here he labored at *Death in the Afternoon, Winner Take Nothing, The Green Hills of Africa, To Have and Have Not,* and the beginning of *For Whom the Bell Tolls.* The study came to be called the "pool house" when in 1937 Pauline had a pool installed in the yard to make Hemingway more comfortable at home and bolster their failing marriage. He

Hemingway's swimming pool, the first on Key West. A penny symbolizing his "last cent" is cemented into the deck.

did swim in the pool but fumed that it had cost him his last cent. The penny that he had cemented into the deck to immortalize his irritation is still there. Hemingway's tantrum about the money seems ironic in view of the fact that it was Pauline's uncle, Gus Pfeiffer, who had bought them the Whitehead Street house with money from his shares in Hudnut cosmetics. But that was part of the trouble: as time went by Hemingway felt undermined by the affluence of Pauline's family.

He could still enjoy it, though, when Uncle Gus staked them to a safari in Kenya and Tanganyika in 1933. Hemingway, Pauline, and Charles Thompson traveled through the Kapiti and Serengeti plains and the hill country below Ngorongoro Crater, shooting gazelle, guinea fowl, buffalo, lion, kudu. Back in New York he went to the shipyards with a $3,000 advance on articles to be written for the new *Esquire* magazine and ordered the boat he had dreamed of ever since he'd been introduced to Key West and the marlin fishing: a forty-foot power cruiser with a black hull, chrome and mahogany trim, two engines—a forty-horsepower and a seventy-five-horsepower—gas tanks that would hold 300 gallons, and sleeping room for seven. On a calm sea it could do sixteen knots. The *Pilar* was more than a boat. It was a way of life.

In the *Pilar* in 1935 he discovered the island of Bimini off Miami, a prime fishing ground for tuna and marlin. There he had an adventure in many respects like that of Santiago in *The Old Man and the Sea*. All afternoon until dark one day he wrestled with a large fish, not a marlin like Santiago's but a tuna, only to have the sharks attack it just before it was hauled into his boat. At Bimini in 1936 he met Marjorie Kinnan Rawlings and discussed with her the importance of an author's keeping a distance spiritually from the rich leisured people with whom he or she might socialize in such settings as Bimini. A failure to distinguish wealth from worth, he was sure, was a factor in the recurrent emotional upheavals suffered by their mutual friend, Scott Fitzgerald. Marjorie Rawlings remembered her last glimpse of him that season at Bimini, punching a 514-pound tuna he had just caught and had hung up on the rack at the island pier.

Through the years of the Depression Hemingway's code of individualism was attacked by writers of the Left, who felt that he ignored the issues of political responsibility and solidarity among people fighting for a common cause. In an era of widespread economic hardship his absorption in big-game hunting, fishing, and travel seemed self-indulgent. In private he expostulated that economics and political ideology had replaced religion as the opiate of the people. But he felt a certain responsibility to answer some of his questioners, and the dialogue helped to crystallize his philosophy of art. *"I cannot be a communist now,"* he wrote, *"because I believe in only one thing: liberty."* A good writer, he added, *"will never like the government he lives under. . . . If he had enough talent, all classes are his province. He takes from them all and what he gives is everybody's property. . . . A true work of art endures forever; no matter what its politics."*

Meanwhile the New Deal was making itself felt on Key West in the form of World War I veterans assigned by the Civilian Conservation Corps to build bridges between the Keys, precursors of the Overseas Highway. In *To Have and Have Not* Hemingway sketched a night at Sloppy Joe's Bar—fictionalized as "Freddy's"—with the vets down from the CCC camps on the upper Keys.

> They were opposite the brightly lighted open front of Freddy's place and it was jammed to the sidewalk. Men in dungarees, some bareheaded, others in caps, old service hats and in cardboard helmets, crowded the bar three deep, and the loud-speaking nickel-in-the-slot phonograph was playing "Isle of Capri." As they pulled up a man came hurtling out of the open door, another man on top of him. They fell and rolled on the sidewalk, and the man on top, holding the other's hair in both hands, banged his head up and down on the cement, making a sickening noise.

Hemingway put into the mouth of one of the characters his views about the politics behind the situation of these men: " '. . . Mr. Roosevelt has shipped us down here to get rid of us. They've run the camp in a way to invite an epidemic, but the poor bastards won't die. They shipped a few of us to Tortugas but that's healthy now. Besides, we wouldn't stand for it. So they've brought us back. What's the next move? They've got to get rid of us. . . .' "

The summer of 1935 gave Hemingway an unforgettable experience in island living and wrote a catastrophic chapter in the story of the CCC veterans. On August 31 Hemingway read in the newspaper that a hurricane was lying off the Bahamas and was expected to hit the Keys in about a day and a half. He rushed to the submarine basin to moor the *Pilar* securely, then returned home to join his neighbors in the hurricane season ritual of "boarding up." While the barometer fell he dragged the lawn furniture and all other movable property indoors and nailed the shutters closed over the tall French windows. At Key West the hurricane hit lightly, blowing down some power lines and trees, including a big sapodilla in the Hemingways' front yard, leaving the *Pilar* intact.

But the worst disaster ever recorded in the area had struck Islamorada and Upper and Lower Matecumbe Keys. On September 2 a passenger train was sent from Miami to evacuate residents of the Keys, including the CCC crews. As the train reached Islamorada a 200-mile-an-hour wind, blowing north from Lower Matecumbe, churned up a seventeen-foot tidal wave that wrecked the train and drowned its passengers. Nearly 1,000 were killed, many of them CCC veterans. Hemingway got Bra Saunders to take him to the devastated islands, where he saw the shoreline jammed with debris and bodies so bloated that they were bursting their dungarees and shirts. This was the end of the line for hundreds of men who had fought their country's war and then been thrown out of work by the ineptitude of the system. Hemingway was furious. "Who sent the vets down here to live in frame shacks during the hurricane season?" he demanded in an article published in the *New Masses*.

As the year went on he wove other comments on Depression time in the Keys into the fabric of *To Have and Have Not*. He set the tone for the death of Harry Morgan's friend Albert by explaining, through dialogue, about the relief programs that put men to work at seven dollars and fifty cents a week, less than a living wage for families. Albert gets shot trying to make extra money to feed his children by helping Harry run a group of men to Cuba in Freddy's boat. The economic desperation of Conchs like Albert and Harry is contrasted with the

Picasso cat, a gift from the artist to Hemingway.

complacency of wealthy tourists relaxing aboard yachts around the Keys. The novel was finished, except for revisions suggested by his editors, in 1936.

By this time Hemingway was close to his peak as a writer, and in the prime of his famous belligerence at any slight against his artistic or personal prowess. He slugged the poet Wallace Stevens, who also liked to vacation on Key West, for telling his sister Sunny Hemingway that her brother's work was "not his cup of tea" and then, when an argument developed, that her literary judgments weren't well informed. After three weeks in the hospital with a broken jaw, Stevens showed up on Hemingway's doorstep. He retracted his reflections on Sunny's taste but stuck to his guns about Hemingway's writing. "Hell," said Hemingway afterward, "a little guy like that sucking soup through a straw for three weeks and still wanting to tell the same story, I invited him in for a drink."

Nineteen-thirty-six was a momentous year for Hemingway. One reason was overt, public, earthshaking. That was the Spanish Civil War, every detail of which he was following with the concern of one acquainted with Spain and its factions. In November, 1936, the North American Newspaper Alliance engaged him to go to Spain the next year and cover the war. The other new development overtook him unaware in Sloppy Joe's one winter afternoon in the person of blond, attractive Martha Gellhorn, an accomplished young journalist and author. Back home at the Whitehead Street house Pauline waited with the Thompsons for him to come home for dinner. She finally sent Charles to Sloppy Joe's—the scene of Hemingway's daily three o'clock stopover, and known as such to everyone on the island—to retrieve him. Charles returned to report that he was talking to a beautiful blond in a black dress and would meet them later at a night spot. He did, but that empty chair at the table marked the beginning of the end of the family life at Whitehead Street.

Hemingway spent most of 1937 and 1938 traveling to and from Madrid. Martha was also in Spain along with other American journalists, John Dos Passos among them. Hemingway, Martha, and their colleagues made forays to the fronts from their headquarters in Madrid, which was under bombardment. He got to know the military personnel, the terrain, the guerrillas, and the people of the countryside, and the way small-scale but savage local feuds fit into the larger picture of the war, all of which he later depicted in *For Whom the Bell Tolls*. Meanwhile, by April, 1937, he and Martha had quietly become lovers, as their fellow journalists discovered one day when a shell burst the hot water tank of their hotel and sent the occupants scurrying from their bedrooms.

Back home at the Whitehead Street house Pauline had begun to accept, though not yet to admit, that as far as her marriage was concerned the handwriting was on the wall. As it became clear that her requests for her husband to disengage himself from the war and from Martha were having no effect, she began to organize her life around her own friends and interests. After 1939 Hemingway's stays at Key West were hardly more than duty visits. He would cross to Cuba, ensconce himself in the Ambos Mundos Hotel in Havana, and fall into a characteristic routine of writing, fishing, tennis, and drinking. In April, 1939, Martha appeared, scouted around, and found a decaying farmhouse about fifteen miles from town, and furbished it up at her own expense. She rousted Hemingway out of the Ambos Mundos and carried him off to "Finca Vigía," Watchtower Farm. That fall a depressing reunion between Ernest and Pauline in Wyoming, where they had spent their summers since the early days of their marriage, made it clear that their break was final.

In 1939–1940 Hemingway was again in passage, as he had been when he came to Key West. At Finca Vigía his life reassembled itself with Martha, whom he married in 1940, his trusted man-of-all-work Toby Bruce, the *Pilar,* and two of his most mature projects, *For Whom the Bell Tolls* and *The Old Man and the Sea.* In the fall of 1940 he moved a sizable portion of his gear—hunting trophies, clothes, papers—out of the Whitehead Street house and into a back room at Sloppy Joe's. The bundles were left there until after Hemingway's death, when his widow, Mary Hemingway, learned about them from Toby Bruce. Many of these mementos of his Key West years are still on the island, at the Monroe County Public Library or in local museums.

Pauline and her two sons lived in the Whitehead Street house until her death in 1951. The house remained in the Hemingway family until 1963, when Mary Hemingway sold it to a local couple. They lived in it

Hemingway's study upstairs in the pool house. Under a hunting trophy, his writing table and cigar maker's chair.

for a short time but were unable to stave off the crowds of people who wanted to see Ernest Hemingway's home. In 1964 they opened it to the public as a house museum. The home is entirely furnished with Hemingway family furniture, including antique Spanish pieces in Circassian walnut. A gate from the courtyard of a Spanish monastery serves as headboard for the bed in the master bedroom. In the same room, atop a Portuguese cabinet inlaid with tile, sits a cat that Picasso sculptured and gave to the Hemingways as a keepsake. Hemingway kept nearly fifty cats on the premises, and their descendants are still there. Visitors may see the pool house study, where Hemingway sat in a wood-and-leather cigar maker's chair and wrote at a small round table.

Legends of Hemingway, authentic and apocryphal, are still alive on Key West; photos and newspaper clippings from his days there line the walls at Sloppy Joe's. To *aficionados* of literature, sport, and travel, to those who still affect his brand of *machismo,* to others who share his passion for the island town with more exotic islands just out of sight over the jade-colored water, he's still "Papa."

6 🏠

Thomas Wolfe, the Angel,
and the Boardinghouse

Carrara angel at Oakdale Cemetery, Hendersonville, North Carolina. It was purchased by local residents from W. O. Wolfe, Tom's father, who imported the angels from Italy. North Carolina Department of Cultural Resources

In the Oakdale Cemetery at Hendersonville, North Carolina, an angel of Carrara marble holds a lily in one hand and raises its other arm, as if in benediction, toward the "distant soaring ranges." The angel was purchased for the site from W. O. Wolfe, engraver and monument maker, the father of Thomas Wolfe. The elder Wolfe didn't make these angels, but he ordered them from Italy to stock his shop on Pack Square in Asheville. They represented his aspiration if not his accomplishment, and became symbols of creative vision to his son. The Wolfe angel stands among the Blue Ridge Mountains in the "Land of the Sky" like a visitor from some mythical country, some motherland of art and epic: incongruous, a bit maudlin, lyrical, haunting.

A rambling prosaic house bearing the sign "Old Kentucky Home"—prototype of the "Dixieland" in Wolfe's novels—still stands at 48 Spruce Street in downtown Asheville. Today visitors to the house, now the Thomas Wolfe Memorial, sit and read *Look Homeward, Angel* on the porch where Mrs. Wolfe's boarders rocked, gossiped, and were entertained by the purple rhetoric of W. O., who would pass the evening chatting with them though he detested the life of the boardinghouse.

Thomas Wolfe and his seven brothers and sisters—from fifteen pregnancies, Julia Wolfe had eight children who survived infancy— were not born in the Spruce Street house, but in a house just a few hundred yards away on Woodfin Street. That house, which no longer exists, had been built and garnished with grapevines and a profusion of flowers and greenery by W. O. Wolfe. It was the Woodfin Street house that Tom ("Eugene"), the baby of the family and a child of four or five in the period described in this passage from *Look Homeward, Angel,* remembered as the setting of a tempestuous but warm and abundant family life centering around the father ("W. O. Gant").

> The family was at the very core and ripeness of its life together. Gant lavished upon it his abuse, his affection, and his prodigal provisioning. They came to look forward eagerly to his entrance, for he brought with him the great gusto of living, of ritual. They would watch him in the evening as he turned the corner below with eager strides, follow carefully the processional of his movements from the time he flung his provisions upon the kitchen table to the re-kindling of his fire, with which he was always at odds when he entered, and onto which he poured wood, coal and kerosene lavishly. . . .
>
> They fed stupendously. Eugene began to observe the food and the seasons. In the autumn, they barrelled huge frosty apples in the cellar. Gant bought whole hogs from the butcher, returning home early to salt them, wearing a long work-apron, and rolling his sleeves half up

his lean hairy arms. Smoked bacons hung in the pantry, the great bins were full of flour, the dark recessed shelves groaned with preserved cherries, peaches, plums, quinces, apples, pears. All that he touched waxed in rich pungent life. . . . The rich plums lay bursted on the grass; his huge cherry trees oozed with heavy gum jewels; his apple trees bent with thick green clusters. The earth was spermy for him, like a big woman.

It wasn't only Tom who saw W. O. as the giver of all good gifts. Later his sister Mabel recalled, "For us Papa always made the grass greener." Besides his generosity with the tangible delights of food and fire, W. O., windy, erratic, a frustrated artist, also furnished food for the boy's mind.

Secure and conscious now in the guarded and sufficient strength of home, he lay with well-lined belly before the roasting vitality of the fire, poring insatiably over great volumes in the bookcase, exulting in the musty odor of the leaves, and in the pungent smell of their hot hides.

Or again, Gant would read to him with sonorous and florid rhetoric passages from Shakespeare, among which he heard most often Marc

In front of the Woodfin Street house (since demolished), the Wolfe family: at far left, Tom, Julia, W. O.; at far right, Ben. North Carolina Department of Cultural Resources

Antony's funeral oration, Hamlet's soliloquy, the banquet scene in Macbeth, and the scene between Desdemona and Othello before he strangles her. Or, he would recite or read poetry, for which he had a capacious and retentive memory.

But home life at Woodfin Street went to pieces in 1906, when Julia felt the time had come for her to branch out into the kind of business enterprise that attracted her: real estate. Tom, her last child, was nearly six. She saw her years of motherhood coming to an end. Feeling a long pent-up need to make money, partly because of her lean childhood in the Reconstruction South, partly because her husband was an alcoholic and, as a provider, more lavish than reliable, she set her sights on the boardinghouse at 48 Spruce Street. According to the novel, it was being put up for sale by a minister whose clerical career had ended abruptly after a tipsy winter evening when he had dashed from the house to the post office in his skivvies, proclaiming the victory of God over the Devil.

> Dixieland was a big cheaply constructed frame house of eighteen or twenty drafty high-ceilinged rooms: it had a rambling, unplanned, gabular appearance, and was painted a dirty yellow. It had a pleasant green front yard, not deep but wide, bordered by a row of young deepbodied maples: there was a sloping depth of one hundred and ninety feet, a frontage of one hundred and twenty. And Eliza, looking toward the town, said: "They'll put a street behind there some day."
>
> In winter, the wind blew howling blasts under the skirts of Dixieland: its back end was built high off the ground on wet columns of rotting brick. Its big rooms were heated by a small furnace which sent up, when charged with fire, a hot dry enervation to the rooms of the first floor, and a gaseous but chill radiation to those upstairs.

When Julia moved into the house she named "Old Kentucky Home" the family split, since W. O. was unwilling to leave Woodfin Street. Julia took Tom while her second daughter, Mabel, stayed with her father. The other children "were left floating in limbo," picking up one meal at the boardinghouse and another at Woodfin Street, sleeping wherever they happened to be at bedtime: "Thus, before he was eight, Eugene gained another roof and lost forever the tumultuous, warm centre of his home. He had from day to day no clear idea where the day's food, shelter, lodging was to come from, although he was reasonably sure it would be given: he ate wherever he happened to hang his hat, either at Gant's or at his mother's. . . ."

Tom wrote in *Look Homeward, Angel,* and his sister Mabel later verified in *Thomas Wolfe and His Family,* that W. O. Wolfe called the boardinghouse "a murderous and bloody barn." He hated the idea that the family's food and shelter should be shared with strangers for profit. As Tom's childhood cornered into puberty, the boardinghouse aroused a kindred feeling in him.

> Eugene was ashamed of Dixieland. And he was again afraid to express his shame . . . he felt thwarted, netted, trapped. He hated the indecency of his life, the loss of dignity and seclusion, the surrender to the tumultuous rabble of the four walls which shield us from them. He felt, rather than understood, the waste, the confusion, the blind cruelty of their lives—his spirit was stretched out on the rack of despair and bafflement as there came to him more and more the conviction that their lives could not be more hopelessly distorted, wrenched, mutilated, and perverted away from all simple comfort, repose, happiness, if they set themselves deliberately to tangle the skein, twist the pattern. . . .
>
> As the house filled, they went from room to little room, going successively down the shabby scale of their lives. He felt it would hurt them, coarsen them: he had even then an intense faith in food, in housing, in comfort—he felt that a civilized man must begin with them: he knew that wherever the spirit had withered, it had not withered because of food and plumbing.

Meanwhile his real home, his Proustian lost paradise, still beckoned from Woodfin Street: "But the powerful charm of Gant's house, of its tacked and added whimsy, its male smell, its girdling rich vines, its great gummed trees, its roaring internal seclusiveness, the blistered varnish, the hot calfskin, the comfort and abundance, seduced him easily away from the great chill tomb of Dixieland, particularly in winter, since Eliza was most sparing of coal."

Yet Julia ("Eliza") was, after all, his mother. She had nursed him until he was three and a half; he slept with her until he was eleven. During the winters she took him to Florida, where she visited her relatives and dreamed of running a guesthouse in the winter season. They explored "the narrow lanes of St. Augustine," "the hard-packed beach of Daytona," "the green lawns of Palm Beach." Among the bric-a-brac in the Spruce Street house today are the coconuts and shells they brought home as souvenirs. This prolonged infantile closeness to the mother with whom he found it impossible to be rationally compatible was a great burden to Wolfe all his life. It loaded every motion of healthy anger toward her, and every attempt to separate from her, with a rending ambivalence.

Thomas Wolfe's home, the "Dixieland" of Look Homeward, Angel.

School years brought Wolfe a measure of diversion from the clamorous egos that inhabited his two homes: from his mother, who was determined to make a go of her boardinghouse regardless of the minor privations it imposed on the family; from his father and his occasional drunken violence; from his sister Mabel, who was often on edge from tending the father and helping out in emergencies at the boardinghouse. He was driven wild by what he described as Julia's "insane niggardliness," and not without reason. Mabel wrote later that Julia's own relatives, who had enjoyed the hospitality of Woodfin Street for years, had to pay room and board when they visited her at Old Kentucky Home.

But because Tom was the youngest, and grew up after Julia felt more secure financially than when the others were his age, he enjoyed the advantage of being able to attend the North State School, a private high school for boys. A building formerly occupied by this school still stands on Ravenscroft Drive in Asheville. There, under the tutelage of Mr. and Mrs. J. M. Roberts—the "Leonards" of *Look Homeward, Angel*—he found forage for his hungry mind in an atmosphere of unaccustomed calm and consistency and, in Margaret Roberts, a spiritual mother. While his brothers and sisters looked for work, married, and groped for paths into adulthood, while his father began his long struggle with cancer, Tom studied. He parsed Latin and Greek, read Cicero, the *Anabasis,* the plays of Friedrich Schiller, and Ben Jonson. He wrote essays and delivered orations.

Against the bleak horror of Dixieland, against the dark road of pain and death down which the great limbs of Gant had already begun to slope, against all the loneliness and imprisonment of his own life which had gnawed him like hunger, these years at Leonard's bloomed like golden apples.

Meanwhile he larked around town with the boys from school, spent hours reading at the public library on Pack Square, and poked his nose in at his father's monument shop. He loved the "brick shack" with his father's name lettered above the door, the flyspecked Carrara marble angel guarding the porch, the rooms filled with gravestones, samples of marble and granite, and stonecutting tools. The shop no longer stands on Pack Square; the Western Carolina Bank occupies its site. But the room at 48 Spruce Street where W. O. Wolfe spent his last years holds the desk from his office at the shop, a photo of the building with his sign over the door, small samples of the types of monuments he engraved and sold, and a collection of his tools: drills, mallets, chisels. These, together with his books in oaken cases—the "hot calfskin" volumes of his son's early memories—are rich with suggestions as to the kind of environment the groping fiery artisan-father created.

After a few years Julia's boardinghouse had become profitable, and she made alterations:

> . . . she had added a large sleeping-porch upstairs, tacked on two rooms, a bath, and a hallway on one side, and extended a hallway, adding three bedrooms, two baths, and a water-closet, on the other. Downstairs she had widened the veranda, put in a large sun-parlor under the sleeping-porch, knocked out the archway in the dining-room, which she prepared to use as a big bedroom in the slack season, scooped out a small pantry in which the family was to eat, and added a tiny room beside the kitchen for her own occupancy.

Julia's additions are easy to see because the floors she put in are clearly distinguishable from the wide-board flooring used in the older parts of the house. Though *Look Homeward, Angel* describes her enlargements in wry tones—"The construction was after her own plans, and of the cheapest material: it never lost the smell of raw wood, cheap varnish, and flimsy rough plastering . . ."—the results were not unpleasant. The rooms she added to the second floor vary in size, but each has its own entrance, one window or more, and a certain coziness and integrity.

But all the while Tom felt keenly what he called the "indecency" of life at the boardinghouse, and squirmed under Julia's efforts to harness him into its squalid service: "Dixieland was the heart of her life. It owned her. It appalled him. When she sent him to the grocer's for bread, he felt wearily that the bread would be eaten by strangers, that nothing out of the effort of their lives grew younger, better, or more beautiful, that all was erased in a daily wash of sewage."

Of all the Wolfe children the closest to Tom in spirit was his brother Ben, eight years older, who had left school after the eighth grade to work for the *Asheville Citizen*. It was Ben who got Tom the paper route that gave him a behind-the-scenes look at the life of the town, particularly the black sections. In *Look Homeward, Angel* Ben emerges as a tough, bitter, tender young man with a flickering blade of a smile and a quick articulation that can trim people's cheap verbal posturings down to size. Ben achieves a special kind of immortality within the novel by the passion with which he hurls his questions, "Where do we come from? Where do we go to? What are we here for?" He is described playfully as living in the company of a satiric angel, with whom he talks over the absurdities of this world. Like Gant's frustrated creativity, Ben's observing ego, with its uncompromising truthfulness, is linked to the imagery of angels that, as its title suggests, forms a poetic motif in the book.

Thin, sallow, weak in the lungs, Ben Wolfe had put his health under a tremendous strain by the time he was twenty, working in the wee hours at the newspaper office on a diet of cigarettes and coffee. *Look Homeward, Angel* shows the fictionalized Ben doing for Eugene's sake what he never did for his own when he cuts through Eliza's self-justifying cant about his family's poverty: ". . . there are people in this town without a fifth of what we've got who get twice as much out of it. The rest of us have never had anything, but I don't want to see the kid made into a little tramp." To Eugene he says often, "You take every damn cent you can get out of them."

Though none of the other Wolfe children had gone to college, it was fairly certain from early on that Tom would go. The family was gaining in prosperity. Tom had the support of Ben and of Mr. and Mrs. Roberts, and his performance as a student was excellent. Just before his sixteenth birthday he entered the University of North Carolina at Chapel Hill, where he eventually earned considerable fame as a humorist. He prepared to become a playwright. His life was being launched.

He still suffered tortures, not unmixed with humor, because of the boardinghouse. *Look Homeward, Angel* contains an anecdote, later corroborated by Mabel, about how his mother embarrassed him during one of her visits to the college. When Wolfe introduced her to some of his friends, she began handing out cards to advertise Old Kentucky Home and promising the young men free lodging there if they would help her "drum up business." The next time he saw Mabel and her husband he took Mabel aside, told her about the in-

At "Dixieland," the upstairs bedroom where Ben died.

cident, and sputtered, "I tell you, M-M-Mabel, Mama's just r-r-r-ruining me over at Chapel Hill."

At home in Asheville after his freshman year, he struck up a romance with one of the boarders, Clara Paul, the "Laura James" of *Look Homeward, Angel.* According to statements made years later by Mabel and by Julia Wolfe, everyone at Old Kentucky Home, including Tom, knew that Clara Paul was planning to be married soon after she returned from Asheville to her home in Virginia. But Tom was brokenhearted about her marriage and in no mood to see humor in the joshings of family and boarders about "calf-love." *Look Homeward, Angel* shows him at this juncture in a hilarious epic frenzy of hatred for the boardinghouse, so beside himself that he tries to pull down the brick columns that prop up its rear: " 'I will kill you, House,' he gasped. 'Vile and accursed House, I will tear you down. I will bring you down upon all the whores and boarders. I will wreck you, House.' "

In October of Tom's third year at Chapel Hill, Ben, then twenty-six, was taken ill with pneumonia. Tom rushed home to find him lying upstairs in the large front bedroom with the bay window, fighting for every breath, clearly dying. The family was frantic with anxiety, grief, and guilt about the years of night work that had tried

Ben's health and the lack of attention that had been paid to him. Even in the first stages of this final illness the mother's preoccupation with her boarders had made it difficult for him to be given proper care. In *Look Homeward, Angel* these feelings prod Helen to a fierce interrogation of the doctor.

> "Has everything been done?" she said again. "I want to know! Is there anything left worth trying?"
> He made a weary gesture of his arms.
> "My dear girl!" he said. "He's drowning! Drowning!"

This passage agrees, almost to the word, with what Mabel, the "Helen" of the story, remembered years later.

> "Aren't you going to do anything for him!" I screamed. "Aren't you going to do anything for him!"
> Dr. Colby looked at me calmly, stood up. "Mabel, there's not a man this side of heaven that can save him," he said evenly. "He's drowning in his own secretions."

Look Homeward, Angel shows Eliza unable to enter the sickroom until the end because Ben can't bear to have her there. Once he sees her approach and turns his face away; another time he actually gasps out, "Get out! Out! Don't want you." Only when he is unconscious can she take her place by him without being rebuffed by that face of rage and truthfulness.

With Ben's death, followed by his father's decline and the sale of the Woodfin Street house, Thomas Wolfe's childhood was over. He was outward bound. Mementos of his later life are gathered at 48 Spruce Street today. His diplomas from Chapel Hill and Harvard hang in the hall on the first floor. The bedroom next to the front room where Ben died has been designated the New York Apartment room because it contains possessions accumulated during his years in New York. Among them is a brass lamp, a gift to Wolfe from Aline Bernstein, the talented stage designer with whom Wolfe shared the greatest romance of his life. This woman, nineteen years older than Wolfe, refused to leave her family for him, but supported him financially and nurtured his talent through the writing of *Look Homeward, Angel*. The intense phase of their relationship was over by 1931, and Wolfe had transferred much of his emotional as well as professional dependence to Maxwell Perkins, his editor at Scribner's.

Meanwhile Asheville, which enjoyed an economic boom in the 1920s, in 1929 was dealt two staggering blows. One was the beginning

The dining room where Mrs. Wolfe served meals to her boarders.

The parlor at "Dixieland"; atop the piano (right) is a photograph of Wolfe.

of the Depression. The other was the publication of *Look Homeward, Angel*. When realism in literature was still relatively new, when the reading public was not yet hardened to the exposé, when novels were held to be works of pure imagination and small towns to be the backbone of the nation, Asheville wasn't ready to see its citizens portrayed recognizably, autobiographically, as human beings with their share— not an inordinately large one—of greed, lust, or stupidity. As Mabel recalled, ". . . for a fact, I do believe, nothing caused such a stir in our town as the publication of *Look Homeward, Angel*. The only thing, I felt, that saved us Wolfes from being tarred and feathered was the fact that in the book Tom had not spared us. He had lambasted the neighbors, but he had pictured his own family also, in no flattering light." The Pack Memorial Library refused to allow Wolfe's novels in its collection until F. Scott Fitzgerald, visiting Asheville while his wife Zelda was a patient at Highland Hospital there, presented the library with a set of Wolfe's works.

During the Depression Julia Wolfe had to sell Old Kentucky Home, but she was allowed to remain in the house and eventually her children were able to buy it back for her. Old Kentucky Home is unusual among house museums in that it passed directly from the Wolfe family to the city of Asheville, with no other ownership intervening. Wolfe's sister Mabel helped to superintend the establishment of the home as the Thomas Wolfe Memorial. The house, almost completely furnished with Wolfe family furniture, is a specimen *par excellence* of an early twentieth-century boardinghouse, from the resourcefully improvised sleeping quarters and bathroom facilities on the second floor to the parlor with its factory-made oak furniture and family pictures, the sun parlor where Wolfe's sisters played the piano in the evenings, and the large dining room, furnished with Julia's oak sideboards, serving accessories, and dishes, where a luncheon is served to visitors each year on Wolfe's birthday.

In two of the bedrooms, glass-front closets display clothing that belonged to Wolfe: a dinner jacket, a brown suit jacket, a huge gray overcoat. He was so tall that when he died—still a young man, not quite thirty-eight—they had to order a special coffin because standard sizes weren't big enough for him. The man who said "You can't go home again" accepted and was evidently comforted by the care of his family during his terminal struggle with tuberculosis of the brain. Once he was even able to joke with his mother about the parsimoniousness that had so infuriated him as a boy. Wolfe is buried with other members of his family at Riverside Cemetery in Asheville. At 48 Spruce Street what remains of Tom, and of W. O. and Julia and the other children, blends, after all the tumult of their lives, in a curious harmony.

7 🏠

Marjorie Kinnan Rawlings:
A Newcomer at Cross Creek

Marjorie Kinnan Rawlings in 1938, the year The Yearling
was published. Courtesy of the *Saturday Review*

When I came to the Creek, and knew the old grove and farmhouse at once as home, there was some terror, such as one feels in the first recognition of a human love, for the joining of person to place, as of person to person, is a commitment to shared sorrow, even as to shared joy. The farmhouse was all dinginess. It sat snugly then as now under tall old orange trees, and had a simple grace of line, low, rambling and one-storied. But it was cracked and gray for lack of paint, there was a tin roof that would have ruined a mansion, and the porch was an excrescence, scarcely wide enough for one to pass in front of the chairs. The yard was bare sand spotted with sandspurs, with three lean Duchess rosebushes left behind to starve, like cats. Inside the house, all the delight of the Florida sunlight vanished. The walls were painted a battleship gray and the floors a muddy ochre. The brick fireplaces were walled over with tin and filled with a year's rubbish. It was four years before the gray of the last room was decently covered with white, money for paint being scarce, and time so filled with other work that an hour with the brush was a stolen pleasure. And even now, the house shining inside and out, roofed with good gray hand-hewn cypress shingles, the long wide screened veranda an invitation to step either inside or out, the yard in lush green grass, there is still a look of weather-worn shabbiness. It is a constant reminder that the wind and rain and harsh sun and the encroaching jungle are about to take over. I suppose that a millionaire, perhaps even just a New Englander, might stand off the elements and maintain a trim tidiness—and a picket fence. But the rest of the Creek would not know what to make of it, and would be made most unhappy.

When she came to the hammock country of central Florida, Marjorie Kinnan Rawlings abandoned picket fences, affluence, and the other trappings of urban middle-class respectability. She arrived in 1928, the same year that Hemingway came to Key West—a coincidence worth noticing because of the similarities between the way these dissimilar individuals used Florida, with its even climate, the primitive character of its waters, lands, and islands, and the unself-conscious intimacy between indigenous Floridians like the Conchs and the Crackers and their natural environment. In short, the vital thing about Florida was its distance from the urban, conventional United States—the United States typified for Hemingway by Oak Park, Illinois, and for Marjorie Rawlings by Rochester, New York, as she knew it when she was a young married woman and syndicated newspaper writer.

Hemingway, of course, did not come to Key West directly from Oak Park, but from Europe after World War I and his years of expatriation. His settling on the island was not so much a repatriation—a return to the mainstream of American life and society—as a compromise with repatriation. In a sense Hemingway never repatriated. He spent the rest of his life on Key West, in Cuba, in Sun Valley, Idaho, never in the kind of middle-class urban environment that he associated with his origins.

Having begun her adult life more conventionally than Hemingway, Marjorie Kinnan Rawlings came to Florida by a different route. She had grown up near Washington, D.C., where her father worked as an attorney in the U.S. Patent Office. His happiest days, and Marjorie's, were spent on his farm in Maryland. Many years later Marjorie recalled "the flowering locust grove; the gentle cows in pasture; Rock Creek, which ran, ten miles away from its Washington park, at the foot of the hill of the locusts, where my brother and I learned to swim and to fish for tiny and almost untakable fishes. . . ." The farm Marjorie later owned in Florida was a spiritual descendant of the Maryland farm, and a material descendant as well, for money inherited from the sale of the latter after her father's death helped pay for the land at Cross Creek.

After high school Marjorie went to the University of Wisconsin, where she majored in English and did, said, and wrote all the things that were expected of a bright, well-bred young woman with literary interests. Her fiction was a little thin, lacking the texture of reality. But success seemed clearly on the horizon for Marjorie.

Over the next ten years it didn't turn out that way. She married Charles Rawlings, who had also served on the staff of the college literary magazine. They moved to his hometown, Rochester, an industrial city full of unassumingly decent people laboring for companies like Kodak under bleak, cloud-ridden skies. They both found their way into newspaper work. Charles developed a specialty covering boating events on the Great Lakes while Marjorie wrote stereotypical Sunday supplement features and poems about the life of a housewife—little lyrics full of what one editorial blurb called "the romance of dishpan and kettle." Meanwhile she worked doggedly but unsuccessfully at fiction. As her pile of unmarketable stories mounted, her dismay began to turn into despair.

She discovered the interior of Florida almost by accident. Early in 1928 she and Charles took a cruise from New York to Jacksonville. For the first time they saw the St. Johns River with its dark brown water, its banks lined with moss-hung trees. "Let's sell everything and move South!" Marjorie exclaimed impulsively. "How we could write!"

They did it. Charles's brothers, who were living in a tiny hamlet in the vicinity of Gainesville, located the Cross Creek property for them that summer. With Marjorie's inheritance and the proceeds from the sale of their home in Rochester, they bought it. They got seventy-four

Marjorie Kinnan Rawlings's Cross Creek home. The uninsulated board-and-batten farmhouse holds the heat in summer and the chill in winter.

acres of land, most of it planted in citrus, an eight-room board-and-batten "Cracker" farmhouse, a smaller tenant house, a barn, chicken houses and a flock of two hundred chickens, two mules, some farm equipment, and a beat-up Ford truck. When they arrived in November and Marjorie walked into the grove she had purchased sight unseen, she knew she had come home.

> Enchantment lies in different things for each of us. For me, it is in this: to step out of the bright sunlight into the shade of orange trees; to walk under the arched canopy of their jadelike leaves; to see the long aisles of lichened trunks stretch ahead in a geometric rhythm; to feel the mystery of a seclusion that yet has shafts of light striking through it . . . . And after long years of spiritual homelessness, of nostalgia, here is that mystic loveliness of childhood again. Here is home. An old thread, long tangled, comes straight again.

She knew from the beginning that life at the Creek would be no tropical idyll. Making the house and grounds habitable, getting the grove to pay, would mean long, exhausting days full of tasks to which the Rawlings could hardly have been less accustomed. Looking around at the life-styles of the older residents of the Creek, Marjorie realized that she would have to readjust her ideas of what constituted a living. She was given a partial initiation into Cross Creek society and values when the black matriarch "Aunt" Martha Mickens came to call. After a short, courteous exchange, Marjorie asked a question that betrayed some of her anxiety.

> I said, "The grove hasn't always made a living then."
> " 'Pends on what you calls a livin'. To get yo' grease and grits in the place you enjoys gettin' 'em, ain't that makin' a livin'?"
> "Yes."
> "Then lemme tell you. Ain't nobody never gone cold-out hongry here. I'se seed the grove freeze to the ground. I'se seed it swivvel in a long drought. But Sugar, they was grove here before my folks crossed the big water. They was wild grove here as long back as tongue can tell. . . . And they'll be grove here right on, after you and me is forgotten. They'll be good land to plow, and mast in the woods for hogs, and ain't no need to go hongry. All the folks here ahead of you has fit cold and wind and dry weather, but ain't nary one of 'em has goed hongry."
> Hunger at the moment was not immediate, but when it menaced later, I remembered the things the old black woman said, and I was comforted, sensing that one had only to hold tight to the earth itself and its abundance. And if others could fight adversity, so might I.

Cooking, mending fences, learning to shoot, overseeing repairs to house and outbuildings, trying to understand how the grove must be protected from sudden freezes, Marjorie tested the strength of her commitment to Cross Creek.

> It is more important to live the life one wishes to live, and to go down with it if necessary, quite contentedly, than to live more profitably but less happily. Yet to achieve content under sometimes adverse circumstances, requires first an adjustment within oneself, and this I had already made, and after that, a recognition that one is not unique in being obliged to toil and struggle and suffer. This is the simplest of all facts and the most difficult for the individual ego to accept.

Time proved that the Creek existence wasn't the life for Charles, though he shared Marjorie's enthusiasm at first. After five years there they separated and she was alone at the grove. She was launched as an author, having enjoyed considerable success with *South Moon Under*, a book about life in the Big Scrub (now the Ocala National Forest). But she was depressed and lonely after the breakup of her marriage.

As she cast about for a way to get a grip on things, a woman friend suggested that the two of them take a trip on the St. Johns. So, like Thoreau and Huck Finn, Marjorie took to the river, navigating *ad lib* through marshes and around spreading nets of water hyacinths, sleeping under tree roots and in deserted cabins, meeting fishermen, riverside squatters, and northern tourists aboard expensive yachts. She had left in a mood of alienation from everything, even the Creek. She came back healed. She took up life on her own, her most basic relationship now with the land and the people who were part of it. Her emotional survival was at stake as she continued to test for the bottom line of her happiness.

Day by sweaty day she worked out her salvation through her physical struggles with the land and livestock. From the other Creek residents she got just the right combination of companionship, help in time of crisis, and for the rest, a benevolent neglect that favored her need for solitude. She lived, as she observed in *Cross Creek,* "within screaming distance" of her closest neighbors. The reminiscence leading from that statement deserves to be reproduced at full length, not only because it shows how the social support system worked at the Creek, but because it conveys the hardship, exasperation, humor, and the peculiar freedom and contentment of her days.

> I was entirely alone on the grove. The summer was one of the two unbearable ones, as to heat, that I have known in my years here. Summer is our unproductive period for vegetables. I had been some time without them, and was afflicted with an itching rash that I recognized too late as nutritional. The Widow Slater and I had been repairing fences together, for I gave her pasture for her milch cow in return for milking my own. We had plowed through long vines of poison ivy along the decrepit fence. Her long black flowing skirts had evidently protected her. I had worked stockingless and in brief voile. The poison ivy had erupted from hips to ankle, from fingertips to throat, overlaying the rash.
>
> Soothing ointments and a prone position might have brought some ease. I was far from ointments and too busy to lie down. My cow broke loose from the pasture and came into the grove, tearing at the low-hanging orange boughs. I drove her out and penned her properly, and returning to the house, found myself in the middle of a patch of sandspurs waist-high. These barbed instruments are all the proof one needs that there is a Devil as well as a God. I was enmeshed with sandspurs, they stuck to voile skirt and to petticoat, creeping up underneath and getting a firm hold with one or two barbs, leaving the others free to grate against my skin. On normal skin they are like arrows. On a skin covered with rash and poison ivy, they were shafts of fire. I plucked at them as I went and came to the house. There the

dogs were waiting for me, shut on the back porch, since they had nothing but chaos to contribute in the matter of penning a cow.

I did not think they had been there very long . . . I can only relate that time is relative, and that what seemed like a short period to me, was evidently a long, long time in the minds of three puppies. Old Sport had become excited at their incontinence and forgotten himself, too. The porch was a shambles. Water for cleansing had to be brought from the outside pump, a bucket at a time. It took twenty buckets, as I remember, and dusk was on me when I finished.

I went then, the porch well cleaned, wet and glistening in the fading light, to water my garden. There were a few carrots that I hoped to bring through the heat, poor things but mine own. I pulled away sandspurs abstractedly as I carried out the watering pot. The mosquitoes descended on me. One would think that exposed neck, arms, and face would suffice the hungriest of insects. But a mosquito is Freudian, taking delight only in the hidden places. They wavered with their indecisive flight up under my skirts and stabbed me in the poison ivy, in the nutritional rash, around the sandspurs, and settled with hums of joy in all unoccupied small spaces. It was too much. I set down the watering pot, and with no thought of help for my distress, for I was past helping, let out shriek after shriek of sheer indulgent frustration . . . I screamed. The screaming satisfied me. I finished the watering, went into the house, fed the dogs, made myself a supper, and went to the veranda to meditate. As I sat, exhausted but content, two figures strolled cautiously up the road and paused in front of my gate. It was Tom Glisson and Old Boss.

Old Boss called, "Everything all right?"

"Why, yes," I said. "Yes, indeed."

Tom said, "Seemed to us like we heard somebody call for help. We just wondered, was everything all right."

I hesitated. After all, there was nothing to be done, and at the moment, it seemed, all was too embarrassing to be told.

"I was singing," I said. "Perhaps you heard me—singing."

"Oh," they said, and turned and walked home again.

So I say that I live within screaming distance of my nearest neighbors.

She lived daily and even nightly with "toady-frogs, lizards, antses, and varmints." She got moccasins in her toilet, after she got a toilet, which she couldn't afford for two years. In 1933 she was out of money and down to a can of tomato soup and a box of crackers when the mail brought a check for $500—the O. Henry Awards prize for "Gal Young Un," a story about a backwoods bootlegger. Another time she fell off a horse, broke her neck, and had to revise her novel *Golden Apples* while wearing a neck brace that gave her, she said, the look of Joan of Arc listening for the heavenly voices.

But whatever the ups and downs of the life she had reached out for so impulsively in 1928, that life nourished her and fed vitality into her writing. From the start her Florida stories had gained the favorable attention of Maxwell Perkins at Scribner's, and Marjorie, like Hemingway, Wolfe, and Fitzgerald, became one of Perkins's protégés. In 1933 Perkins suggested that she write a boy's story in the vein of *Huckleberry Finn* or *Kim,* but other projects kept her from becoming involved with the idea until it crystallized all at once in 1936. For years she had brooded on the beauty and mystery of the Big Scrub, her home for two and a half months in 1931 together with a hunter and his family, applying her retentive memory to the details of their life and the cadence of their talk. Suddenly she envisioned, not a written-down story "for" boys, but a story about a boy—about boyhood and its end— that would draw on the lore of hunting and farming life in the Scrub. From the old hunter she had heard the story of a fawn his brother had kept as a pet when they were children. Remembering his tale, she began to conceive *The Yearling,* a story of the boy Jody Baxter, his love for a dependent animal, and the conflict between that love and the greater imperatives of survival. At the conclusion Jody's father, Penny Baxter, tells him, "You figgered I went back on you. . . . Boy, life goes back on you . . . ever' man's lonesome. What's he to do then? What's he to do when he gits knocked down? Why, take it for his share and go on."

This philosophy, and the way it is fleshed out through the relationship of characters to a certain place, link Marjorie's novel to the work of such contemporaries as Ellen Glasgow and Margaret Mitchell, both of whom Marjorie knew personally. The national and international success of *The Yearling* brought to Marjorie's home at the Creek other famous visitors: Dylan Thomas, James Branch Cabell, Wallace Stevens, Robert Frost. Among the attractions of the Creek was Marjorie's cooking, which she had refined into an art, drawing on Cracker recipes and the bounty of the countryside to serve her guests alligator or turtle steak, succulent swamp cabbage, mango ice cream homemade with thick Jersey cream.

In 1941 Marjorie married Norton Baskin, owner of the Castle Warden Hotel in St. Augustine. From then on she divided her time between St. Augustine and the Creek. On the whole this change seems to have nurtured the woman in her at the expense of the artist, probably because she felt less in touch with herself in town than at the grove. Her writing suffered because of other stresses that set in in the '40s. After the great success of *The Yearling* she unfortunately developed a fear of being tagged a "regionalist" that led her to start her next novel, *The Sojourner,* on a new tack. She would base it on the character of her maternal grandfather and his life as a farmer in Michigan after the Civil War. The success that *The Yearling* met with abroad as well as at home should have proved to her that she had touched sensitively on universal themes, and the stature of Willa Cather's Nebraska novels should have ended the use of "regionalist" as a term of belittlement in American letters. But Marjorie was intimidated by it, and determined to show that she could employ a different setting in *The Sojourner*. On this story, which clearly lacked the inspiration of her Florida narratives, she spent ten laborious years.

Meanwhile in 1946 she went through a trouble to which some observers attributed a partial failure of her creativity for some years afterward. Early in her Creek days Marjorie had got to know the area by accompanying the census taker, Zelma Cason, on her rounds. After the publication of *Cross Creek* Zelma sued Marjorie for portraying her in a manner she claimed was libelous. Nearly all the other residents of Cross Creek, including many that had been surprised to read about themselves in a nationally famous work of literature, rallied to Marjorie's defense. She had lived at the Creek for eighteen years; she had used her resources and influence to help them fight their battles in time of sickness, financial need, or trouble with the law, even as they had helped her fight hers. The years they had considered her an outsider had been few and long since past. Marjorie won out in the first trial at Gainesville, but the plaintiff appealed, and in 1947 the state supreme court reversed the original verdict. Marjorie only had to pay token damages of one dollar, but she was also liable for $18,000 in court costs.

On the witness stand at her trial, Marjorie spoke of her deep involvement with the Creek and its influence on her life and writing. In her earlier years, she explained, she had been "unhappy, living in the North and in cities." She had struggled with her writing to little avail, trying rather academically to approach her stories through plot and character, until she moved to Florida and began simply to allow her responses to "this lovely country" to guide her choice and treatment of subjects.

That her commitment to Cross Creek represented no affectation but a profound and permanent bond was emphasized by her burial in the lonely peace of Antioch Cemetery, some nine miles from her house. After the thankless years of work on *The Sojourner,* she was just beginning to enjoy research for a biography of Ellen Glasgow when coronary thrombosis struck her down in 1953. She willed her Cross Creek home to the University of Florida. Now leased to the Florida Department of Natural Resources, it has been restored with the aid of convict labor from the state penitentiary at Raiford. Much of the atmosphere described in *Cross Creek* still survives in the house with Marjorie's informal furniture and other personal effects, on the porch where her round writing table with its palm log base still sits, in the grove and the undisturbed swath of hammock filled with palmetto, live oak, and citrus trees. Though Marjorie didn't neglect to make legal provision for her home, a different kind of testament concerning its destiny—a statement consistent with her ultimately trustful and optimistic naturalism—comes from *Cross Creek*.

Who owns Cross Creek? The red-birds, I think, more than I, for they will have their nests even in the face of delinquent mortgages. And after I am dead, who am childless, the human ownership of grove and field and hammock is hypothetical. But a long line of red-birds and whippoorwills and blue-jays and ground doves will descend from the present owners of nests in the orange trees, and their claim will be less subject to dispute than that of any human heirs. Houses are individual and can be owned, like nests, and fought for. But what of the land? It seems to me that the earth may be borrowed but not bought. It may be used, but not owned. It gives itself in response to love and tending, offers its seasonal flowering and fruiting. But we are tenants and not possessors, lovers and not masters. Cross Creek belongs to the wind and the rain, to the sun and the seasons, to the cosmic secrecy of seed, and beyond all, to time.

8 🏠

John Steinbeck:
Salinas and the Long Valley

The Steinbeck home at 132 Central Avenue, Salinas. Amid a colorful ethnic mix, another leg of Main Street.

In the sun-splashed waters of the bay off Monterey, California, marine life abounds; the shallows are a rich pasture for the biologist. Inland a little way to the east rise the Santa Lucia mountains. Farther east and roughly parallel to the northern Santa Lucias stands the Gabilan Range. Over these mountains, whose name means "hawk" in Spanish, the sun rises for those who live in the fertile valley between the two ranges. The river, the valley, and the town about ten miles inland from the mouth of the river all have the same name: Salinas. The name recurs like a tonic chord through the stories of John Steinbeck.

It is under a sycamore tree beside a green pool formed by the river that the reader first meets George and Lennie in *Of Mice and Men.* The foothill ranches above the valley are the settings for "Chrysanthemums," "The Harness," "The Red Pony," "The Leader of the People," and one is the home of the Hamiltons in *East of Eden.* Salinas the town is prominent in *East of Eden,* remote in the "long valley" stories. Here people come to barter, to play, to settle scores. The town is the source of law, order, and social justice, or what passes for them.

In quiet contrast to the glittering mirages of the forty-niners and the boom-and-bust glamour culture of Hollywood, Steinbeck's long valley embodies what is most enduringly fabulous about California. There is the topographic drama of ocean, mountains, and valley. There is the diversity of food crops grown in the black soil of the lowlands: lettuce, beets, cauliflower, artichokes, grain, fruit. There is the richness of the total ecology: the teeming marine microcosm of the bay; the ranches and forests sheltering cattle, horses, and small game; the human mix of Anglos, Orientals, *paisanos,* middle-class townsfolk, ranch hands, prostitutes, and drifters that Steinbeck observed in his early life and recreated in his stories.

Salinas had a population of 3,000 when Steinbeck was born in 1902. It had its Chinatown and its Mexicans; it had its row of bordellos, unforgettable to readers of *East of Eden;* it had, and still has, a colorful annual rodeo with a Spanish flavor that attracts visitors from far beyond the locality. But in many other respects Salinas was Main Street, and had its affinities with the Red Clouds and Sauk Centres of its day. For families like the Steinbecks, social life centered around school dances and concerts and church poetry readings and covered dish suppers. Mrs. Steinbeck was active in the Altar Guild of the Episcopal church; her son was engaged in a promising career as an acolyte until he failed to fasten securely a tall crucifix that he had carried in a procession, so that it fell during the sermon and hit the bishop on the head. Around the town a few automobiles, like Will Hamilton's Ford in *East of Eden,* were making uncertain maiden voyages through streets full of horse-drawn buggies and surreys, as they were doing then on Main Streets the country over. Small ranchers and farmers worked the land outside town, which had not yet been transformed by refrigeration and collectivization into the Eden of "agribiz."

Steinbeck was born and grew up in a gabled and turreted mid-Victorian house at 130 (now 132) Central Avenue in Salinas. At the time of his birth the second floor was unfinished inside, and all the family slept downstairs. He was born in the first-floor front room with the bay window, which later became a formal parlor. Eventually he and his two older sisters had bedrooms upstairs. John's was the front bedroom, overlooking Central Avenue. Many years later, when he and his first wife, Carol Henning, were helping to care for Mrs. Steinbeck during her last illness, John did much of the writing of *The Red Pony* and *Tortilla Flat* in that room.

John Steinbeck was the third child, and the only boy, born to second-generation Californians whose parents were immigrants from Ireland and Germany. The picture of Steinbeck's family in *East of Eden*—an authentic account, according to Steinbeck's own testimony in *Journal of a Novel: The East of Eden Letters*—is dominated by the image of his maternal grandfather, Samuel Hamilton, who farmed a barren tract of 1,760 acres near King City. Hamilton was a warmhearted Irishman with a gift for figurative speech and a genius for improvising and repairing tools and machines. In *East of Eden* Steinbeck reconstructed a picture of his grandfather in his blacksmith shop with his cronies, sharpening plows, shoeing horses, and taking a nip of whiskey between stories: "It was a bad day when three or four men were not standing around the forge, listening to Samuel's hammer and his talk." In his letters Steinbeck mused about the portrait of his grandfather in the book: *"I wonder if I got the aliveness of his brain, his mechanical ability and the curious poetry he put about him."*

Hamilton never made money, but he made friends, and raised a large, close-knit family. Their stories were Steinbeck's family history: Will, who had the Midas touch when he speculated on anything from Ford cars to beans for the army; vivacious Dessie, whose dressmaking business went to pieces after her mysterious love affair ended unhappily; Tom, whom Steinbeck later described as *"shy, and silent, and good—very good and confused,"* who committed suicide after inadvertently causing Dessie's death. Their sister Olive—Steinbeck's mother—started out in life as a country schoolteacher. She taught at Peachtree, Pleyto, and in the wilderness of Big Sur, cramming the

three R's down the gullets of rough ranch boys twice her size. After a
few years of teaching she married John Ernst Steinbeck of King City.
They settled in Salinas, where her husband became manager of the
Sperry Flour Mills. Brisk, spunky, Olive detested sloppiness—her son
later called her "a passionate sewer-on of buttons"—and had a horror
of debt. "She planted that concept so deeply in her children," Steinbeck wrote in *East of Eden,* "that even now, in a changed economic
pattern where indebtedness is a part of living, I become restless when a
bill is two days overdue."

Olive Steinbeck was never more herself than in her reaction to
World War I, which made itself felt in Salinas by the time John was
about fifteen. Though she was not of a political turn of mind, the fact
that a war was going on struck home with her when a neighbor boy was
killed in battle. "If the Germans had been sensible," wrote her son,
"they would have gone out of their way not to anger her."

She sold so many war bonds that she was singled out for a special
award: a ride in an army airplane. Olive, who had not yet acknowledged
the existence of the airplane, made her will before she entered the one
sent to do her honor. After she was flown three times over the Spreckels Beet Sugar Factory, where her husband was then employed, the
pilot looked back at her and yelled, "Stunt?" "Stuck" was the word
she thought she heard. Trying to keep him from panic, she smiled and
nodded. Time after time the watchers saw the airplane loop and roll,
then it flew upside down across the field. They had to put Olive to bed
for two days afterward. Said the flier, "I tore up the rule book and she
wanted more. Good Christ, what a pilot she would have made!"

For all her pluck, Olive was conservative. She wanted John to be
"something decent, like a banker." It was the reticent German father,
whom John described as *"a man intensely disappointed in himself,"*
who supported his son in his desire to become a writer *"in spite of
mother and hell."* The Steinbeck family was not exceptionally literary,
but books were in evidence in the Central Avenue house. After supper
the mother and father read to the children in the sitting room to the
right of the front entrance hall, where the family spent its leisurely
hours. Steinbeck recalled that "in the great dark walnut bookcase with
the glass doors, there were strange and wonderful things to be found.
My parents never offered them, and the glass doors obviously guarded
them, and so I pilfered from that case. It was neither forbidden nor
discouraged. I think today if we forbade our illiterate children to touch
the wonderful things of our literature, perhaps they might steal them
and find secret joy. Very early I conceived a love for Joseph Addison

which I have never lost." Besides Addison, Steinbeck also read George Eliot, Flaubert, Dostoievsky, Hardy, Milton, the Bible. He got Malory's *Morte d'Arthur* for his ninth birthday, and it became one of the major influences on his work. Like Twain, he used it both reverently and irreverently. In books like *Tortilla Flat,* it served both as a wellspring for his sense of myth and epic, and as the butt of a jocular picaresque. As children, Steinbeck and his younger sister Mary evolved a secret language composed of Middle English expressions that they used even as adults when they wanted to communicate privately.

Mary and John were close companions. Together they paddled rafts over the pond near their house and fought mud fights with the kids from down the block. Mary wanted to be a boy. In *East of Eden* she quizzes their uncle Tom Hamilton about how she could turn into one, only to find that he liked girls and didn't regard the proposed change as an improvement. In Mary's esteem Uncle Tom lost ground that he never recovered. Steinbeck wrote in *Journal of a Novel,* "All yesterday's work about Mary trying to be a boy is true to the smallest detail."

Steinbeck's education at West End Elementary School and Salinas High School was conventional, his performance satisfactory. What is outstanding about his early life is that even as a boy he was developing characteristic ways of exploring California's land and people. As a grade school student he evinced a fascination with biology. He brooded over the thousands of preserved bird skins and books on ornithology in the collection that belonged to the father of his chum, Ed Silliman. As a boy he learned to handle animals. He had a horse of his own; years later he remembered his excitement on the day she foaled, an excitement like Jody's in *The Red Pony.* During his high school years he began working as a ranch hand. He swam in the Salinas River, went through the Corral de Tierra to Pacific Grove for vacations with his family, and hiked and fished on the Monterey Peninsula. After many years he remembered climbing Fremont Peak and finding "cannon balls and rusted bayonets . . . among dark granite outcroppings." The fragments of old artillery filled his imagination with visions of General Frémont standing off armies of Mexicans.

That he learned early about racial tension is suggested by the autobiographical account of the B.A.S.S.F.E.A.J. (Boys' Auxiliary Secret Service For Espionage Against the Japanese) in *The Pastures of Heaven.* It was actually a very young John Steinbeck who, like Robbie in the story, organized his schoolmates into a spy ring for the purpose of putting the local Japanese under surveillance. An early meeting of this clandestine confederation was held in a barn where a couple of

John Steinbeck and his sister Mary on "The Red Pony."
Courtesy of Mrs. Beth Ainsworth

tramps had slept the night before, and the next morning some of the boys, including John, were infested with lice. Mr. and Mrs. Steinbeck reacted more promptly and decisively to the invasion of their household by vermin than the Defense Department did some thirty years later to the bombing of Pearl Harbor. From the bathroom, where his father was scouring him with a stiff brush, blistering water, and skin-tingling disinfectant, John screamed, "But I *want* lice!"

The B.A.S.S.F.E.A.J., when it reconvened, pursued the problem of defending the national security. In the immediate neighborhood the

Yellow Peril was represented by the family of little Takashi Kato, a good friend of the boys in the B.A.S.S.F.E.A.J. Groups of boys began to follow Takashi everywhere. One evening Takashi's father, jittery at having seen a face at the window of his house, fired his shotgun into the dusk. After such a frightening episode, the B.A.S.S.F.E.A.J.'s days were numbered.

> The Boy Auxiliaries received their death blow when Takashi, who had in some way learned of their existence, applied for admittance.
> "I don't see how we can let you in," Robbie explained kindly. "You see you're a Japanese, and we hate them."
> Takashi was almost in tears. "I was born here, the same as you," he cried. "I'm just as good American as you, ain't I?"
> Robbie thought hard. He didn't want to be cruel to Takashi. Then his brow cleared. "Say, do you speak Japanese?" he demanded.
> "Sure, pretty good."
> "Well, then you can be our interpreter and figure out secret messages."
> Takashi beamed with pleasure. "Sure I can," he cried enthusiastically. "And if you guys want, we'll spy on my old man."
> But the thing was broken. There was no one left to fight but Mr. Kato, and he was too nervous with his shotgun.

Formal scholarship never absorbed much of Steinbeck's interest. His career at Stanford was very much like Sandburg's at Lombard College. He took a few courses that were very important to him, eventually dropping out without obtaining a degree. Between stays in school he worked at jobs, usually manual, that kept him close to the land and the bases of the economy. He worked with a surveying crew on a road-building project near Big Sur, and as a bench chemist at the Spreckels Beet Sugar Factory in Salinas. He did odd jobs in small towns and bucked grain on ranches from San Francisco to Salinas. After he left Sanford for good in 1925 he worked as caretaker at an estate near Lake Tahoe, then at the fish hatchery in Tahoe City.

His major novels grew naturally out of his long-standing patterns of relationship to California. In the early 1930s he and his first wife, Carol Henning, lived in Pacific Grove, where notoriously conservative Republicans and Methodists coexisted with flamboyant *paisanos*. Steinbeck mingled with both extremes, absorbing material for a novel that he named after the pine-covered ridge in Monterey where *paisanos* lived in small frame houses: *Tortilla Flat*. Around the same time he met Ed Ricketts, proprietor of the Pacific Biological Laboratories on Monterey's Cannery Row. Ricketts became the prototype of Doc in *Cannery Row* and *Sweet Thursday*—the shrewd, reticent, patient biologist, "whose sympathy had no warp." Together he and Steinbeck ranged Monterey Bay and the Gulf of California collecting marine specimens and studying the life systems of marine animals. By extension, by analogy, Steinbeck related his knowledge of marine life systems to the human ecology. Meanwhile a drama was about to unfold in the western United States that no one was better equipped to comprehend than a native of California's food-producing regions like John Steinbeck.

Willa Cather's description of the Nebraska corn crop as "one of the great economic facts . . . like the wheat crop of Russia" was and is applicable to the fertile valleys of California, particularly since the development of refrigeration early in this century gave the farmers of that region a national market. As recently as 1972 the Salinas area was the scene of a confrontation between the United Farm Workers, led by Cesar Chavez, and the local growers' associations, with lettuce as the disputed commodity. How the stage was set for power struggles in this rich agricultural area is suggested by one of the subplots in *East of Eden:* the story of Adam Trask's attempt to open new markets by shipping lettuce east in refrigerated freight cars. Steinbeck wrote in *Journal of a Novel*, ". . . *refrigeration was the reason for the great change in the Valley. And out of that Valley came a large part of the pioneering which has changed the food supply of the world. And the crazy part of it is that the men who worked at it first all failed.*"

With the expansion of markets and profits came the danger that the profit motive would unbalance the system, whose proper workings, in Steinbeck's view, involved a balance between sound economics and the need of human beings for dignity. In the mid-1930s the balance was catastrophically upset when the droughts in the Great Plains sent thousands of people to California in search of work and food. In the summer of 1936 Steinbeck was living with migrant workers in camps around northern California, working on a series of articles called "The Harvest Gypsies" for the *San Francisco News*. He wrote a friend, ". . . *the labor situation is so tense just now that the* News *is scared and won't print the series. . . . There are riots in Salinas and killings in the streets of that dear little town where I was born.*" In 1937 Steinbeck followed a group of migrant workers headed west from Oklahoma, documenting their living conditions and the repression and brutality with which they were treated. By 1938 he was working on *The Grapes of Wrath* and continuing to follow developments in the migrant camps. In February he wrote a friend,

> *I must go over into the interior valleys. There are about five thou-*
> *sand families starving to death over there, not just hungry but ac-*
> *tually starving. The government is trying to feed them and get medi-*
> *cal attention to them with the fascist group of utilities and banks and*
> *huge growers sabotaging the thing all along the line. . . . Do you*
> *know what they're afraid of? They think if these people are allowed*
> *to live in camps with proper sanitary facilities, they will organize and*
> *that is the bugbear of the large landowner and the corporation*
> *farmer.*

Even heavy rains were calamities to undernourished people without shelter, as Steinbeck showed in the dramatic final chapters of *The Grapes of Wrath.* Later that February he wrote, "*Four thousand fam- ilies, drowned out of their tents, are really starving to death.*"

Steinbeck the biologist was furious that the proper order of things had been violated, that a peaceful, healthy, working ecology had been devilishly skewed. It is his sense of outrage that lends such power to this passage from *The Grapes of Wrath:*

> There is a failure here that topples all our success . . .

> The people come with nets to fish for potatoes in the river, but the
> guards hold them back; they come in rattling cars to get the dumped
> oranges, but the kerosene is sprayed. And they stand still and watch
> the potatoes float by, listen to the screaming pigs being killed in a
> ditch and covered with quicklime, watch the mountains of oranges
> slop down to a putrefying ooze; and in the eyes of the people there is
> the failure; and in the eyes of the hungry there is a growing wrath.

The Grapes of Wrath represented the culmination of Steinbeck's California experience. After a period of transition during the '40s, he settled permanently in New York. In 1951, when he was beginning *East of Eden,* Steinbeck wrote that the novel was for his sons, John and Thom. "*I shall tell them this story against the background of the county I grew up in and along the river I know and do not love very much. For I have discovered that there are other rivers.*"

This refusal to sentimentalize old places was consistent with his refusal to sentimentalize old times:

> Even while I protest the assembly-line production of our food, our
> songs, our language, and eventually our souls, I know that it was a
> rare home that baked good bread in the old days. Mother's cooking
> was with rare exceptions poor, that good unpasteurized milk touched
> only by flies and bits of manure crawled with bacteria, the healthy

old-time life was riddled with aches, sudden death from unknown causes, and that sweet local speech I mourn was the child of illiteracy and ignorance. It is the nature of a man as he grows older, a small bridge in time, to protest against change, particularly for the better.

But though there may have been other rivers, the opening chapter of *East of Eden,* with its impassioned description of the moody stream below the shaggy brown hills, the valley covered with lupine and poppies, gives an equivocal turn to Steinbeck's remark about not loving the Salinas very much. The voice in the novel is that of a man who never lost touch with his early years, when "there was no world beyond the mountains."

9 Willa Cather, the Prairie, and Red Cloud

Willa Cather at sixty-three. Cather Pioneer Memorial

A great change came into Willa Cather's life when, as a little girl of nine, she left behind the hills and meadows of her birthplace near Winchester, Virginia. The green of budding woods in spring, the winding creeks and waterfalls, the small valleys where horses grazed in neatly fenced pastures, the brick farmhouses whose classical architecture gave even the shabby ones a touch of stateliness—all this landscape full of domesticated detail was obliterated by days of overland travel to a new home in Nebraska.

By the time she and her family reached the Divide, a wide tableland near the Kansas-Nebraska border, the mountains and farms of northern Virginia were irrecoverable. The prairie stretched before her, empty and forbidding, immense and shaggy as a great beast. The vast silence of the land and sky extinguished her. But by the end of her first autumn in the new country, the land had taken hold of her. Among the long reaches of wine-colored grass, the sunflower-bordered roads, the river bluffs, the cottonwood trees shining like brass against blue skies "hard as enamel," she found the permanent home of her imagination.

For a year Willa lived out on the Divide in a farmhouse that belonged to her grandparents, the William Cathers, prototypes of the Burdens in *My Ántonia*. This house, which no longer exists, was built on two levels, with a basement kitchen entered from a ravine, like the Burden house. Grandmother Cather, like Grandmother Burden in the novel, carried a rattlesnake cane with a pointed tip whenever she walked to the garden. During these first seasons Willa, full of a child's fierce eagerness, absorbed the language of the land, its colors, its textures, its weathers.

In winter the landscape was monotonous, forbidding, starving to the eye and to the soul.

> The variegated fields are all one color now; the pastures, the stubble, the roads, the sky are the same leaden grey. The hedgerows and trees are scarcely perceptible against the bare earth, whose slaty hue they have taken on. The ground is frozen so hard that it bruises the foot to walk in the roads or in the ploughed fields. It is like an iron country, and the spirit is oppressed by its rigour and melancholy. One could easily believe that in the dead landscape the germs of life and fruitfulness were extinct forever.

Spring was a burst of light blown about the big sky.

> There were none of the signs of spring for which I used to watch in Virginia, no budding woods or blooming gardens. There was only— spring itself; the throb of it, the light restlesssness, the vital essence

of it everywhere; in the sky in the swift clouds, in the pale sunshine, and in the warm, high wind—rising suddenly, sinking suddenly, impulsive and playful like a big puppy that pawed you and then lay down to be petted. If I had been tossed down blindfold on that red prairie, I should have known that it was spring.

The prairie acclimated her to a new way of seeing; her eyes grew accustomed to great spaces and to the sparseness of focal points. "It was the scarcity of detail on that tawny landscape," she wrote in *My Ántonia,* "that made detail so precious." In the strict aesthetic economy of the prairie, each object—each tree or distant house—created its own field of force, and the artist in Willa was being trained to the selective use of detail.

The huge, lonely land peopled itself for her as she became acquainted with other homesteaders on the Divide. Like Sandburg with his milk route and Marjorie Kinnan Rawlings accompanying the census taker around Cross Creek, Willa got a peek inside the doors of her neighbors in Webster County by helping with a routine job: delivering the mail on horseback. Within a few hours' ride up the county were clusters of Bohemians, French Canadians, Germans, Danes, Norwegians, Swedes, many of them living in sod dugouts. Willa became, and never ceased to be, profoundly involved with these people and what they brought to the prairie.

They brought their troubles—poverty, illness, homesickness—and many American settlers, looking at the foreigners, saw only their miseries. The Americans, Willa wrote years later, "were kind neighbors— lent a hand to help a Swede when he was sick or in trouble." But few bothered to know the individuals, to distinguish between one overworked, poverty-stricken Czech or Swede and another, to realize that some of the newcomers had been people of refinement and distinction. As Jim Burden says in *My Ántonia,* "If I told my schoolmates that Lena Lingard's father was a clergyman, and much respected in Norway, they looked at me blankly. What did it matter? All foreigners were ignorant people who couldn't speak English."

In the homes of immigrants Willa saw hardship, and she saw dignity, courage, and resourcefulness. She saw the force of ritual and custom, from religious ceremonies to special ways of canning plums, in holding families together under stress. In its own way, habit was as much of a saving influence on the frontier as its opposite, flexibility, as Willa illustrated in this portrait of a Swedish woman in *O Pioneers!:* "Habit was very strong with Mrs. Bergson, and her unremitting efforts to repeat the routine of her old life among new surroundings had done a great deal to keep the family from disintegrating morally and getting careless in their ways. The Bergsons had a log house, for instance, only because Mrs. Bergson would not live in a sod house.''

Willa noticed the immigrants' Old World tricks of thrift and husbandry. She sampled the delicacies that came from their kitchens: fruits and preserves put up with mysterious spices, hot fragrant kolaches stuffed with plums or apricots. She saw the specially cherished objects they brought to America, like Mr. Shimerda's gun in *My Ántonia,* with the stag's head on its hammer. He had been given the gun in Czechoslovakia by '' 'a great man, very rich, like what you not got here; many fields, many forests, many big house.' '' Mrs. Shimerda had brought along another kind of treasure, savory dried mushrooms, ''gathered, probably, in some deep Bohemian forest. . . .''

In the fall of 1884 Willa and her family moved to the nearby town of Red Cloud, a division point on the route of the Burlington and Missouri Railroad. They rented an unpretentious frame house at Cedar Street and Third Avenue, which still looks very much the way Willa remembered it in *Song of the Lark:* ''. . . a low storey-and-a-half house, with a wing built on at the right and a kitchen addition at the

Willa Cather's childhood home at Third and Cedar streets, Red Cloud. The Cather family lived here from 1884 to 1904.

back, everything a little on the slant—roofs, windows, and doors."
The house was really too small for Willa's parents, her maternal grandmother, and the seven Cather children. But the Cathers lived in it until
1904, nine years after Willa had finished at the University of Nebraska
and moved to Pittsburgh. In "Old Mrs. Harris" she drew on her recollections of the interior of the house. Some of its rooms were small
and bare and perpetually covered with the jackets, toys, and other gear
of seven children. But the good taste and hospitality of the family asserted itself in the parlor. As seen through the eyes of a neighbor in the
story, ". . . the parlour was neat and comfortable—the children did
not strew things about there, apparently. The hard-coal burner threw
out a warm red glow. A faded, respectable Brussels carpet covered the
floor, an old-fashioned wooden clock ticked on the walnut bookcase.
There were a few easy chairs, and no hideous ornaments about."

In "The Best Years," written when she was forty-five, Willa recalled the children's quarters in the Cedar Street house, where she and
her brothers and sisters slept in a second-floor loft. Her imagination
transformed the loft into an elves' lair, a "baronial hall" out of
Grimm's Fairy Tales.

> Their upstairs was a long attic which ran the whole length of the
> house, from the front door downstairs to the kitchen at the back. Its
> great charm was that it was unlined. No plaster, no beaverboard lin-
> ing; just the roof shingles, supported by long, unplaned, splintery raf-
> ters that sloped from the sharp roof-peak down to the floor of the
> attic. . . .
>
> The roof shingles were old and had curled under hot summer suns. In
> a driving snowstorm the frozen flakes sifted in through all those little
> cracks, sprinkled the beds and the children, melted on their faces, in
> their hair! That was delightful. The rest of you was snug and warm
> under blankets and comforters, with a hot brick at one's feet. The
> wind howled outside; sometimes the white light from the snow and
> the half-strangled moon came in through the single end window. Each
> child had his own dream-adventure.

Like her heroines in "The Best Years" and *Song of the Lark,* Willa
eventually had a room of her own, in the north wing of the house under
the eaves. Its walls are still decorated with paper in the pattern described in *Song of the Lark,* "small red and brown roses on a yellowish
ground," which Willa paid for by working after school at Cook's Drug
Store.

After Willa Cather had become a novelist of wide reputation, she
wrote, "The ideas for all my novels have come from things that hap-

Willa Cather's attic room, with the original wallpaper that she paid for by working at Cook's Drug Store.

pened around Red Cloud when I was a child. I was all over the country then, on foot, on horseback and in our farm wagons. My nose went poking into nearly everything.'' Next door to the Cathers lived the Miner family—a Norwegian merchant and his wife, with several children—who became the prototypes for the Harlings in *My Ántonia*. The Miners owned a ranch southwest of Red Cloud, and Willa and the Miner children spent long days riding over the prairie and picnicking on the shores of the Republican River. Their hired girl, Annie, was the Ántonia of the novel. Ever since Willa had moved to Webster County she had heard the story of Annie, whose father, a refined elderly Czech, had killed himself during a period of despair with the alien prairie. Afterward Annie had drudged in the fields, side by side with her brother, to keep the family farm going. After she came to town to work, she paid her wages over to her brother for the support of her widowed mother and little sister.

Through the years Willa kept up with Annie. She knew when Annie left Red Cloud to marry a brakeman on the Burlington, and that she came home soon afterward, unmarried and expecting a baby. In time she married a young Czech named Pavelka, and they built up a farm like that of the Cuzaks in *My Ántonia,* rich with orchards and overrun with healthy, cheerful children. Outside the house was a fruit cave full of canned fruits and preserves, exactly like the one in the novel. The Pavelkas' neighbors, like the friends of the Rosickys in "Neighbour Rosicky," used to ask them why they didn't sell their choice, thick cream for profits to invest in more land. The Pavelkas always replied that color in the children's cheeks was more important than property or money in the bank, a sentiment that Willa immortalized in her story. The Pavelka farm buildings now belong to the Willa Cather Pioneer Memorial.

Among the leading citizens of Red Cloud in Willa's day was Silas Garber, former governor of Nebraska. In his army days Garber had been one of the founders of Red Cloud, and he had established the Farmers' and Merchants' Bank (now the headquarters of the Willa Cather Memorial). His wife Lyra, a diminutive woman of extraordinary charm, furnished the inspiration for *A Lost Lady,* as Willa confirmed after the novel was written: "*A Lost Lady* was a woman I loved very much in my childhood. Now the problem was to get her not like a standardized heroine in fiction, but as she really was, and not to care about anything else in the story except that one character. And there is nothing but that one portrait. Everything else is subordinate."

Like Marian Forrester in the novel, Mrs. Garber was from California. She was much younger than the governor, but devoted in her role as his wife and stepmother of his son. She visited often in Colorado,

Anna Pavelka's farmhouse with fruit cave. This was the prototype of the Cuzak farm in My Ántonia.

but when she was at home she frequently entertained young people from Red Cloud for her stepson's sake. Willa was among those who attended her parties and picnics, and her description of the landscape around the Garber home—the cottonwood grove, the creek where the bridge washed out in floodtime, the tree-lined avenue leading to the house—was true to the actual setting except that in reality box elders, not poplars, grew along the road to the house. Recalling Mrs. Garber, Willa often said, "Wasn't she a bright flash against a grey background, that lady?"

The bank failed and the Garbers lost their money, as the Forresters did in the story. The years that followed put Mrs. Garber under an increasing strain as she tried to nurse her failing husband. Her story ended very much like that of Willa's heroine. After a period of confusion following her husband's death and the loss of even more of their means, she went back to the West Coast, married another wealthy man, and was herself again.

Willa Cather's novel based on the portrait of Mrs. Garber was the only book she ever sold to Hollywood. Warner Brothers paid her $10,000 for it. At the Nebraska premiere of *A Lost Lady* in 1925, all the townspeople agreed that the film gave a recognizable and faithful representation of the Garbers, whom everyone knew to be the prototypes of the couple in the story. In the 1930s *A Lost Lady* was made into another movie, this time less true to the book. These were the days when it was becoming increasingly lucrative for major novelists to sell to Hollywood; Hemingway got $100,000 for *For Whom the Bell Tolls* in 1940. But Willa Cather was so upset about the second film version of *A Lost Lady* that, heedless of possible profits, she refused ever again to sell a story to Hollywood, and stipulated in her will that no work of hers could ever be sold for performance on the screen, on radio, on television, or through any medium yet to be developed.

Many of Willa's minor characters, as well as major figures like Marian Forrester, were drawn from people she knew in Red Cloud. Wick Cutter, the notorious moneylender of *My Ántonia,* was modeled on a man named Bentley who actually shot his wife, just prior to his own suicide, to keep her relatives from inheriting any of his money. The Cathers' hired girl, Margie, was the prototype of Mandy in "Old Mrs. Harris" and Mahailey in *Song of the Lark*. Professor Wunsch, the German musician in *Song of the Lark,* was Professor Schindelmeisser, Willa's piano teacher. Schindelmeisser found Willa a frustrating pupil because she was so much more interested in his tales of the splendors of the Continent than in her piano lessons. "Vat vill I do mit dat Villie

Cader?'' he would exclaim. "Her folks vants her to haf some music, but all she vants to do is sit on mine lap und ask qvestions!'' Finally her mother convinced him that the education Willa was getting from listening to his memories of European life and culture was more important than strict adherence to the lessons.

A near neighbor of the Cathers in Red Cloud was Mrs. Charles Wiener, a cultivated Frenchwoman whose husband was a local merchant. The Wieners, reproduced as the Rosens in "Old Mrs. Harris,'' realized that Willa's capacities were extraordinary, and they gave her the freedom of their house, with its fine pictures and excellent library. On warm afternoons when her own house seemed unbearably cramped and cluttered, Willa, like Vickie in "Old Mrs. Harris,'' would go over to bask in the shadowy silence and refinement of Mrs. Wiener's living room.

The influence of people like the Wieners grew in importance as Willa moved out of childhood and into young womanhood. As a high school student she began to feel oppressed by the limited social and cultural life of her hometown. Studying to be a doctor, signing herself "William Cather, M.D.,'' and vivisecting frogs in order to pursue her anatomical inquiries, she was bound to exhaust the tolerance of some of her fellow citizens. At one point in her life she went so far as to call Red Cloud "bitter'' and "dead.''

Rather than expressing a rational judgment about Red Cloud, or a reversal of her early affection for the town, such feelings were just symptomatic of the fact that she needed a more expansive environment and had to generate a certain amount of anger in order to separate herself from a place where so much of the intense feeling of childhood had been invested. Some of the emotional energy that she had poured into the prairie after the journey from Virginia years before, she had to take back in order to pursue her mature concerns, and irritation and claustrophobia were useful in the process. Not that her negative feelings about the town, expressed in their more reasonable form, didn't include some truth. Much later she admired Sinclair Lewis's *Main Street,* with its reflections on the pettiness of life in small towns. She evokes an atmosphere similar to that in Lewis's novel in this passage from *My Ántonia* about the homes of "Black Hawk'' (Red Cloud):

> The life that went on in them seemed to me to be made up of evasions and negations; shifts to save cooking, to save washing and cleaning, devices to propitiate the tongue of gossip. This guarded mode of existence was like living under a tyranny. People's speech, their voices,

On the prairie northwest of Red Cloud, the Dane Church, which was built by hardy Scandinavian settlers.

their very glances, became furtive and repressed. Every individual taste, every natural appetite, was bridled by caution. The people asleep in those houses, I thought, tried to live like the mice in their own kitchens; to make no noise, to leave no trace, to slip over the surface of things in the dark.

Only during a brief interval between graduation from the University of Nebraska and acceptance of a post as editor of the *Home Monthly* in Pittsburgh did Willa Cather have to struggle with the possibility of being stranded in Red Cloud. After Pittsburgh the setting of her life shifted permanently to the Eastern seaboard and Europe. She visited Red Cloud periodically until her mother died in 1931. After that she never went back. But her relationship with Nebraska endured in her correspondence with friends like Annie Pavelka and in her commitment to the prairie, and the human stories that were lived out upon it, as material for her art.

In 1921 Willa Cather, then forty-eight, said that the "years from eight to fifteen are the formative period in a writer's life, when he unconsciously gathers basic material. He may acquire a great many interesting and vivid impressions in his mature years . . . but his thematic material he acquires under fifteen years of age." What she herself internalized during those formative years was the struggle of human beings to nest in an alien land. In her novels the bare prairie is contrasted with something that is usually implied, suggested, remembered, rather than actually portrayed. That remembered something is the world of civilization and domesticated detail: the world of cities, of historic Eastern regions like Virginia, or of Europe. In the end the prairie is contrasted with itself. The old, barren plain that killed hardworking settlers is replaced by miles of generous corn and wheat land, with "all the human effort that had gone into it . . . coming back in long, sweeping lines of fertility." She emphasizes the universality of this vision in a remark from *My Ántonia* about Nebraska corn, which became "one of the great economic facts, like the wheat crop of Russia, which underlie the activities of all men, in peace or war."

But her vision didn't begin on the grand scale. It began inductively, in the particulars observed by the little girl who rode a bumpy wagon from the Burlington depot at Red Cloud to a new home in 1883. As a mature artist, she knew the story she had to tell, and the vast poise of her style, the control of innuendo as well as of statement, the satisfying sense of form without contrivance, are related to her profound acceptance of the material she recognized as rightfully hers. In her novels we see not only regionalism raised to the level of universality, but representation raised to the level of distinguished art. H. L. Mencken wrote of *My Ántonia* in *Prejudices: Third Series,* "It proves, once and for all time, that accurate representation is not, as the campus critics of Dreiser seem to think, inimical to beauty. It proves, on the contrary, that the most careful and penetrating representation is itself the source of a rare and wonderful beauty."

10 🏠

Mark Twain:
A Connecticut Yankee at Home

Mark Twain's home at 351 Farmington Avenue, Hartford, Connecticut:
filling out the spaces of his dream.

In 1868 Sam Clemens, Confederate army deserter, gold and silver prospector, riverboat pilot, and maverick newspaper correspondent, paid his first visit to Hartford, Connecticut. He succumbed instantly to the tree-lined respectability of Hartford, just as he had succumbed the year before to the charms of Miss Olivia Langdon of Elmira, New York, as depicted in the miniature carried by her brother. His growing public read this description of Hartford in the *Alta California:*

> I think this is the best built and the handsomest town I have ever seen. They call New England the land of steady habits, and I can see the evidence about me that it was not named amiss. . . . At the hospitable mansion at which I am a guest, I have to smoke surreptitiously when all are in bed, to save my reputation, and then draw suspicion upon the cat when the family detect the unfamiliar odor.
>
> They have the broadest, straightest streets in Hartford, that ever led a sinner to destruction, and the dwelling houses are the amplest in size, and the shapeliest, and have the most capacious ornamental grounds about them. This is the centre of Connecticut wealth. Hartford dollars have a place in half the great moneyed enterprises of the union. All those Phoenix and Charter Oak Insurance Companies, whose gorgeous chromo-lithographic show cards it has been my delight to study in far-away cities, are located here.

"To live in this style," he added in another letter to the *Alta,* "one must have his bank account of course."

Of course. But Clemens was no Nathaniel Hawthorne, courting the Muse while contemplating the rents in his dressing gown. At the age of thirty-three "Mark Twain" was already acclaimed as the author of "The Celebrated Jumping Frog of Calaveras County" and on his way to being able to command his own fees on the lecture circuit. He was shortly to become the wealthiest American author—that is, the wealthiest by virtue of his earnings as a writer and lecturer—in American history up to his time. In defense of his contention that writers should be guaranteed an equitable share in the proceeds from their work, he, like Longfellow and Emerson, joined in the battle for more stringent laws of international copyright that was carried on in this century by other world-renowned writers, such as Margaret Mitchell.

Before Clemens's day few authors had been able to support themselves at all by their writings, much less in a style that allowed for expansiveness, experiment, indulgence. The history of Mark Twain in Hartford is a history of warm family life and rich literary productivity; during this period his three daughters were born, and he wrote *The*

Gilded Age, Tom Sawyer, Huckleberry Finn, and *A Connecticut Yankee in King Arthur's Court.* But it is also a history of money, of a fortune made and lost, of grandiose prosperity followed by an appalling succession of disasters.

Things began promisingly. Sam and Olivia Clemens moved to Hartford in 1871 and took up residence at Nook Farm, a neighborhood inhabited by such accomplished people of letters as Harriet Beecher Stowe and Charles Dudley Warner. William Dean Howells, then editor of the *Atlantic Monthly,* and Thomas Bailey Aldrich, author of *The Story of a Bad Boy,* visited Nook Farm frequently. To some of the New England literati Mark Twain was an *enfant terrible,* with his Midwestern origins and his whopping tall tales, of which the story of his own life seemed the most egregious. In the Nook Farm community, though, he was immediately and warmly accepted. The early days in Hartford were marred by one tragic event, the death of the Clemenses' twenty-two-month-old son, Langdon. But though the parents grieved, they were young and conscious that their best years lay ahead.

In 1873 they bought a lot on Farmington Avenue, near the Stowe and Warner properties. They commissioned the architect Edward Tuckerman Potter to design a house for them—something different in design from the decorous foursquare houses of the period. Potter gave them the "English violet": an asymmetrical structure lavish with gables, chimneys, wooden trim, and geometrical borders of polychromatic brick. There were nineteen rooms, including a conservatory, a billiard room, and five bathrooms. Many of the upper rooms had balconies, which furnished charming views of the nearby hill and river and places for the master of the house to hide when the butler brought up the calling cards of unwelcome visitors. Clemens put the kitchen toward the street so that, as he said, the servants could watch the circus go by without having to run outside. The newly built house didn't fail to receive mention in the *Hartford Times* (March 23, 1874): "The novelty displayed in the architecture of the building, the oddity of its internal arrangements, and the fame of the owner will all conspire to make it a house of note for a long time to come."

It was, and is, a festive house. In the octagonal entrance hall the chandeliers hang like diamond pendants from the polished walnut rafters. In the library, under the mantel piece that Sam and Olivia imported from a castle in Scotland, a brass plate bears the inscription, "The ornament of a house is the friends that frequent it." When his children besieged him with demands for stories, Clemens gathered them in the library and improvised tales incorporating the bric-a-brac that decked its shelves. He always had to include each ornament in the

*The entrance hall at
the Mark Twain home,
with decor by Tiffany.*

same order, from the picture of the cat to the portrait of "Emmeline."
"These bric-à-bracs," he recalled in his *Autobiography,* "were never
allowed a peaceful day, a reposeful day, a restful Sabbath . . . they
knew no existence but a monotonous career of violence and blood-
shed." Off the library is the opulent mahogany-paneled guest room,
where Olivia spent weeks preparing for the extravaganza that was
Christmas. On the third floor is the billiard room, with cues, balls, and
pipes stenciled in red on the ceiling above the green-covered table.
There Clemens spent the late evenings with his cronies, telling stories
into the wee hours and knocking balls about with a crooked cue in a
haze of cigar smoke and fumes of hot Scotch. Clemens, who had a
lifelong fascination for gadgets, put in an intercom system so that the
girls could call George, the butler, from the farthest reaches of the third
story.

In 1881 the Clemenses hired Tiffany and Associated Artists to re-
decorate the first floor. Today the restored entrance hall is brilliant with
geometrical borders accented by walnut timbers converging in star patterns; the drawing room exudes a softer splendor, with its silver sten-

Mark Twain's billiard room and study. On the table, his crooked cue.

ciling on walls of pale salmon. The Mark Twain home is the only house decorated by Tiffany that is open to the public today. On the first floor one actually feels closer to Tiffany and to the "gilded age" than to the Mark Twain of Hannibal, the creator of Tom Sawyer and Huckleberry Finn. A reason is suggested by William Dean Howells's observation about Clemens: "He was never a man who cared anything about money except as a dream, and he wanted more and more of it to fill out the spaces of this dream."

Howells, Aldrich, George Washington Cable, Bret Harte, General William T. Sherman, the explorer H. M. Stanley who discovered Livingstone in Africa, Rudyard Kipling, and other illustrious guests visited the Clemenses in Hartford. Years later the Clemenses' maid, Katy Leary, recalled the dinner parties where family and visitors sat down to fillet of beef or canvasback duck, with sherry, claret, and champagne, and, for dessert, charlotte russe, Nesselrode pudding, or ice cream molded into flowers and cherubs. Afterward Clemens would play the piano in the drawing room and sing Negro spirituals or such favorites of the period as "In Days of Old When Knights Were Bold."

He regaled the company with spooky stories—an after-dinner classic was "The Golden Arm"—or jokes with a point.

> Minister, about to christen baby: "Well, it's a little mite of a thing, but it *may* be wonderful, it may grow up to be a great member of Parliament, it may be a great President. . . . And what is his name?"
> Mother: "Mary Ann."

The Clemenses' butler, George, had a habit of laughing loudly at dinner table repartee before anyone else had a chance to laugh. This disturbed Olivia for her guests' sake, and she was even more distressed by his incorrigible tendency to lie in a pinch, and by his inveterate gambling. Once George's crimes so exhausted Olivia's patience that she fired him. The next morning he reported for work as usual, claiming that he was indispensable to the Clemens household. And he was— at least to its master, who instantly rehired him.

By the time he settled in Hartford Clemens was, as William Dean Howells put it, "at the crest of the prosperity which enabled him to humor every whim or extravagance." He was so famous that letters addressed to "Mark Twain, Anywhere" reached him at the Farmington Avenue house. A consummate speaker, he nevertheless abhorred the lecture circuit and avoided it except when the income from it was absolutely necessary. After his marriage he went on few platform tours; a notable exception was the reading tour he took in 1884 with George Washington Cable, whose *Old Creole Days* and other New Orleans stories he admired. It was Cable who introduced him to Malory's *Morte d'Arthur,* which he read reverently and irreverently for the rest of his life, meanwhile deriving inspiration for the book that was to become *A Connecticut Yankee in King Arthur's Court.*

Clemens was never the man to let work interfere with his friendships or his romps with his three daughters. His favorite was Susy, the oldest, a brilliant girl who at the age of thirteen began writing a biography of her father. "He is," she wrote, "the loveliest man I ever saw or ever hope to see— and oh, so absent-minded." She continued, "He doesn't like to go to church at all, why I never understood, until just now, he told us the other day that he couldn't bear to hear any one talk but himself, but that he could listen to himself talk for hours without getting tired, of course he said this in joke, but I've no dought it was founded on truth." "If I am as transparent to other people as I was to Susy," her father wrote in his old age, "I have wasted much effort in this life."

The second daughter was Clara, a determined miss who at the age of six was convinced by the family's coachman that if she curried his calf every morning it would turn into a pony. For weeks each morning found Clara in the smelly barn, brushing and combing her pet, then walking it up and down Farmington Avenue in a brilliant green blanket made of a cast-off cover from her father's billiard table. The youngest of the girls was Jean, born in 1880. In his *Autobiography* Clemens recalled the days in the schoolroom when Susy and her friend Daisy Warner would act out plays based on the lives of queens, usually Elizabeth I and Mary Queen of Scots. Little Jean would always be given the same job: sitting at a desk and writing out death warrants.

The girls and their mother were Clemens's first audience and critics-in-chief when a new story was in the works. At home in Hartford, he wrote at a desk in his billiard room after the girls annexed his study for their schoolroom. Much of his writing was done at Quarry Farm near Elmira, New York, where the family spent the summers with Olivia's relatives. At a distance from the main house, which still stands, Clemens's sister-in-law, Susan Langdon Crane, had a study built for him. He described it to a neighbor in Hartford as ". . . the loveliest study you ever saw. It is octagonal, with a peaked roof, each face filled with a spacious window, and it sits perched in complete isolation on the top of an elevation that commands leagues of valley and city and retreating ranges of distant blue hills." There he wrote large portions of *Tom Sawyer, Huckleberry Finn,* and the children's favorite, *The Prince and the Pauper.* At Quarry Farm, or in the Hartford house, the family would gather around in the evenings and listen as he read them the day's harvest of manuscript. The library at the Hartford house was often the scene of elaborately staged theatricals acted by the Clemens and Warner children; one of the most memorable productions was *The Prince and the Pauper,* which they performed many times, using the conservatory as the palace garden.

It took Clemens seven years, off and on—mostly off—to write *Huckleberry Finn.* For that story, as for *Tom Sawyer,* he turned to autobiography, recollecting from a distance in time and space his childhood in Missouri. Tom Blankenship, son of the town drunkard of Hannibal, was the model for Huck. Clemens wrote in his *Autobiography:*

> In *Huckleberry Finn* I have drawn Tom Blankenship exactly as he was. He was ignorant, unwashed, insufficiently fed; but he had as good a heart as ever any boy had. . . . He was the only really independent person—boy or man—in the community, and by consequence he was tranquilly and continuously happy, and was envied by all the rest of us. . . . I heard, four years ago, that he was justice of the peace in a remote village in Montana, and was a good citizen and greatly respected.

Clemens himself was Tom Sawyer, and his mother was Aunt Polly, with modifications in both cases. Young Clemens really did feed Painkiller to the cat, and his brother Harry exposed him one day when he had gone swimming illegally and resewed his collar with black thread instead of white, as Sid exposed Tom in the book. There was an actual Injun Joe, and once he was trapped in the cave in the ridge between Hannibal and the river. But he didn't starve to death. He caught bats and ate them, and lived to tell his story to a curious young Sam Clemens. A boyhood home of Clemens, and other landmarks related to his novels, may still be seen in Hannibal today. Visitors may explore the cave in which Tom Sawyer and Becky were lost on the day of the fateful picnic. The terrain around Hannibal and the river at the foot of the town recreate the atmosphere of Clemens's novels, since his descriptions of the countryside were so realistic.

Too often stereotyped as a humorist, Mark Twain was a major figure in the rise of American realism. This was because, first, his fiction was built on factual material, on minimally transmuted autobiography. Secondly, it was because he tried to strip his writings of dogma, sentiment, and illusion. His European readers understood his fundamental seriousness better than his American audiences, who never seem to have dealt with the implications of such remarks as:

> Everything human is pathetic. The secret source of Humor itself is not joy but sorrow.

or

> There are many humorous things in the world; among them the belief of the white savage that he is less savage than the other savages.

Clemens had other business interests besides his writing. Like his Connecticut Yankee, he was permanently addicted to patents and inventions. He himself invented a vest buckle, a bed clamp, and a self-sticking scrapbook. He was the first to try out new contrivances of his day, like the phonograph and the typewriter. During the 1870s he invested in a steam generator, a steam pulley, a marine telegraph, and a watch company, and lost over $60,000. In the year 1881 alone he lost $40,000 in investments. He never could resist loaning money to an inventor or buying stock in a new gadget—except once. In 1877 he met a young fellow at the *Hartford Courant* office who urged him to buy stock in a new communication device. Clemens, still feeling burned from his last run of losses, declined. The man begged him to invest, and said he could have a whole hatful of stock for $500. Clemens sent him packing, congratulating himself on his refusal to sink money into another doubtful contraption: the telephone. No spoilsport, he later had a telephone line run from his house to the *Courant* office—the first telephone line in a private house in the world.

He never really learned to be on his guard. In 1884 he invested in a complicated automatic typesetting machine, the Paige compositor. Over eleven years he poured $190,000 into this colossus, which, he said, "would do everything that a human being could do except drink and swear and go on a strike." By 1891 his financial situation was ominous. The typesetter was draining money from the publishing company he had set up to market his books, and all in all his expenses were exceeding his income. Olivia bolstered the publishing company over a period of time with more than $60,000 of her own money, but as 1893 came on the approaching panic damaged the book market, forced the publishing company out of business, and threatened the Langdon family businesses that were the source of Olivia's capital. Everything went to smash in 1894, when the typesetter finally proved itself a failure even to Clemens. In 1891 the family had closed the Hartford house and gone to Europe in order to economize, fully expecting to return and take up their accustomed life after the storm was ridden out. Now their return was postponed indefinitely, and, as it proved, permanently.

The rest of Mark Twain's life was a race to the finish between good luck and bad, with time calling the race before happiness could regain its lead. Firm in their determination that his creditors must be paid a hundred cents on the dollar, though he could have got away with fifty, he and Olivia embarked on a lecture tour around the world in 1895. He was sixty and in poor health, and she had been a semi-invalid since her teens, but they completed the tour and by 1896 were well on the way to the solvency that they finally achieved in 1898. To a sympathetic American public all this made Mark Twain more of a hero than ever. But just as they were ready to sail home from the global tour, Susy, who had remained behind in the United States, fell ill suddenly and died of meningitis. She died in the mahogany room of the Hartford house, and Olivia would never enter the house again. Soon afterward Jean was discovered to be epileptic. In 1902 Olivia was bedridden with exhaustion and heart trouble, and the following year Clemens sold the Hartford home. In 1904 he lost Olivia, who had been his trusted editor as well as companion and *mère de famille* for thirty-four years—the woman to whom he once wrote, *"I am notorious, but you are great— that is the difference between us."* In 1909 Clara married and went to live in Europe. That same year, on Christmas Eve, Jean died.

Mark Twain was alone, an old man writing at a desk or dictating in the ornate Venetian bed with cherubs mounted on its posts that may be seen in the Hartford house today. He railed against the absurdity of life and the hopelessness of the damned human race; he grieved for his rich past.

> The spirits of the dead hallow a house for me. It was not so with other members of my family. Susy died in the house we built in Hartford. Mrs. Clemens would never enter it again. But it made the house dearer to me. I have entered it once since, when it was tenantless and silent and forlorn, but to me it was a holy place and beautiful. It seemed to me that the spirits of the dead were all about me and would speak to me and welcome me if they could: Livy and Susy and George and Henry Robinson and Charles Dudley Warner. . . . In fancy I could see them all again, I could call the children back and hear them romp again with George—that peerless black ex-slave and children's idol who came one day—a flitting stranger—to wash windows and stayed eighteen years.

But his public never abandoned him, and neither did his humor. During his last illness he composed a set of pointers for persons about to enter the pearly gates:

> Upon arrival do not speak to St. Peter until spoken to. It is not your place to begin.
> Do not begin any remark with "Say."

He had come into existence in 1835, the year of Halley's comet. In 1910, the year of its return, he left.

The story of the restoration of Mark Twain's Hartford home is a saga in itself. In 1903 the Clemenses sold the house to a private family and auctioned off the furniture. In 1917 it became a private school, in 1922 a warehouse; as the years passed, coat after coat of alien paint covered the Tiffany-stenciled walls. At one point it was converted into apartments. The original room divisions and configurations of walls were all but lost as new partitions were built and holes cut so pipes could be attached to plumbing fixtures and appliances. The house would have been torn down if the Friends of Hartford hadn't raised $150,000 to buy it in 1929. For a time afterward the building earned its keep by housing a branch of the Hartford Public Library. Hartford citizens were unwilling to abandon the house, but restoration promised to be formidably laborious and expensive.

It wasn't until 1955 that the board of trustees of the Mark Twain Memorial voted to begin restoring the home. They marshaled all known documents containing descriptive references to the house, stereopticon views of it in the Library of Congress, and information collected in interviews with contemporaries of the Clemenses, to reconstruct a detailed picture of the premises during the Clemenses' occupancy. Twenty years and more of detective work went into the tracing of Clemens family furniture through auction numbers so it could be repurchased and returned to the home. Within the building, layer after layer of paint had to be removed from the walls, and woodwork stripped away, to reveal the original wallpapers and finishes. It was a dramatic moment when the silver stencilings on the drawing room walls were discovered under seven coats of paint.

Each year some sixty thousand people visit the restored house, which contains a collection of rare Victoriana in addition to Clemens family property. Besides the furniture and other effects distributed throughout the rooms, the basement contains such unique objects as Mark Twain's high-wheel bicycle; an intricate model of a Mississippi steamboat that a burglar who stole the silver from Mark Twain's last home made while he was serving a ten-year sentence for the robbery; and a Paige typesetting machine, the enemy of Clemens's prosperity, now a harmless relic of nineteenth-century technology. Across a wide lawn from the Mark Twain Memorial is the Harriet Beecher Stowe house, which is also open to the public. These two houses are the only remains of the Nook Farm community, now reduced to an island of continuity with the past within a changing neighborhood of apartment buildings and small businesses.

11 🏠

Emerson in Concord

Ralph Waldo Emerson, by Mathew Brady. National Archives

Not many people today remember when every American home with any pretensions to bookishness boasted a shelf full of the works of Emerson. But the major liberal movements of this century—notably the civil rights and the antiwar movements—have fed on Emersonian thought like trees on an underground stream. Emerson's views on civil disobedience, essentially similar to Thoreau's, are clearly implied in his reaction to the Fugitive Slave Law, which required people who discovered the whereabouts of runaway slaves to return them to their owners. "This filthy enactment," Emerson wrote in his journal, "was made in the nineteenth century, by people who could read and write. I will not obey it, by God." In those words, and in Thoreau's "It is not desirable to cultivate a respect for the law, so much as for the right," there is the same radical individualism.

Other statements of Emerson's might have been written in the twentieth century, in reaction to the assembly line and the sterile collectivism of bureaucracy and corporation. The specialization of functions in society, he said, should not go so far that a laborer, lawyer, or scholar becomes a mere tool of his own trade and no longer a total person. In an era of creeping gray asphalt and gray flannel, his books still "smell of pine and resound with the hum of insects"; his rural imagery actually gains rather than loses from being carried over into an urban context. His thought is like his French alabaster clock, exquisitely antique and impeccably up-to-date, which still sits on its shelf in his dining room, keeping perfect time.

Still owned and maintained by the Emerson family, Emerson's house is a biography of the man. He lived in it for forty-seven years and died in the four-poster in the master bedroom in 1882. In the downstairs hall hang small portraits of his parents: his father, a Boston minister born of a long line of clergymen; his mother, who ran a lodging house to support her children and eventually put four sons through Harvard. His family was at times so poor that he and a brother had to share a winter coat. In her old age his mother lived with him; her favorite chair still sits in the downstairs guest room.

The parlor, and the bedroom above it, were built onto the house to accommodate Emerson's brother Charles and his bride. But before his wedding Charles died of tuberculosis, as another of Emerson's brothers had two years before. "Consumption" plagued Emerson himself for six years, until he was able to shake it off around the age of thirty. It also took his first wife, Ellen Tucker, in 1831.

In 1835 he moved into the house with his second bride, Lydia Jackson, and his mother. Lydia's portrait hangs near his over the stairway by the side entrance, and her small summer suit with shirred bodice is displayed in the master bedroom. In an alcove in that bedroom stands a superb Queen Anne highboy used by the Emersons. In a closet hangs one of the heavy blue house robes they wore in the winter, when the temperature of the bedroom was down to fifty degrees. On their washstand are two heavy silver pitchers, lined inside so water brought up by maids in the morning would stay warm. A curving window commands a view of the garden at the rear of the house, with its grape arbor, pear trees, and flower beds. Here Lydia, or Lidian—her husband changed her name to keep Bostonians from calling her "Lydiar"—sat to do her sewing, which she stored inside the window seat.

Emerson had no children during his first marriage. He and Lidian had four, all born in the downstairs bedroom that was ordinarily used as a guest room ("Pilgrim's Room"). Over a mantel in the master bedroom hangs a portrait of two little girls, their daughters, Ellen and Edith. Full-sized portraits of the daughters, painted in their adulthood, hang in the parlor. Ellen, named for Emerson's first wife, is shown as a dignified woman with a braided crown of bright golden hair and a serene face rather like her father's. After her parents died she became mistress of the house and lived there until her death in 1909.

A portrait of the Emersons' younger son, Edward, hangs in the downstairs hall. Their first child, Waldo, a sensitive boy whom Emerson adored, died of scarlatina at the age of five. Simple but deeply moving was the short letter Emerson wrote to notify Mary Moody Emerson, the aunt who was a second mother to him, of Waldo's death: *"My boy, my boy is gone."* The loss tried Emerson's faith in the healing processes of the human psyche, and added a dimension of personal pain to his meditations on the question of immortality.

As his son Edward observed many years later, Emerson's favorite study was the outdoors—the pastures, pine woods, and Walden Pond, which gave such a crystal-like ring when rocks were thrown on it in the winter that he called it the "ice-harp." When he did work at home, it was in a study next to the parlor, at a revolving round table with drawers in which he stored the journals that he called his "savings-bank." In one of the windows is an Aeolian harp he put there because he loved the strain of music it gave forth when the wind blew into the room.

Above the black Italian marble fireplace in the study is a painting, in tones of black and rose, of the Fates drawing out, measuring, and cutting the thread of human life. Today there is some difference of opinion as to who painted the original of this picture—Michelangelo or one of his apprentices. Emerson believed the work was Michelangelo's, and during a visit to Florence commissioned an artist friend to do a copy, which he

Emerson's study, with the picture of the Fates, and the round table in which he stored the journals he called his "savings bank."

hung in his study. The picture fascinated Emerson, no doubt because of his interest in the problems of fate and free will. His formulations of those issues were revolutionary to his American audiences because he moved the great questions about freedom out of a Calvinistic context and analyzed fate in nonmystical terms. He pointed out that much of what was called "fate" merely stemmed from "unpenetrated causes," and that so-called "acts of God"—for instance, typhus epidemics—could be averted, once their causes were understood, by such practical and even mundane means as good drainage. Mind, will, and the resistance of the human being to destructive forces, he reminded his hearers, were as much a part of fate as the destructive forces themselves.

Emerson's study and most of the rest of his house are lined with his books, placed in free-standing shelves so they could be thrown out, shelf by shelf, in case of fire (books at the Manse were stored the same way). Seeing the profusion of books with which Emerson surrounded

himself reminds one not to take out of context certain statements from
"The American Scholar":

> Books are the best of things, well used; abused, among the
> worst. . . . They are for nothing but to inspire. I had better never see
> a book than to be warped by its attraction clean out of my own orbit,
> and made a satellite instead of a system.

> Books are for the scholar's idle times. When he can read God directly,
> the hour is too precious to be wasted in other men's transcripts of
> their readings.

In the master bedroom hangs Emerson's black ministerial gown, a
reminder of his conflict about his vocation as a clergyman. That conflict was eventually settled by his leaving the Unitarian ministry. Emerson's attitude toward religious institutions was all of a piece with his
attitude toward political institutions; he renounced the authority that
stultified, and insisted on the right of the individual and the body politic
to experiment. Hence his pride in the United States as a nation with
"no castles, no cathedrals, and no kings." It seemed to him that commitment to any doctrinal system precluded freedom to change, to keep
up with the felt truths of the spirit: "A foolish consistency is the
hobgoblin of little minds. . . . Speak what you think now in hard
words and to-morrow speak what to-morrow thinks in hard words,
though it contradict everything you said today." By the time of his
second marriage Emerson was seeking the truth of his age in his own
way, feeding his ideas through his journals and into finished form in his
books and lectures.

Emerson was one of the pioneers in the development of public lec-
turing as a major medium in the nineteenth century. From the mid-
1830s until the 1870s he was one of the most sought-after lecturers in
American history. He lectured not only in Concord and other parts of
New England but all over the nation. His was a day when belief in the
power of ideas and of the spoken and written word to solve human
problems was very strong; witness the heights of oratory and the quan-
tities of literature inspired by the issue of Abolition. Emerson was,
incidentally, an early and eloquent Abolitionist. In his time the lecture
was replacing the church service for many hearers. Emerson was no
mere entertainer but a philosopher-soldier of the platform, braving bad
weather, bad food, long absences from home, and even actual danger
to lecture in nearly inaccessible parts of the newly developing Midwest. Once he had to escape with luggage in hand from a burning hotel;
three times he had to cross the frozen Mississippi on foot. But what he

had to say about education, about slavery, about the worth of the individual, in a context removed from religious doctrine, was news. The responses of his audiences seem to have been well summed up by James Russell Lowell, who spoke of Emerson as "the man who made us worth something for once in our lives."

He was so universally reverenced, even by those who were capable of satirizing the extreme fads of Transcendentalism, that to rehearse people's reactions to him would be monotonous if they had not been occasionally mixed with humor. A Concord lady, on her way to one of his lectures, was asked if she understood what he said. "Not a word," she replied, "but I like to go and see him stand up there and look as if he thought everyone was as good as he was." Wags parodied the incantatory opening lines of "Brahma"—

> If the red slayer thinks he slays,
>   Or if the slain think he is slain,
> They know not well the subtle ways
>   I keep, and pass, and turn again.

to

> If the gray tom-cat thinks he sings,
>   Or if the song think it be sung,
> He little knows who boot-jacks flings
>   How many bricks at him I've flung.

When Emerson, at seventy, had returned from a trip abroad that included a visit to Egypt, he wrote in his journal:

> Mrs. Helen Bell, it seems, was asked, "What do you think the Sphinx said to Mr. Emerson?" "Why," replied Mrs. Bell, "the Sphinx probably said to him, 'You're another.' "

It was once reported that Emerson's course of lectures during the winter of 1856–1857 was attended by "the *effete* of Boston."

Concord people seem to have felt a loyalty to him that was sometimes manifested in droll ways. Once a man who owned a lot that bordered on Emerson's property put up an ugly shed that spoiled the view. A bunch of boys came in the night with ropes and pulled the building down.

In 1872, Emerson's house partially burned. His fellow townsmen collected enough money to rebuild the house and to send Emerson abroad while the work was in progress (it was during that tour that he visited the Sphinx). The house as it stands today is a memorial not only to Emerson but to the Concord of his day, and to many other people, some remembered, some forgotten, in whose lives his was invested. Thoreau lived with the Emersons in their house for two years, and a souvenir from his visit still remains. In the front hall is a set of three small side chairs, all identical except that one has a drawer built in above the rung under the seat. Thoreau added the drawer because Emerson, when chided about being late for church, complained that he never could find his gloves in time for services. Rumor has it that the amiable renegade from the despotism of cathedrals didn't become much more punctual at church even after he started tucking his gloves in the drawer.

In a hall upstairs is a photograph of Tennyson, whom Emerson knew, and one of Emerson's friend Charles Sumner, the fervent Abolitionist senator who was once beaten senseless by a furious member of the proslavery faction in Congress. In the dining room is a photograph of Carlyle, a gift to Emerson from the author of *Sartor Resartus,* who once wrote to his friend in America, *". . . there is no voice in this world which is completely human to me . . . but your voice only."* Carlyle also gave Lidian Emerson, as a wedding gift, an engraving of Aurora ushering in the dawn, which now hangs in the parlor in the Emerson house. Emerson often invited May Alcott, the daughter of his friend Bronson Alcott and younger sister of Louisa May, to come to his house and spend time among the pictures and engravings there, since the Alcotts, always short of money, had few such amenities. A copy of the Aurora engraving, made by May, who was an artist, now hangs in Orchard House, one of the Alcotts' homes in Concord. In the study at the Emerson house is a small panel painting of asters and goldenrod done by May as a gift for Emerson.

Probably no literary figure in American history has ever provided more nurture for other aspiring and gifted people than Emerson. He superintended the publication of Carlyle's books in this country; he took time from his own work to promote the writings of Thoreau and Margaret Fuller. The appreciation of posterity for Bronson Alcott is due in large part to him, and he assisted Louisa May Alcott with her literary business dealings until she was sufficiently experienced to manage them for herself. It was Emerson who gave Whitman the only significant commendation he received when he published the first edition of *Leaves of Grass* in 1855. *"I greet you,"* wrote Emerson, *"at the beginning of a great career."* This endorsement, used without asking Emerson's permission, made an excellent advertisement for Whitman's second edition.

So deeply rooted was Emerson's life in Concord that in order to see all that remains of it, one must visit other homes than his own. At several periods of his life he lived in the old Emerson family home, the Manse. On the piano in the parlor at Orchard House sits a silver pitcher that he gave Anna Alcott as a wedding present. The house in which Thoreau was born, and the house in which he died, still stand in Concord. One certainly has not finished with Emerson in Concord without seeing Walden Pond, where a cairn now marks the site of the cabin built by Thoreau, that "self-appointed inspector of snow-storms and rain-storms." The furniture from Thoreau's Walden hut is now preserved at the Museum of the Concord Antiquarian Society.

Ralph Waldo Emerson House, Concord, built in 1828. Filled with eloquent memorabilia of his family, friends, and work, Emerson's home is his biography.

Next to the Manse is the North Bridge, where a monument commemorating the first battle of the Revolution was dedicated on July 4, 1837. At the ceremony the townspeople sang to the tune of the Doxology Emerson's "Concord Hymn":

> By the rude bridge that arched the flood,
> Their flag to April's breeze unfurled,
> Here once the embattled farmers stood
> And fired the shot heard round the world.

No cemetery in the nation can boast a more distinguished gathering of literary people than Concord's Sleepy Hollow. There, on Authors' Ridge, Emerson, his two wives, and many of his relations are buried just up a slight elevation from Thoreau and his family. A little farther away are the Alcotts and Nathaniel Hawthorne. In another part of Sleepy Hollow lies Daniel Chester French, the sculptor of the Minuteman in Lexington and the seated figure of Lincoln at Lincoln Memorial. As a boy French had his first sculpting lesson from May Alcott, and later made a bust of Emerson that is now at the Concord Library, while a copy is on display at the Emerson home.

The preservation of a literary community such as nineteenth-century Concord is unfortunately rare; it is the result of an unusual set of conditions. One is the long, continuous residence of authors and their families in a given area; another is the existence, within the community, of sufficient energy and means to preserve landmarks. Concord is large enough to have those resources, yet small enough to be relatively free from the forces that work against preservation in large cities. Partly because of his generous care for his literary friends in the village, and partly just because of his long connection with the town, Emerson is the ruling spirit of the historic Concord. In his life and thoughts, in his home and its contents, all the other lives meet.

12 🏠

Edgar Allan Poe:
Empty Shrines on the
Eastern Seaboard

Edgar Allan Poe, by Mathew Brady. National Archives

In search of an opportunity to establish the literary magazine of his dreams, Edgar Allan Poe haunted the eastern corridor of the nation, moving from city to city with his young wife; the mother-in-law whom one observer described as "a kind of universal providence for her strange children"; and Catterina, the cat, whom Poe's letters mention in almost human terms. Any household, no matter how poor, has its *lares* and *penates,* objects that reveal something of the habits and tastes of their owners. Of the Poes' personal property and home life we have only a few sketchy descriptions written by other people, and almost no concrete remains. Indeed the striking thing about Poe's homes is that they are so empty, not of period furnishings, and not of information and concern about the painful enigmas of his life, but of actual memorabilia of him and his family. This is not attributable to anything about the way the houses have been maintained, but rather to the conditions of Poe's life, particularly to his poverty.

Five of the major cities on the East Coast contain memorials to Poe, the most enshrined and the most elusive of American authors. A plaque in Boston commemorates his birth in that city in 1809. A cottage in the Bronx, a house in Philadelphia, and another in Baltimore are preserved as landmarks because he lived in them at various stages of his itinerant career. Each of these cities also has an active Poe Society. In his home city, Richmond, a Poe Museum is maintained in a diminutive stone house that, though never a residence of the poet, has its own claim to distinction as being the oldest building in the city and occupying a lot shown on a map of the area made by William Byrd. This museum houses a small collection of Poe's personal effects—only a handful, but more than any other house museum.

Many of the mementos in the Richmond museum relate to Poe's early life and family connections. It is well known that his parents were traveling actors, that they both died before he was three, and that he and his sister Rosalie were raised by prominent Richmond families, the Allans and the Mackenzies. What is less often mentioned is that Poe had a large and perfectly respectable set of relatives in Baltimore. The head of that family was the poet's paternal grandfather, David Poe, who had rendered distinguished service as a quartermaster-general with the rank of major during the Revolution, and was in later years treated as a personal friend by Lafayette. By the time Poe's mother died, his grandfather had already taken over the upbringing of her older son, Henry Poe, born in 1807. Correspondence between the Poe and Allan families shows that the Poes were concerned about the infant Edgar's welfare after his mother's death, but assumed that as a ward of the Allan family, he was in good hands. The Poe Museum in Rich-

*Poe House, 203 Amity
Street, Baltimore.*

mond contains furniture from the Allans' homes, none of which exist today. Also in the museum are portraits of the Allans, the only known photograph of Poe's sister Rosalie, and a portrait of Rosalie's foster mother, Jane Scott Mackenzie.

Thanks to the Allans, Poe had an excellent early education, including five years at schools in England. But John Allan never adopted him. After the year Poe spent at the University of Virginia at Charlottesville, where his room is still preserved as a memorial, he and Allan became permanently estranged. Poe enlisted in the army for a brief time, spent a few months at West Point, then settled in at Baltimore. By this time he had published two small volumes of poems and had decided on a literary career.

From 1832 to 1835 Poe lived on Amity Street in Baltimore with his aunt, Maria Poe Clemm, and her daughter Virginia, who in 1832 was ten years old, some thirteen years younger than Poe. Little is known of the details of life in the Amity Street house except that Mrs. Clemm was poor, and that Poe became deeply attached to her and to Virginia. When a wealthier member of the family offered to take them in and educate Virginia, Poe was desperate in his pleas that the two women make their home with him instead. From Richmond, where he had gone to work for the owner of the *Southern Literary Messenger,* he wrote to Virginia, *". . . think well before you break the heart of your cousin. Eddy."* In 1836 he and Virginia were married in Richmond.

The Poe Museum in Richmond houses a desk and chair from the offices of the *Southern Literary Messenger,* and a portrait of Thomas White, the owner of the magazine, who was Poe's employer. Poe's career in literary journalism began with his editorship of the *Messenger,* which gave him an outlet for his energy and talent as a critic. Within two years the magazine's circulation grew from 500 to 3,500. But here Poe first faced the fact that without capital an editor, however brilliant, was only an employee. When a magazine's circulation increased it was the investors, not the salaried personnel like Poe, who realized the gains. In addition Poe often had to accede to the wishes of his employers about what contributions should be accepted for the magazine, even when their tastes were admittedly inferior to his. These were major reasons for the series of dramatic journalistic triumphs followed quickly by ruptures with employers that marked Poe's career.

In 1838 Poe moved to Philadelphia, where he lived for six years. It was his longest residence in any city during his adult life. There he wrote several of the short masterpieces for which he is remembered today—"Ligeia," "The Fall of the House of Usher," "William Wilson"—and was paid about ten dollars apiece for them. There, too, he first produced his "tales of ratiocination," which gave rise to the modern detective story. Auguste Dupin, hero of Poe's "Murders in the Rue Morgue," was the prototype of such classic detectives as Sherlock Holmes, Chesterton's Father Brown, and Agatha Christie's Hercule Poireau. The *Philadelphia Dollar Newspaper* awarded Poe a prize of $100 for "The Gold Bug," whose popularity was proof of his genius for sizing up and meeting the demands of the reading public.

Poe once summed up his views on the state of American writing in a letter to James Russell Lowell: *"How dreadful is the present condition of our Literature! To what are things tending? We want two things, certainly:—an International Copy-Right Law, and a well-founded Monthly Journal, of sufficient ability, circulation, and character, to control, and so give tone to, our Letters."* While serving as editor, first of *Burton's Gentleman's Magazine* and later of *Graham's Magazine,* Poe strengthened his position as the leading critic of his time and developed plans for a journal of his own, to be called the *Penn Magazine.* But just as he had secured enough investors, the project fell apart because of bank failures in Philadelphia.

Poe's associations with Philadelphia were memorialized through

Poe's Fordham cottage, in his time a country retreat, now in the midst of the densely populated north Bronx.

the zeal of a noted Poe collector, Colonel Richard Gimbel. Not only did Colonel Gimbel search down and purchase letters, manuscripts, and first editions of Poe's works; he also bought a former home of the Poe family to house them. Located at 530 North Seventh Street, it was the residence of the Poes from 1843 to 1844, when they left Philadelphia for New York. In that house Poe wrote "The Gold Bug" and "The Black Cat." Ownership of the house is now in the process of being changed from the city of Philadelphia to the National Park Service, which will administer it as a national historic site.

Colonel Gimbel's collection of Poeana, which includes manuscripts of "Annabel Lee," "Murders in the Rue Morgue," and the only surviving manuscript of "The Raven," is now at the Philadelphia Free Library. "The Raven" was not written in Philadelphia, though literary Philadelphians cherish the notion that it was conceived there. Poe wrote it in New York, and got twenty dollars for it. Today that manuscript alone would be worth enough to have relieved the poet's chronic poverty. "The Raven" made the greatest sensation in Poe's career, topping even the success of "The Gold Bug." Afterward Poe wrote a friend that his *"bird"* had beaten his *"bug,"* *"all hollow."* But he also lamented, *". . . I am as poor now as ever I was in my life."*

Virginia was now ill with tuberculosis, and in New York Poe fought his despair over her deteriorating condition to put in fifteen hours a day as editor of the *Broadway Journal*. He continued to write his own poems and stories; among the products of this period are "The Purloined Letter" and "The Cask of Amontillado." When he became proprietor of the *Journal,* his dream of having his own magazine seemed on the brink of fulfillment. But capital failed, and his depression deepened. Meanwhile the Poes moved from one house to another in search of a situation that would be beneficial to Virginia.

In 1846 they moved to a cottage on a farm in Fordham, located in what is now a densely populated area at Kingsbridge and Grand Concourse. Poe used to take quiet country walks to get the view of the East River from over the hills and to talk with scholars at St. John's College, now Fordham University. From this time comes one of the few descriptions we have of the Poes at home, written by an intimate friend of the family, Mrs. Mary Gove:

> We found him, and his wife, and his wife's mother—who was his aunt—living in a little cottage at the top of a hill. There was an acre or two of greensward, fenced in about the house, as smooth as velvet and as clean as the best kept carpet. There were some grand old cherry trees in the yard, that threw a massive shade around them. The house had three rooms—a kitchen, a sitting-room, and a bed-chamber over the sitting-room. There was a piazza in front of the house that was a lovely place to sit in summer, with the shade of cherry-trees before it. There was no cultivation, no flowers—nothing but the smooth greensward and the majestic trees. . . .
>
> The cottage had an air of taste and gentility that must have been lent to it by the presence of its inmates. So neat, so poor, so unfurnished, and yet so charming a dwelling I never saw. The floor of the kitchen was white as wheaten flour. A table, a chair, and a little stove that it contained, seemed to furnish it perfectly. The sitting-room floor was laid with check matting; four chairs, a light stand, and a hanging bookshelf completed its furniture. There were pretty presentation copies of books on the little shelves, and the Brownings had posts of honour on the stand.

At Fordham Virginia's illness reached its crisis. Near the end she was nursed by Marie Louise Shew, who painted a miniature of Poe that is now at the Philadelphia Free Library. Mrs. Gove described the situation in the cottage as the year drew to its close:

In the Fordham cottage, the room and the bed in which Virginia died.

     The autumn came, and Mrs. Poe sank rapidly in consumption, and I saw her in her bed chamber. Everything here was so neat, so purely clean, so scant and poverty-stricken, that I saw the sufferer with such a heartache as the poor feel for the poor. There was no clothing on the bed, which was only straw, but a snow white spread and sheets. The weather was cold, and the sick lady had the dreadful chills that accompany the hectic fever of consumption. She lay on the straw bed, wrapped in her husband's great-coat, with a large tortoise-shell cat on her bosom. The wonderful cat seemed conscious of her great useful- ness. The coat and the cat were the sufferer's only means of warmth, except as her husband held her hands, and her mother her feet.

The very bed in which Virginia died early in 1847 was not the Poes', but was brought in by Mrs. Shew and Mrs. Gove. It is still in the tiny bedroom off the sitting room at the Poe cottage in Fordham. Next to nothing is known about the woman who married Poe when she was hardly more than a child except that she sang—Poe kept a piano for her when he could scarcely afford any other furniture—and was said to be a beauty and a loyal wife. Poe was evidently sincere when he wrote to her in 1846, "*. . . you are my greatest and only stimulus now to battle with this uncongenial, unsatisfactory and ungrateful life. . . .*"

    After her death he floundered, became involved in abortive court- ships with two other women, and produced some poems of merit, including "Eldorado" and "Annabel Lee." He once attempted suicide, and struggled with a host of nervous symptoms—anxiety, depression, paranoia—partly alcohol-induced, partly simply the result of stress. He went to Richmond, where success as a lecturer together with warm receptions from old acquaintances led him to form a plan to move there with his mother-in-law. But a few days after he had left Richmond to return north, he was found half-conscious on a sidewalk in Baltimore. He was recognized, taken to a hospital, and carefully tended, but died on October 7, 1849, of what one newspaper called "congestion of the brain."

Poe's trunk, which was not found for some time after he died, is now in the Poe Museum in Richmond, along with its few contents: a mirror and a jewelry box that had been Virginia's, and some button-hooks. There is, as well, Poe's walking stick. The poet was buried in the Presbyterian Cemetery, now the yard of Westminster Presbyterian Church, near his grandfather, the Revolutionary officer. A cousin, the same one who had nearly convinced Mrs. Clemm and Virginia to come and live with him years before, ordered a stone for Poe's grave, but it was broken on its way to the site. In 1875 a group of Baltimoreans erected a handsome monument in the front of the churchyard, had Poe's body moved from among the graves in the rear, and reburied Virginia and Mrs. Clemm along with Poe under the new stone. The dedication of this monument was attended by one writer of note, Walt Whitman.

Near the end of his own life Whitman spoke with feeling of Poe, whose work he had not always admired: "Poe was morbid, shadowy, lugubrious—he seemed to suggest dark nights, horrors, spectralities—I could not originally stomach him at all. But today I see more of him than that—much more." Whitman, who knew what it was to live near the bottom line financially, mused on the question of whether security may be better than poverty, even for artists:

> As a general rule it is true that we need something substantial at the foundation—all men—every man—but we can't set the same bounds for all men. There's Poe, for instance—poor Poe—to whose poverty, struggles, death at last in the gutter—sad, tragic, as it may seem—all his work, his quality, seems owing.

13

Edith Wharton "at Home": The Mount in Lenox, Massachusetts

The Mount, Lenox, Massachusetts, home of Edith Wharton.

In her autobiography, *A Backward Glance,* Edith Wharton wrote that even after she had become an acclaimed novelist, "none of my relations ever spoke to me of my books . . . the subject was avoided as though it were a kind of family disgrace, which might be condoned but could never be forgotten." Born Edith Jones, a descendant of the aristocratic "New York 400," she grew up in a milieu where a woman lived in her role as in a house of ornately carpeted and tapestried rooms. At any moment, in any room, the door might close, locking one away from freedom and the means of emotional survival.

In 1885, when she was twenty-three, Edith married Edward ("Teddy") Wharton, twelve years her senior, son of a prominent family of Boston bankers. Genial, gracious, a lover of sport and hospitality, literate but decidedly not intellectual, he was her devoted attendant, carrying a thousand-dollar bill around as mad money in case she should want something.

In the early years of her marriage, Edith was outwardly absorbed in the fashionable life she and Teddy led in New York and Newport. As one observer remarked, "she dressed, she furnished her house, she fed her guests, she laid out her garden, all better than anyone else." But by 1899 she was suffering from nervous symptoms caused by her demanding but trivial social routine, and by what she eventually identified as a lack of intellectual stimulation. In the early fall of that year, desperate to get out of Newport, she visited her mother-in-law's country home at Lenox, Massachusetts, in the Berkshires. Here she discovered historic small villages clustered around high-spired white churches between tiers of mountains, the deep green of hemlock forests on their slopes shading off into blue in the distances.

Besides exquisite scenery, this section of Massachusetts was and is rich with cultural and literary associations. In the mid-nineteenth century Longfellow and Holmes had resided there. Hawthorne had lived at Lenox in 1850 and 1851 and had named his *Tanglewood Tales* for the Tanglewood Estate, where the Boston Symphony concerts are now held in the summer. Arrowhead, from 1850 to 1863 the home of Herman Melville and now preserved by the Berkshire Historical Society, is some eight miles away at Pittsfield. Near Stockbridge is the Chesterwood Studio, at the turn of the century the summer home of the sculptor Daniel Chester French. When Edith began building a home at Lenox she consulted with French, who was well known as the creator of the Minuteman statues in Lexington and Concord and would later build the statue of Lincoln in the Lincoln Memorial.

In 1901 Edith purchased in her own name 113 acres of property in southwestern Lenox (a small part of her holding was actually located in the adjoining town of Lee). From a fairly broad elevation her land sloped downward for two miles through woods and fields to a large pond called Laurel Lake. At the top of the slope she and Teddy built what she later described as "a spacious and dignified house," modeled after Sir Christopher Wren's Belton House in Lincolnshire. The Whartons named their house "The Mount," after the Long Island home of Edith's great-grandfather, Ebenezer Stevens. It was sufficiently completed for them to move in at the end of September, 1902. As Edith put it in *A Backward Glance*, ". . . at last I escaped from watering-place trivialities to the real country. . . . The Mount was my first real home."

At the front of the house a small walled court formed an entranceway from which guests were ushered into a long gallery with a graceful barrel-arched ceiling. Typical of the artistic detail with which the house was finished was the marble bas-relief of a cherub over the door at the end of the gallery nearest the library. The gallery opened into the drawing room, where gilt mirrors and tapestries were set into large framed panels above marble fireplaces. Off one end of the drawing room was the dining room, similar in design but smaller. Off the other end was the library, its handsome dark paneling trimmed with carved garlands corresponding to those in the drawing room. Each of these three ground-floor rooms opened onto a wide terrace, with a majestic double staircase leading down to the gardens below.

Doorway leading from the gallery to the library at the Mount, with bas-relief and marble moldings.

The gardens no less than the house Edith meant to make her masterpiece. During 1903 she was engaged in writing *Italian Villas and Their Gardens,* and became enamored of the principle that gardens, like houses, should make use of enclosed space. Layering the slope below her house into steep terraces, creating intricate divisions with trees, hedges, and walls, complementing the ruggedness of stone walls and columns with the delicacy of early spring flowers, she fashioned gardens that could respond to every variation in the seasons, or in the moods of those who walked, read, or carried on tête-à-têtes there.

After wintering in New York or Europe, the Whartons generally arrived in Lenox early in the summer. They would remain through the colorful Berkshire autumns and long enough into the early winter to enjoy sleigh rides over the snow-sprinkled hills. At the Mount they entertained a continuous stream of visitors, many of them literary people, European as well as American. The most notable of their regular guests was Henry James, whom Edith's memoir reveals as a genius, a humorist, and an occasionally nervous, vulnerable human being. During long evenings on the terrace he would hold Edith and other listeners spellbound with his masterly reminiscences of an older New York, the families and the manners that regulated it, and their counterparts in French and English provincial towns. He had a gift for reading poetry aloud; he and Edith discovered that, somewhat surprisingly, they both revered Whitman as "the greatest of American poets." But James the purist couldn't resist a characteristically worded quip about Whitman's habit of pressing French words into service in *Leaves of Grass:* "Oh, yes, a genius; undoubtedly a very great genius! Only one cannot help deploring his too-extensive acquaintance with the foreign languages."

Extremely hot summer weather would reduce James to helpless prostration. *A Backward Glance* preserves a humorous picture of him laid up with an "electric fan clutched in his hand" and "a pile of sucked oranges at his elbow." At such times nothing could give him relief except a ride through the hills in the Whartons' automobile. "Motor-flights" were a favorite diversion at the Mount. The Whartons showed a real spirit of adventure as they raced around the Berkshires in the days when mountain roads were apt to prove too much for the far-from-perfected automobile engine. Edith recalled "penetrating the remoter parts of Massachusetts and New Hampshire . . . and coming back weary but laden with a new harvest of beauty, after sticking fast in ruts, having to push the car up hill, to rout out the village blacksmith for repairs, and suffer the jeers of horse-drawn travellers trotting gaily past us."

A favorite destination of the Whartons' automobile was Ashfield, where Charles Eliot Norton, then retired from the presidency of Har-

Walled garden with columns and fountain, the Mount.

vard, made his home. Norton held Edith and her work in the highest esteem, but after the publication of *The House of Mirth* in 1905 he admonished her that "no great work of the imagination was ever based on a tale of illicit passion"—an incredible remark from a Dante scholar. His statement seemed doubly ironic years later, when Edith had lived long enough to see her treatment of sex viewed as timid and reticent by a franker postwar generation.

No matter how full her house, or how crowded the afternoons might be with social engagements, drives, or gardening, Edith wrote every morning until eleven. To the rest of the household her work schedule was unobtrusive, but it was unvarying. During her years at the Mount she wrote *Italian Villas and Their Gardens, The House of Mirth,* and *The Fruit of the Tree,* began *The Custom of the Country,* and absorbed details of the Berkshire area that she transmuted into background material for *Summer* and *Ethan Frome*.

The story of Edith Wharton's life at the Mount is the story of a woman's determined effort to create herself—to bring herself to birth as an artist and a self-nurturing person. She was trained as rigidly as a thoroughbred animal to put tradition and good taste ahead of all forms of self-assertion, and was left to teach herself the art of survival. By the time she was in her forties—the period of her residence at the Mount—she had been considerably aided in her struggle by her talent and her inherited wealth, which was substantially greater than her husband's. Her nervous tone, a bit shaky in her thirties, improved in middle age, while Teddy began to develop alarming mental symptoms as he approached his sixties. By 1909 he was clearly manic-depressive, no longer competent to handle Edith's estate, and unable to deal with the fact that its management, which had been one of his chief functions for twenty-five years, was being taken away from him. Meanwhile Edith had become firmly rooted in Paris, where they had long spent a part of each year. In 1912, when her affairs were heading up toward divorce from Teddy and permanent residence in Paris, they sold the Mount to a Connecticut couple. On the eve of World War I Edith settled in Paris, and at the end of the war was decorated by the French government for her exertions on behalf of refugees. She resided in France until her death in 1937.

The later history of the Mount, as an instance of the preservation of a literary landmark, shows that substantial and aesthetically impressive buildings do not have an unmixed advantage over more modest ones. On the contrary, the expense of their maintenance may make them more likely candidates for the auction block and the wrecking ball, since, with the exception of the properties that belong to the states, the Department of the Interior, or the National Trust for Historic Presvation, most literary and historic landmarks in this country are maintained on shoestring budgets with volunteer labor. In their way, too, the Mount's changing fortunes serve as an index to changing times. Like the much more elaborate mansions at Newport, the Mount outlived the days when a lavishly hospitable domestic life was carried on in many quarters by people with the money to support it and the leisure to enjoy it. It weathered the Depression and served for thirty-five years—from 1941 to 1976—as a dormitory of the Foxhollow School for Girls. In 1976 a tight economy together with an apparent decline in the demand for the classic college-preparatory institution brought about the closing of Foxhollow School. The school's setting is now the property of a newly developing resort called the Center at Foxhollow. Because the Mount is a national historic landmark, the government contributes $10,000 a year toward its exterior maintenance. Even with that subsidy the resort, whose main building is on an adjoining ridge about a quarter of a mile away, has not yet been able to integrate the Mount as a profitable facility. It is now being leased to a theatrical company as a center for study and performances. Managers of the Center at Foxhollow plan to supervise the continued use of the Mount as a facility for cultural and artistic enterprises.

14 William Faulkner and Rowan Oak

Rowan Oak, William Faulkner's home near Oxford, Mississippi.
Faulkner lived from childhood in Lafayette County,
the "Yoknapatawpha" of his fiction.

Born male and single at early age in Mississippi. Quit school after
five years in seventh grade. Got job in Grandfather's bank and learned
medicinal value of his liquor. Grandfather thought janitor did it. Hard
on janitor. War came. Liked British uniform. Got commission
R.F.C., pilot. . . . Returned to Mississippi. Family got job: postmaster. Resigned by mutual agreement on part of two inspectors; accused
of throwing all incoming mail into garbage can. How disposed of out-
going mail never proved. Inspectors foiled. Had $700. Went to Eu-
rope. Met man named Sherwood Anderson. Said, "Why not write
novels? Maybe won't have to work." Did. *Soldiers' Pay.* Did. *Mosquitoes.* Did. *Sound and Fury.* Did. *Sanctuary,* out next year. Now
flying again. Age 32. Own and operate own typewriter.

In Oxford, Mississippi, where he had lived since he was five, they
called William Faulkner "Count No 'Count." Even Major Lem Old-
ham, who treated him like a son, and whose daughter Estelle had
marked him for her husband when he was six, refused his request to
marry her when he was twenty, believing that Bill, who had as yet
produced nothing but moody verses in imitation of the Symbolists,
would never amount to anything. Bill watched as Estelle was married
and carried off to Honolulu and Shanghai, where her husband pros-
pered as an attorney, while he himself became the most inept, trifling
postmaster the University of Mississippi ever had.

But all was not lost. On a sweltering June day in 1929 Faulkner,
thirty-one, drove his mother's Chevrolet to the courthouse in Oxford
to get a marriage license. Then he picked up Estelle, now divorced and
waiting in a wedding gown for the man she had offered to elope with in
1918. Irritably but incurably filial, he turned the car toward her father's
law office, climbed the stairs to ask once more for the paternal benediction, and was again met with anger but with a passive consent: they
were too old to be forbidden. Since the minister of Estelle's Episcopal
church had refused to marry a divorced woman, the ceremony was
performed by the Presbyterian minister, whose wife left off making jam
to stand up as witness with blackberry-stained arms. They loaded their
ready-made family into the car—Estelle had two children—and as her
five-year-old son shouted his jubilation that "Mama and Mr. Bill got
married," they drove to Pascagoula for a honeymoon belated by
eleven years.

A year later they bought the old Shegog place, a little less than a mile
from town on Old Taylor Road, where they had both played when they
were little. The white frame mansion with its stately pillared portico rose
like a mirage of the old South from behind a jungle of ancient magnolias.
A winding avenue of cedars teased the eye by obscuring the house so that
from no angle was an unobstructed view of it possible. "Colonel" Robert

Shegog, a wealthy Irishman, had built the house in the 1840s on a hilly tract of land owned earlier by a Chickasaw Indian. From her girlhood Estelle had heard the legend of Colonel Shegog's daughter Judith, who fell to her death from the front balcony as she attempted to elope with a Yankee lieutenant during the Civil War. Whenever notes sounded in the dead of night from Estelle's much-traveled piano, the children were sure it was Judith's ghost.

Meanwhile Faulkner drew on lore from another source to choose a name for his home. According to Sir J. G. Frazer's *The Golden Bough,* Scottish peasants placed branches of the rowan tree, a type of ash, over the thresholds of houses to keep out evil spirits and insure peace and security to the inhabitants. Hoping to appropriate a little of that beneficent magic, Faulkner named his homestead "Rowan Oak."

For the rest of his life Faulkner put his own labor and most of the money from his books into Rowan Oak. During the first summer he and a few helpers jacked up one section of the house after another and replaced the foundation beams. Then he painted, put in new screens and a new roof, and got the house ready for plumbing and wiring. Eventually he added the study where he worked on his masterful tales of Yoknapatawpha County: *As I Lay Dying, Light in August, Absalom, Absalom!,* the Snopes trilogy, and others.

Yoknapatawpha, the name of the mythical region in which Faulkner's characters played out their dramas of passion, avarice, cunning, and endurance, was the early name of the river southwest of Oxford in Lafayette County now called the Yocona, but designated on older maps as the Yocanapatafa. Oxford, the county seat of Lafayette County, corresponded roughly to the "Jefferson" of Faulkner's Yoknapatawpha. His fiction was more thoroughly transmuted from reality, less overtly representational, than that of Thomas Wolfe, whom he admired; the anatomy of Faulkner's home community cannot be traced in Jefferson and the Yoknapatawpha country, or the exact identity of its citizens in his characters, as Asheville and its people could in *Look Homeward, Angel.* But the human types and the passions of which Faulkner wove his fiction were there in the town and in its past: landholders of grandiose vision, grasping poor whites, half-breeds who could live neither in the black world nor in the white.

Exaggerating, playing on alternative possibilities and outcomes, Faulkner drew on real situations occasionally. He knew of a retiring spinster in Oxford who was courted by a Yankee named Barron, as Miss Emily Grierson was in "A Rose for Emily"; in real life the two were married and the outcome of their relationship in no way resembled the macabre denouement of Faulkner's story. An actual case in which a site in Lafayette County was dug up in a search for buried money is believed to be the prototype of the incident in *The Hamlet* in which Henry Armstid and V. K. Ratliff dig up the yard at the Old Frenchman place in search of a buried fortune. As a metropolitan area to play off against the smaller towns and rural settings of the Yoknapatawpha country, Faulkner used Memphis, where his characters went on occasional forays to gamble and carouse. "Miss Reba's" place, which figures in *Sanctuary* and *The Reivers,* was a real brothel on Mulberry Street in Memphis. On one of their visits to the city Estelle asked her husband to take her to see it. "It simply wouldn't be right," he protested. But when she insisted he took her to see the house and its madam, who fell all over herself to be cordial and respectable, exclaiming, "I'm so glad you come along with Bill, dearie."

At Rowan Oak Faulkner pursued the active hobbies he had engaged in since he was a boy, hobbies that furnished vivid background for such stories as "The Bear." He rode horseback—more recklessly as he grew older, some said—and went off alone or with other men on long hunts for deer, bear, fox, coon, and possum. In 1938 he bought Greenfield Farm, northeast of Oxford, where he grew cotton, corn, and hay, and raised cattle and mules. From his early years Faulkner had plenty of background for his fictional statement that a mule would work for ten years for the chance to kick its master once. The farm is still managed by a member of the Faulkner family.

The living room at Rowan Oak, with portraits of Faulkner (left) and his great-grandfather (right), prototype of John Sartoris.

For twenty years after he began writing novels, Faulkner was rewarded with critical acclaim but very little money. From the '30s through the middle '40s he was almost constantly strapped. Besides keeping up the payments on Rowan Oak, he had to provide for a large household. In addition to his wife and stepchildren, there were his old nurse, Caroline ("Aunt Callie") Barr; the children's nurse, Narcissus McEwen; and his yardman, Uncle Ned Barnett. His daughter Jill was born in 1933, and after his father's death he took on partial responsibility for his mother. He was trying perpetually to arrange for small loans from his chief publisher, Random House. His importunities were sometimes humorous and sometimes bitter, like this letter to Robert K. Haas of Random House:

> *Beginning at the age of thirty I, an artist, a sincere one and of the first class, who should be free even of his own economic responsibilities and with no moral conscience at all, began to become the sole, principal and partial support—food, shelter, heat, clothes, medicine, kotex, school fees, toilet paper, and picture shows—of my mother . . . [a] brother's widow and child, a wife of my own and two step children, my own child; I inherited my father's debts and his dependents, white and black without inheriting yet from anyone one inch of land or one stick of furniture or one cent of money. . . .*

To keep the sheriff away from Rowan Oak, he would go to work in Hollywood, writing and overhauling screenplays. He detested the work and was fidgety after a few weeks away from home. *"I dont like this damn place any better than I ever did,"* he would write. *"That is one comfort: at least I cant be any sicker tomorrow for Mississippi than I was yesterday."* Or again: *"I wish I was at home, still in the kitchen with my family around me and my hand full of Old Maid cards."*

But when financial security finally came, it came in large part from Hollywood. In 1948 MGM bought *Intruder in the Dust* for $50,000. Meanwhile the publication of *The Portable Faulkner* in 1946 had made a consolidated, coherent version of the Yoknapatawpha stories available to the public, and Faulkner began to reap financial returns as well as learned compliments. He and his family remained secure in their ownership of Rowan Oak, which his daughter Jill inherited after his death and leased to the University of Mississippi. In 1973 the university purchased the house and thirty-two acres.

Today Rowan Oak, though absolutely uncommercialized, is opened regularly to scholars and other visitors. Estelle's piano and a sofa and chairs that the Faulkners bought in New Orleans remain in the parlor. Decorative objects that Estelle collected in the Orient may be seen in the parlor and the dining room. The living room to the left of the entrance hall is lined with Faulkner's books. The Bible and Shakespeare are conspicuous, flanked by Dickens and Alexandre Dumas. Over the fireplace is a portrait of Faulkner painted by his mother. On the opposite wall hangs one of Faulkner's great-grandfather, Colonel William Falkner, a soldier, a railroad builder, and the author of a popular novel of 1881 called *The White Rose of Memphis*. Faulkner once wrote a friend that his great-grandfather was the prototype of John Sartoris. Off the living room is Faulkner's study, with the casually improvised combination desk and bookshelf at which he wrote his manuscripts in longhand. On a shelf are a bottle of horse liniment and an ashtray made of an artillery shell casing, which brings to mind the yarn Faulkner often told about having seen active duty with the RAF during World War I (he trained with the Royal Canadian Air Force, but was never in a battle).

The outline for *A Fable* that Faulkner wrote on the wall over the daybed in the study is still there. The study looks out on a stable built of logs chinked with clay, the oldest building on the premises. Behind the big house is the smokehouse, originally the kitchen, where the Faulkners cured their own bacon, ham, and sausage.

Traces of Faulkner may be found in other places around Oxford. After World War II, angry at the injustices experienced by black pilots in the war, he watched with sardonic humor as white supremacists in Lafayette County protested the inclusion of black soldiers' names on a plaque to be placed in the courthouse yard in memory of the war dead. The names of the seven local blacks who had died in combat were put on the plaque, though under the heading, "Of the Negro Race." The inscription on the plaque was written by Faulkner: "They held not theirs, but all men's liberty / This far from home, to this last sacrifice." And on the outer west wall of the library at the University of Mississippi is engraved an excerpt from the acceptance speech Faulkner gave when he was awarded the Nobel Prize for 1949: "I decline to accept the end of man. . . . I believe that man will not only endure, he will prevail."

15 🏠

Sinclair Lewis:
No Castles on Main Street

Sinclair Lewis at thirty (1915). Sinclair Lewis Foundation

Harry Sinclair Lewis was born in the village of Sauk Centre, Minnesota, population 2,807, in 1885. His birthplace was only some twenty years older than he. It had three or four blocks of storefronts, wooden sidewalks where there were sidewalks at all, and unpaved streets, like the streets of "Gopher Prairie," that covered pedestrians with dust in dry weather and mud in wet.

Like Hemingway, Lewis was the son of a physician to whom respectability was the cardinal virtue. The people of Sauk Centre set their clocks by the pendulum-like figure of Dr. Lewis walking from home to office at seven o'clock each morning. So important were time-consciousness and regularity to the doctor that he once knocked seventeen-year-old Harry down right in the front hallway for coming home after curfew, though it was a debating society meeting that had kept the boy out. The red-haired, blue-eyed mother whom Harry so closely resembled—her picture hangs in the parlor of the Lewis house today—died when he was six. He was raised from the age of seven by a friendly stepmother whose sensibilities were no match for his own, but who read to him "more than was the village custom."

As a grown man Sinclair Lewis once remarked that the only reason for his youthful discontent with his hometown was that it had no ruined castles. In 1931 he wrote a brief reminiscence called "The Long Arm of the Small Town" for the fiftieth anniversary issue of his high school yearbook. In it he recalled ". . . the fun which I had as a kid, swimming and fishing in Sauk Lake, or cruising its perilous depths on a raft (probably made of stolen logs), tramping out to Fairy Lake for a picnic, tramping ten miles on end, with a shotgun, in October; sliding on Hoboken Hill, stealing melons, or listening to the wonders of an elocutionist at the G.A.R. Hall. It was a good time, a good place, a good preparation for life."

In both the self-satirizing quip about the ruined castles and the graciously worded reminiscence for the yearbook, there is probably more gallantry (and perhaps defensiveness) than truth. Young Harry Lewis was no Tom Sawyer. He was too fidgety to enjoy fishing, and couldn't compete with his father and brothers in hunting quail, ducks, and rabbits. At the age of ten he ventured into a swimming hole with his older brother, Claude, and a gang of Claude's buddies. He nearly drowned. Claude had to pull him out of the water. As if that weren't enough, it was written up in the *Sauk Centre Avalanche* for all the town to read.

Harry again made the local paper when at thirteen he ran away to enlist as a drummer boy in the Spanish-American War. Leaving a note for his parents, he walked with fifty cents in his pocket to the town of Melrose, ten miles away, where he waited for an eastbound train. Dr.

Lewis found him there and they rode home in a buggy, the crestfallen boy and the irate father. Much later Lewis said, "The only people I ever wanted to impress were my father and brother Claude. I never succeeded."

When he was in his teens, love broke out in the boy like a disease—like a case of the acne that plagued him for years to come. The object of his affections was one Myra Hendryx, daughter of the editor of the *Sauk Centre Weekly Herald*. Of Myra he rhapsodized: "What a waist, what a head, what arms, what shoulders, and what legs!" And again, "She is dearer to me even than my books and God knows that they are very dear and near to me." Meanwhile at weekly dances and other social events it was his fate to see Myra's attention going to all the other fellows except "ole Doc Lewis's youngest boy, Harry."

His passions for Myra and for print sent him poking his nose into the *Herald* office when he was fifteen. To his duties as janitor and typesetter he added heroic visions of breaking a never-to-be-forgotten news story. From the second-floor bedroom that he shared with his brothers he saw lights flashing on and off at night in a cottonwood thicket called Stabler's Grove about two miles away. He debated as to whether it could be German spies or a ring of horse thieves, and concluded that it must be counterfeiters: "Now naturally you could capture criminals only by night. Who ever heard of closing in on Professor Moriarty on a prairie afternoon, with meadow larks piping? But at Doc Lewis's you went to bed before nine-thirty." But it came—the night when his father was out on a call and his stepmother at a membership committee meeting for the Eastern Star. He lit out for the grove. As he crouched among the cottonwood trees his trembling vigilance was rewarded by the sight of Farmer Stabler walking to his barn to bed his horses down for the night, the glare of his swinging lantern flashing signal-like among the tree trunks.

> Next morning, in the *Herald* office, Mr. Hendryx inquired, "Did you get any news about the Eastern Star membership from your mother this morning?"
>
> "Gee, I forgot to ask her."
>
> "That's all right. That's perfectly all right. Let me see, Harry. How much am I paying you now?"
>
> Wild expectations leaped in young hopeful. "Why, just now, you're paying me nothing a week."
>
> "Well, my boy, I'm afraid you aren't worth that much. You're fired, and I hope this will be only the first of many such journalistic triumphs."
>
> It was.

Through all these bruising and funny extracurricular fiascoes—the humor and the heartbreak of them would deepen as long as the man lived—he was a good student. He persuaded his father to send him to Yale instead of his own *alma mater,* the University of Minnesota. Lewis's Sauk Centre boyhood ended when he went to Yale, though for vacations he still came home to the plain white frame house at 812 Third Avenue where he had lived since he was four.

It was on one of those vacations, in the summer of 1905, that his first major novel, *Main Street,* was conceived. During that hot, dull summer he found himself accepted—indeed rather an important person, a "Yale man"—among the local young people who got up picnics, cruises, fudge-making parties, and summer flirtations. He realized, ironically, that the sense of belonging had come too late. He was no longer of Sauk Centre, if indeed he ever had been. He was bored and stifled. His parents were disgruntled when he suggested returning to New Haven early, so he stayed in Sauk Centre, holing up in the carriage house in his family's backyard, drinking and reading stacks of books. One of them, Hamlin Garland's *Main-Travelled*

Sinclair Lewis's boyhood home, 812 West Sinclair Lewis Avenue, Sauk Centre. Though his stepmother enjoyed his success, Lewis felt that his father disapproved of Main Street.

Main Street, Sauk Centre, Minnesota. Dr. Lewis's office was over the drugstore.

Roads, drew a hard realistic picture of life in the rural Midwest that reinforced Lewis's sense of Sauk Centre's "atmosphere of August heat and lack of sympathy."

Just as that atmosphere became almost unbearable he met a young lawyer, Charles Dorion, who had just moved to Sauk Centre to set up a practice. Lewis went walking and rowing with Dorion and joined him in arguing with the local pastors on behalf of socialism and other liberal heresies. Dorion left Sauk Centre after less than a year, but he gave Lewis a sense of the way such a person would react to a conservative village environment. Years later Lewis said that the idea for his novel *Main Street* first solidified, not around its heroine Carol Kennicott, but around the lawyer Guy Pollock, "who started practice in a prairie village and spiritually starved." In the *Sauk Centre Herald*, not long after the novel was published, he admitted that one character in the novel, "a young man," was "suggested by an actual person" who had left the village years before. This was Dorion, the prototype of Guy Pollock.

Into *Main Street* Lewis poured the details of his early life in Sauk Centre. His memory gave him the landscape: the wheat lands studded with lakes around the town; the prairie, like Willa Cather's prairie, thickly settled with Scandinavians who survived dirt poverty and the condescension of Americans to achieve a solid prosperity within a generation or two of their immigration. Observation of his father the doctor taught him the ins and outs of a country medical practice. He once assisted his father, as Carol Kennicott assisted her husband, with an operation in which the patient had to be given ether instead of the preferred anesthetic, chloroform. The doctor worked by the light of a lantern that might have caused the ether fumes to explode at any minute.

As a child, Lewis had sometimes hung about his stepmother's parlor listening to the deliberations of the Gradatim Club, a local women's club that engaged in community improvement projects. Mrs. Lewis was one of the guiding spirits of this club, which was named after a poem written by J. G. Holland, a friend of Emily Dickinson's. The message of the poem was that we rise to heaven by stages. In the novel Lewis created a women's club, the Thanatopsis—also named after a famous poem—that sponsored projects exactly like those initiated by the Gradatim. Both were responsible for beautification projects and fly exterminating campaigns. Both ran a public rest room for wives and children of farmers in town for a day on business.

Sauk Centre became "Gopher Prairie," whose Main Street, as Lewis put it in his introduction to the novel, "is the continuation of Main Streets everywhere. The story would be the same in Ohio or Montana, in Kansas or Kentucky or Illinois. . . ." *Main Street,* published in 1920, made Lewis famous overnight. Like Sherwood Anderson's *Winesburg, Ohio* (1919), and Edgar Lee Masters's *Spoon River Anthology* (1915), it challenged the myth that small towns were citadels of honesty, good fellowship, and the wholesome virtues. Lewis's Gopher Prairie had some of those virtues. There was a middling average of honesty, industry, and neighborliness. But he exposed the conflicts under the surface—the way local businessmen undercut each other, the vicious gossip that could drive aspiring newcomers out of town, the informal conspiracy to keep servants at subsistence wages and to charge farmers steeply for the services of the town, the startlingly effective hostility that ordinarily decent people could muster if progressive ideas seemed to threaten their interests, the utter indifference to aesthetics. More than all these things, Lewis attacked, and attacked most effectively by mimicking as only a native could do, the complacency of Main Street, which amounted to a kind of quasi-religious faith. "Main Street," he declaimed with tongue in cheek, "is the climax of civilization. That this Ford car might stand in front of the Bon Ton Store, Hannibal invaded Rome and Erasmus wrote in Oxford cloisters. . . ."

The initial reaction of Sauk Centre to the novel was rather like that of Asheville, North Carolina, to Wolfe's *Look Homeward, Angel.* The citizens were shocked and hurt, torn between a wish to be identified with the towering success of the novel and the novelist and mortification at the image of the town that the book presented. But within two years, while other towns around the nation were changing the names of their Main Streets to avoid the negative connotations created by the book, Sauk Centre had proudly renamed its central thoroughfare "The Original Main Street." Third Avenue, where Lewis's boyhood home stands across the street from his birthplace, is now Sinclair Lewis Avenue. The original furnishings in the Lewis boyhood home are few but significant, chiefly as reminders of the differences between the novelist and his father. Lewis felt proud in 1905 when the house got a bathroom, but the doctor continued to take baths in his bedroom. In the downstairs back room where Dr. Lewis saw patients before he rented an office downtown across the street from the Palmer House Hotel is a crystal radio set that his son gave him in 1920, the year *Main Street* was published. Dr. Lewis didn't like the book.

During his lifetime Lewis knew his hometown's rejection, then its acceptance and its admiration. Before she died his stepmother expressed her satisfaction at what her temperamental son had made of himself. But he was never to experience that fundamental sense of approval from his father.

> My father has never forgiven me for *Main Street*. . . . *Main Street* condemned me in his eyes as a traitor to my heritage—whereas the truth is, I shall never shed the little, indelible "Sauk-centricities" that enabled me to write it. . . .

Today Lewis lies in Sauk Centre. With him are buried his unresolved ambivalences, his poses, self-deprecations, and reserves, all of which deepen the essential enigma of what Main Street meant to him.

16 🏠

Laura Ingalls Wilder:
The House at the End of the Road

Rocky Ridge Farm, home of Laura and Almanzo Wilder.

A covered wagon bumping across the prairie with two sunbonneted little faces peeping out the back; the strains of a fiddle under the stars where the wagon halts; these are the images that have given millions of children their first sense of pioneer life since 1932, when Laura Ingalls Wilder published the first of her "Little House" books. *Little House in the Big Woods* was written when its author was a mature woman of sixty-three. Nostalgia, reconciliation, and a disarming simplicity are the hallmarks of its style.

Laura Ingalls Wilder, Hamlin Garland, Willa Cather, and Sinclair Lewis all grew up on the Midwestern prairies, in the raw new post–Civil War settlement towns or on farms near them. Garland, born in 1860, was only seven years older than Laura. The routes taken by the Garland and Ingalls families while the two future authors were growing up actually crossed, for both lived briefly in the Iowa settlement of Burr Oak, which figures in Garland's *A Son of the Middle Border*. Garland, with his bitter directness; Cather, with her evocative nostalgia; and Lewis, with his gadfly ambivalence and satire, provided adult readers with a range of perspectives on the prairie and on the pioneers, whom all of these very divergent authors respected as a disappearing breed of large-souled people.

Wilder's stories for younger readers present, on the surface, relatively simple conflicts, no irony, nothing of the exposé. But though the tone, attitude, and level of presentation of her stories are different, the times, places, and conditions are essentially similar to those in Garland's work. Both could describe the beauty of the pristine, undeveloped prairie. Both convey a sense of the epiphany-like experience a child could have spending hours alone among the blowing grasses under a sky filled with the songs of meadowlarks. But both were also acquainted with the drudgery of farm work, the heat, droughts, and grasshoppers that attacked the prairies like the plagues of Egypt, the isolation of pioneer homes, the devastating emotional effects of continuous moving, the scarcity of time and money for intellectual pleasures.

It is still possible to follow the route of the Ingalls family and to see many of the places that were home to Ma and Pa and the girls. A plaque marks the site of the Little House in the Big Woods near Pepin, Wisconsin. The dugout that sheltered the Ingallses on the banks of Plum Creek, near Walnut Grove, Minnesota, is still there. Laura's parents and her three sisters are buried in the cemetery at De Smet, South Dakota, where the Ingalls family settled after its journeyings.

It was in De Smet that Laura came of age and married Almanzo Wilder. Almanzo was a vigorous young homesteader who had a certain

Left to right: Carrie, Mary, and Laura Ingalls in De Smet, South Dakota, in 1881. Laura was fourteen. Wilder Home and Museum

reputation for heroism around De Smet because, during one especially brutal winter, he had helped to save the town from starvation. With a friend he had ventured out across the ice-covered prairie and found a settler with some wheat to spare. Farming was in Almanzo's blood, as homesteading had been in that of Laura's father. Laura wasn't sure she wanted to be a farmer's wife, since farmers worked their fingers to the bone and never made any money. But she married Almanzo and went to live on the claim north of town where he raised wheat, timber, and livestock.

During the first four years of their married life, she and Almanzo had every kind of bad luck in the book. "Everything evens out," Almanzo used to say. "The rich man gets his ice in the summer, the poor man gets his in the winter." The proverb turned into a grim joke when a summer hailstorm wiped out their first wheat crop. The next year's crop was passable but didn't bring enough extra money to pay off notes on farm machinery and a mortgage on the house. They caught diphtheria. Almanzo, forcing himself to work before he was sufficiently recovered, had a stroke that impaired his vigor for the rest of his life. Their first baby, Rose, was healthy and pretty and smart. Their second child, a boy, died when he was twelve days old. Two weeks later their house burned down. Since the cold winters were hard on Almanzo, they decided on a radical change. They traveled far south and settled in the tiny community of Westville, on the panhandle of Florida. But the humidity didn't agree with Laura, and after two years they went home to De Smet.

They worked and waited, saving what they could from Laura's earnings as a dressmaker's assistant and the pay Almanzo collected from doing odd jobs around town. They also had a secret hoard: $100 they got by selling a flock of sheep that Laura had bought with money she made from selling the colt she had bought with money she earned by teaching before she got married. They had seen pictures of a town named Mansfield in Missouri, the "Land of the Big Red Apple," a country with beautiful blue grass, cool clear water, and abundant trees, where the poor man didn't get so much ice in the winter.

In 1894 Laura, Almanzo, and Rose said good-bye to Ma and Pa and the rest of the family and set out for Missouri in a black wagon with an oilcloth top and curtains. In company with another couple, a Mr. and Mrs. Cooley, they traveled south to Nebraska, their experienced farmers' eyes assessing the quality of crops, soil, and water. On the way to Lincoln Laura wrote, "The oats and wheat are good here and the corn does not look bad but of course it needs rain so people are blue and cross and stingy." Laura didn't like Nebraska, didn't like the look of the farms or the countryside.

They saw colonies of foreign settlers like those described by Willa Cather. They passed through a Russian settlement, where the people, who could speak only a few words of English, pressed them to accept milk and biscuits. In Stanton, Nebraska, there were so many Germans that, as Laura noted, there were "German signs on the stores and German texts on the churches."

When there were no roads, they followed railroad tracks or telegraph wires. They traveled in a straight line south from Lincoln to Beatrice, Nebraska, and crossed over into Kansas some one hundred miles east of Red Cloud. On the way to Topeka Laura wrote, "It is *terribly* dusty. We breathe dust all day and everything is covered with it." From Topeka they traveled southeast in an uneven line, crossing the border into Missouri near Fort Scott, and making their way toward Springfield. Laura wrote, "Parts of Nebraska and Kansas are well enough but Missouri is simply glorious." She saw grassy hills above fertile bottomlands, woods of oak, hickory, and walnut, and plums, persimmons, and blackberries beside the stony roads—"a lavishness of fruit growing wild."

After six weeks on the road they came to Mansfield, full of the hope of finding a home after the discouragements of the past nine years. They made camp in the woods near Mansfield and for days Almanzo

The living room at Rocky Ridge Farm. The fireplace is made of native stone, the rafters of oak from the Wilders' woods.

scoured the countryside, looking for the right farm at the right price. One day he and Laura left Rose with the Cooleys and went out together. They came back full of excitement. They had found a place on a hill, forty acres, with a log house and a spring and 400 little apple trees that needed to be planted. That afternoon they had to meet the banker and sign the papers. Laura did up her hair and put on her best black dress, her wedding dress. She opened the polished wooden lap desk that Almanzo had made for her, where she had carefully tucked the precious hundred-dollar bill.

The money was gone.

It was several days before they found the bill, in a crack in the desk. They hurried back to the bank and bought the farm. That was Rocky Ridge Farm, Laura's home for sixty-three years. Eventually the forty acres grew into 200. After the first year Almanzo built a two-room frame dwelling that became the kitchen of the large, comfortable house they created over the next twenty years. Today the house is full of the Wilders' handiwork and the materials they took from the earth around them to do the building. In the parlor, for instance, the timbers are hewn from oak trees on the farm, the fireplace is made of stones from the property, and the rugs from the skins of the Wilders' own goats.

Much of the furniture was made by Almanzo, who couldn't look at a forked tree without seeing a table or lamp base in his mind's eye.

On their farm Laura and Almanzo raised wheat, corn, oats, cattle, hogs, and sheep. Almanzo bred Morgan horses, and Laura's leghorn chickens were famous. Her first writing experience came about because of the leghorns. She was often invited to speak at meetings in the area, and once a paper that she wrote came to the attention of an editor of the *Missouri Ruralist*. Laura became head of the *Ruralist*'s household department, and later poultry editor for the *St. Louis Star*. Meanwhile Rose grew up, went into journalism, and became a foreign correspondent during World War I. She was, in fact, a famous writer long before her mother, and it was partly at Rose's instigation that Laura began writing the "Little House" books when she was in her sixties.

Rocky Ridge farmhouse and the museum next door are full of beautiful things made by Laura, who, long before she ever thought of herself as a writer, nourished her imagination with the work of her hands. In the museum is a "Sunbonnet Girl" quilt that she designed and made; the pattern is women's faces, varied, coquettish, arresting. A dress of Hawaiian piña cloth and another of white Persian lawn, both made by Laura, also exemplify her gifts as a craftswoman. The exhibits in the museum are well laid out for younger viewers, for they are displayed in cases so as to be seen easily without having to be handled, and the labels and notations are extraordinarily clear.

Most memorable of all to devotees of Laura's books are mementos of the Wilder and Ingalls families. Among the Ingalls furniture in the house is the organ that Laura's sister Mary played at the home in De Smet after she was blind. In the museum is the glass bread plate with the motto, "Give us this day our daily bread," that was saved when Laura and Almanzo's house burned on the claim in De Smet. There too is the lap desk where the precious hundred-dollar bill was lost and found again. Now resting silently in its glass case is Pa's fiddle, the symbol, for Laura, of all wanderings and homecomings.

17 Walt Whitman and the Mickle Street House

Walt Whitman, by Mathew Brady. National Archives

The interior of Walt Whitman's unpretentious row house on Mickle Street in Camden is bountifully adorned with photographs of the poet, whose picture photographers delighted to take. Most are variations on the familiar image: loose coat, shirt open at the neck, bare head or broad-brimmed hat, free-flowing hair and beard. But one is different, out of key with the others and with the surroundings: with the plain house in the row of dwellings straggling down toward the Delaware River, with the legend of the crippled old poet carrying a knapsack or market basket, hawking *Leaves of Grass* around Camden and Philadelphia.

The odd photograph is an oval daguerreotype of a young man, his expression urbane and slightly aloof, one cheek resting on a graceful hand while an almost dandified wave of hair hangs above the right eye. He is dressed with conventional elegance in a dark coat, vest, and tie. This was Whitman in his late twenties or early thirties, probably when he was editor of the *Brooklyn Eagle*. The picture is rich with suggestions as to the nature of Whitman's options in life—with negative suggestions, because it seems to represent what was rejected but possible among his potential identities. Whitman's conversations with Horace Traubel, who first met the poet as a little boy on the streets of Camden and grew up to become his Boswell, reveal his sophistication and urbanity, the breadth of his acquaintance with people and with issues. Had it been worthwhile to him, Whitman could have played the game, and would no doubt have come in for his share of social and professional success in the literary milieu of his day. As it was, he retained permanently one taste from his youth: a love of the opera, unexpected in one so avowedly intolerant of "upholstery," convention, and artifice. But around 1855, when he was thirty-six and had just published the first edition of *Leaves of Grass,* he started down a road of commitment to individualism, to proletarianism, that finally led to Mickle Street. With that course of action and its results he seems to have been, right up to the end, supremely content.

Whitman came to Camden in 1873, after he had been stricken with paralysis in one leg. He wanted to be near his mother, who was terminally ill at the home of his brother George in Camden. After she died Whitman remained at his brother's, confined to one room a good deal of the time because of his leg. Later he moved with his brother and sister-in-law to another house on Stevens Street. Then, as now, Camden was an industrial town, muddy in wet weather, dusty in dry, full of the noise of street, river, and railroad traffic.

When Whitman was able to move about, he roamed the streets, striking up acquaintances with newsboys, horse car drivers, vendors,

The Walt Whitman home at 330 Mickle Street, Camden: "a little wooden house of two stories near the Delaware River . . ."

and anyone else who would talk to him, including boys like Horace Traubel. To some he was just an aging eccentric—a "gasbag," one policeman called him. To others he was a kind of saint. He particularly enjoyed taking the ferries to Philadelphia, finding objects of contemplation in the gulls and the ships, which he called "floating poems." Through a lawyer friend he got free passes on the ferries. He became a familiar figure on the boats and on the streets of Philadelphia—Market, Broad, Chestnut. When his brother moved his family to Burlington in 1884, Whitman refused to go, though his brother and sister-in-law were determined to take him. With $1,250 from royalties and $500 borrowed from a wealthy friend, he bought a two-story home on Mickle Street, in a working-class neighborhood just two blocks from the ferry stop.

The new house—the only home Whitman ever owned—came complete with tenants, a Mr. and Mrs. Lay, who agreed to board their new landlord in return for a reduction in their rent. But they soon moved out, perhaps because Whitman was incorrigibly irregular in his eating habits. Whitman, who had no furniture except one broad-armed rocking chair and a brass lamp, scraped together a bed, an oil stove, and some wooden crates to serve as tables and chairs. Sixty-five years old, alone and partially disabled, he was in a rather pathetic situation until he met Mrs. Mary Oakes Davis while he was walking around Camden, trying, according to some accounts, to peddle *Leaves of Grass* from door to door.

Mrs. Davis, the widow of a sea captain, had made it her life's work to care for people; at the time Whitman met her she was raising an orphan girl. Whitman persuaded her to bring her furniture and move in with him, which she did, bringing the orphan girl, a dog, a cat, some chickens, a pair of turtledoves, and a robin she had saved from a cat. In return for rent-free shelter under his roof, she cooked—often paying for the food out of her own pocket—kept house, and functioned as his personal servant for the rest of his life. Many a noon hour would see the crippled poet emerging from his house on the arm of Mrs. Davis, who tried to ignore the knowing looks and waggish whispers of the neighbors. After a few hours she would leave dinner simmering or burning on the stove while she hurried to the ferry stop to help him home, sometimes meeting three boats in an afternoon because she never knew which one would bring him.

Indoors, Whitman usually sat in his fairly spacious and airy upstairs front room, amid a profusion of papers that astonished visitors and exasperated Mrs. Davis. To him it wasn't chaos; he could retrieve anything he wanted in one motion. He saw the room as "a sort of result and storage collection of my own past life":

> Today in the upper story of a little wooden house of two stories near the Delaware River, east shore, sixty miles up from the sea, is a rather large 20-by-20 low ceiling'd room something like a big old ship's cabin. . . . There are all around many books, some quite handsome editions, some half cover'd by dust . . . some maps, the Bible (the strong cheap edition of the English crown), Homer, Shakspere, Walter Scott, Emerson, Ticknor's *Spanish Literature,* John Carlyle's *Dante,* Felton's *Greece,* George Sand's *Consuelo,* a very choice little Epictetus, some novels, the latest foreign and American monthlies, quarterlies, and so on. There being quite a strew of printer's proofs and slips, and the daily papers, the place with its quaint old-fashioned calmness has also a smack of something alert and of current work. . . . I have here various editions of my own writings, and sell them upon request; one is a big volume of complete poems and prose, 1,000 pages, autograph, essays, speeches, portraits from life, &c. Another is a little *Leaves of Grass,* latest date, six portraits, morocco bound, in pocket-book form.

On view in the upstairs room today are many souvenirs of Whitman's occupancy, including the bed in which he died, a knapsack that he

Whitman's bedroom, with the Whitman family clock and Mrs. Davis's horsehair sofa. On the back of the wicker rocker, a protective pad lifts to reveal a photograph of the poet.

Among rhododendron in a wooded dell, Walt Whitman's tomb in Harleigh Cemetery, Camden.

carried when he went out for walks, a waistcoat of red knitted silk sent to him by an English admirer, Lady Mount Temple, and a rocking chair with his photograph set into the back under a little protective pad, which he gave to some friends as an anniversary present.

In the downstairs front room sits Whitman's rocker, aptly described by one visitor as "a curious great cane-seat chair, with posts and rungs like ship's spars; altogether the most imposing heavy-timbered, broad-armed, and broad-bottomed edifice of the kind possible." In this room Whitman received the visitors who arrived in a steady stream, coming like mountains to Mohammed because, poor and nearly immobilized, he could not come to them. A young labor agitator came because he saw in *Leaves of Grass* the Scripture of a "new dispensation"; a study group in Bolton, England, appointed a representative to travel to America and visit Whitman; the great English critic Sir Edmund Gosse came to Mickle Street, as did Oscar Wilde.

In 1885 a group of thirty-seven friends of Whitman, Mark Twain and John Greenleaf Whittier among them, contributed ten dollars apiece to buy him a horse and phaeton. Whitman greatly enjoyed his equipage, and when the horse began to grow shaky in the knees, he bought himself a faster one. The stepping-stone that he used to enter the phaeton, engraved with his initials, may be seen on the sidewalk in front of the house today.

The horse and buggy were, indirectly, the cause of Whitman's last illness. In 1888, after a pleasant sixty-ninth birthday party given by local friends, he drove out to a nearby pond and sat on the shore to enjoy the sunset. The evening air chilled him and made him so ill that he became even less mobile than before. Until he died four years later, he was confined indoors most of the time. Horace Traubel became his constant companion, recording exhaustively all his expressions on any subject. Whitman admitted to Traubel that he was disappointed with his country's lack of achievement in the arts; evidently he still held the view he had expressed in *Democratic Vistas* some twenty years before, that the nation was "an almost complete failure in its social aspects, and in really grand religious, moral, literary, and esthetic results." But he insisted on the strength and resilience of America's institutions and the essential soundness of its people. "I love America, I believe in America, because her belly can hold and digest all—anarchist, socialist, peacemakers, fighters, disturbers or degenerates of whatever sort—hold and digest all," he asserted. And again, "I trust humanity; its instincts are in the main right: it goes false, it goes true, to its interests, but in the long run it makes advances. . . . When we get a real democracy, as we will by and by, this humanity will give a fuller report of itself.''

Whitman held the hand of Traubel as he died in the upper room of the Mickle Street house in 1892, while such a crowd clamored outside the door for news of the poet's condition that the attending physician had to post a bulletin on the door to keep the house from being overrun. One of the posted notices hangs in the house today, over the deacon's bench where close friends sat until they were invited to make their way upstairs. Whitman is buried in Harleigh Cemetery in Camden, in a grotto-like tomb he designed himself so that it would be large enough for his parents and four other members of the family. Among the pilgrims who have found their way there was Carl Sandburg, a lover of Whitman, and, like Whitman, a lover of Lincoln. On a lecture tour in the East in 1904, Sandburg wrote his sister Mary, *"I was in Walt Whitman's old home last Sunday, and on Memorial Day threw a rose in his tomb at Camden."*

Today the Whitman house, owned by the state of New Jersey, stands with the neighboring dwellings in its old row on the south side of Mickle Street, which is paved with cobblestones for some three feet beyond the curb. At that point asphalt and urban blight take over; the houses on the other side were leveled so the street could be widened. If Whitman could look out his front windows today, he would see a weed-filled vacant lot stretching to the Campbell Soup plant, which is topped with two towers painted red and white to look like cans of soup. But even urban renewal couldn't take away the river just past the end of the street, and the chunk of Philadelphia skyline across the water is steep and thrilling. Rooted as unaccountably in this traffic-wracked industrial area as ivy in a cranny full of soot are Whitman's house, and Whitman's faith.

18

Sherwood Anderson's
Vanishing Winesburg

Sherwood Anderson as a schoolboy (tintype circa 1890).
Clyde Public Library

Born in Camden, Ohio, in 1876, Sherwood Anderson was the third'
child of a harness maker who moved, as another of his sons said, whenever the rent came due. Anderson sketched his earliest recollections in
his fictional memoir, *Tar: A Midwest Childhood:* "For Tar Moorehead
life began with a procession of houses. They were at first very dim in
his mind. They marched. Even when he grew to be a man the houses
went across the walls of his fancy like soldiers in a dusty road. As
when soldiers marched some few were sharply remembered."

Around 1884 the Andersons settled in Clyde, Ohio. A much older
Sherwood Anderson recalled Clyde as "a fair and sweet town" with
maple-lined streets and small white frame homes. The Andersons were
very poor and changed houses frequently. Sherwood wrote later that
they sometimes got shelter by staying in "haunted" houses ("It is a
system—I recommend it to poets with large families"). But continuous residence in the town gave stability to his life and coherence to his
impressions. He recalled

> Ohio, race horses trotting on a race track, corn growing in fields,
> little streams in narrow valleys, men going out in the spring to plow,
> in the fall, the nuts getting ripe in the woods about an Ohio town.
> There were horse races in our main street on winter afternoons,
> the streets cleared for them, and on winter nights, dances in country
> barns. Maple trees shedding their winged seeds on spring days when
> a breeze sprang up, creeks near town where boys went to swim.

Between 1884 and 1895 the Andersons had about six different residences in Clyde. One of them, a small white frame house, still stands,
slightly altered, at 129 Spring Avenue. It is now privately owned. In
that house, in 1895, Mrs. Anderson died of tuberculosis and overwork.
Years later Anderson wrote a friend, *"I presume I shall never in my
life see a working woman without identifying her with my mother."* For
some ten years she had taken in washing to help support her family of
six children (a seventh baby, Fern, born in Clyde, died at the age
of two). In his *Memoirs* Anderson described ". . . a bitterly cold winter during which she continued to toil as a washwoman, running constantly in and out of the house, her clothes wet with the warm wash
water in the tub by the kitchen stove and often freezing on her body as
she went to hang the washed clothes on the clothesline strung across
the back yard, her bony hands growing thinner and bonier, her gaunt
body continually more gaunt." Her death the next May was doubly
devastating because the children knew their father could not be de-
pended on to keep the family together without her. Irwin Anderson, a
skilled harness maker before machinery had begun to render his craft

The Andersons' home at 129 Spring Avenue, Clyde, Ohio. Here the death of Sherwood's mother brought their family life to an end.

obsolete, drank up a good bit of the little he made as a house and sign painter in Clyde. Civil War veteran, amateur actor, and *bon vivant*, the father "flew in and out" of his children's lives "as a bird flies in and out of a bush," sometimes leaving the family without any money for weeks on end. In *Tar* Anderson told how his mother once acquired a winter's supply of cabbages for nothing, by pretending to bluster at the local boys who were throwing them at people's front doors for a Halloween prank. Delighted at seeing her dance in mock fury on the front steps, the youngsters doubled their assault on the house while the Anderson children carefully stored the cabbages in a trench dug in the backyard.

All the children worked from the time they were old enough to earn pennies doing odd jobs. Sherwood was known around Clyde as "Jobby" because he was always hustling. During the winter he contracted to mow lawns in the spring. He worked as a farmhand and as a livery stable helper. He served as water boy for men working on local street and sewer projects. He met every train that came into the Clyde depot to pick up and sell the daily shipments of the *Cleveland Plain Dealer* and the *Toledo Bee*. He put in several monotonous months in a bicycle factory. He drove a delivery wagon for the local grocery store, whose proprietor, Thaddeus Hurd, was the father of his chum, Herman Hurd.

Unlike the skimpily provisioned Anderson household, the Hurds' kitchen abounded with food, fragrance, and buoyant good humor. As

Main Street in Clyde, Ohio, Sherwood Anderson's "Winesburg."

Sherwood sat at the Hurds' dinner table, facing mounds of mashed potatoes, chicken, baked beans, and fresh pies, the force of his mother's admonitions not to "be a pig" weakened in the face of Mr. Hurd's repeated command: "Pass your plate, boy."

Sometimes on a summer afternoon the gray-bearded grocer would load the boys into his wagon and drive them to his farm outside town, philosophizing as he eyed the landscape: " 'There is a God, boy. Don't doubt it. . . . But he is not the God of the churches. He is in the field here, in that wheat stacked in that field there. He is in every growing stalk of corn. He is in the grass, in these weeds growing here beside the road. . . . He is in you, in me, in the trees.' " At such times Anderson remembered feeling "a kind of awe before the facts of life in meadows, in the corn and wheat fields, in men and women and even in the flies being whisked away from her sides by the tail of the grocer's old black mare. . . ."

This mood, this sense of impending illumination, colors his accounts of the sensations the countryside evoked in him. In *Tar* he recalled, "The corn, when it grew high, was like a forest down under which there was always a strange soft light." A vision of "God in you and me" breaks through at the conclusion of "Hands," the first story of *Winesburg, Ohio*. "Hands" is the story of a gifted teacher who was run out of a Pennsylvania town because his habit of touching his students gave rise to rumors that he was homosexual. He takes refuge in

Winesburg, where his prowess at picking strawberries makes his hands a source of local pride. After developing the peculiar qualities of this character who has been bent out of shape by life, Anderson again focuses on his hands: "The nervous expressive fingers, flashing in and out of the light, might well have been mistaken for the fingers of the devotee going swiftly through decade after decade of his rosary." Anderson used his mythical "Winesburg" country very much as Faulkner, whom he influenced, used "Yoknapatawpha." It is not so much in specific characters as in the setting and background details of his fiction that the evidences of his life in Clyde are traceable. The portrait of the artist Telfer in *Windy McPherson's Son* is unusual in that it was based on the life of John Tichenor, a self-taught artist from an old Clyde family. Anderson's evocative short story, "Death in the Woods," about a woman whose otherwise stark and drudging life found meaning in the feeding of men and animals, seems to have been based on an incident that occurred in Clyde when he was a boy: the discovery of a woman's dead body in a snow-filled wood, with her clothing partly torn away by dogs.

The countryside around Clyde, as Anderson described it in all his autobiographical works, had the same features as the rural landscape in *Winesburg*. There were the fields of berries, corn, wheat, and cabbage. There were the woods—he mentions beech groves in particular—where children gathered nuts. Like Winesburg, Clyde had and still has a creek, Raccoon or Coon Creek. At Clyde Community Park, just west of town, the creek runs into a small reservoir that is still called Waterworks Pond, although the old waterworks of Anderson's day are no longer there.

The railroad crosses Main Street at the northwest end of Clyde's central business district, which is still only about three blocks long. Clyde's old railroad hotel, the St. Vincent House, was located near the tracks some half a block over from Main Street, as was the New Willard House in Winesburg. The St. Vincent House is gone now, as is the depot of Anderson's day.

In Clyde, as in Winesburg, there was, and is today, a Buckeye Street, a sedate residential street that crosses Main one long block south of the railroad tracks. West of town is a residential area, Piety Hill, where the Anderson family lived for a time. It is situated in the same relation to Waterworks Pond that "Gospel Hill" is in the novel. In his *Memoirs* and in *Winesburg*, Anderson described the town fairgrounds as being up a low hill from the pond. The fairgrounds and racetrack, where he spent countless dusty but exciting hours with horses and the men who trained them, no longer exist in Clyde. They were located on what is now the property of South Main Street Elementary School, in the southwestern part of town.

For Anderson Clyde was a benevolent environment. Though his father's improvidence and alcoholism were well known, his mother was respected as a hardworking, devoted family woman. Sherwood was not only accepted as one of the boys by townspeople like the Hurds, but was regarded as an exceptionally good worker. Like many of his friends, he didn't complete high school, partly because his mind was always on making money. When he went to work in Chicago after his mother died, Clyde still considered him one of its own. The weekly *Enterprise* described him as "one who had left a lucrative position in Chicago"—he was actually working for low wages in a warehouse—to enter the Spanish-American War with a company of National Guardsmen from his hometown. He returned to Clyde briefly after his discharge, then left for good.

In later years, particularly after his first divorce and the publication of *Winesburg* had made him *persona non grata* in Clyde, Anderson came back only at long intervals to visit Herman Hurd and his family. The townspeople evidently disliked the book, not because they felt personally libeled as did residents of Asheville when Wolfe published *Look Homeward, Angel,* but because they thought it was obscene and negative.

"Sherwood Anderson made the modern novel," said John Steinbeck, "and it has not gone much beyond him." Yet it has been true in Anderson's case, as with many other American authors, that the prophet is without honor in his own village, particularly in his own generation. As an older citizen of Clyde once remarked, "I think Sherwood would have been a much more successful author if he hadn't written such gloomy things."

19 Flannery O'Connor: Redemption in Slash Pine Country

Flannery O'Connor's home in Milledgeville. The house once served briefly as the governor's mansion.

It was not in the world familiar to readers of her fiction—a backcountry world of clay hills, pine woods, sharecroppers, itinerant swindlers, and hand-painted "Jesus Saves" signs—that Mary Flannery O'Connor was born in 1925. She was born in the historically elegant coastal city of Savannah, and lived in a high brownstone house facing the Cathedral of St. John the Baptist, a house that still stands. She was educated at Sacred Heart parochial school and at St. Vincent's school for girls.

At the age of five, as she recalled later in "The King of the Birds," she had a pet chicken, a Colchin Bantam, that could walk backward. Pathé News once sent a photographer all the way from New York to take a picture of the chicken. Perhaps this incident sparked Flannery's lifelong alertness to oddities and revelations. Anyway, the pleasure she got out of raising fowl seems to have been what led to her later passion for peacocks.

The long tragedy of the O'Connors began when Flannery was about twelve years old. Her father was stricken with lupus, an incurable degenerative disease of the connective tissues that is sometimes hereditary. He died in 1941, leaving Flannery, an only child, and her widowed mother profoundly reliant on one another. In the early '50s the manifestations of lupus in Flannery would intensify that relationship, as the two women, the younger gradually becoming disabled, worked out their courageous partnership at Andalusia Farm. But when Flannery's childhood in Savannah ended, it was still a long way to Andalusia.

When it became clear that Major O'Connor's condition was hopeless, the family moved to Milledgeville, the antebellum capital of Georgia, a community of white pillared houses sprayed with dogwood in the spring, where Mrs. O'Connor's maternal relatives, the Treanors, had lived for generations. It was in the home of a Treanor that the first Mass in Milledgeville was held in 1847. The O'Connors lived in the white frame house on Green Street where Flannery's mother, the former Regina Cline, had grown up—a house with huge fluted columns surmounting a high front stair, which had once served briefly as the governor's mansion.

The house had been built in 1820, the bricks for its garden walls believed to have been made by hand by slaves. From the mid-1880s it was the home of Peter Cline, mayor of Milledgeville and father of sixteen children, including Regina. Even today the twin drawing rooms on either side of the entryway, the Victorian furniture and antique grand piano, the dark-paneled dining room with the carved medallion in its ceiling, convey a sense of something now past its prime but established and formidably durable. Here Flannery lived from the time she was thirteen until she went to graduate school at the University of Iowa. She wrote fiction steadily when she was a student at Peabody High School, and while she was attending Georgia State College for Women, just a few blocks away from her home, she gained a reputation as a writer and cartoonist.

Full of purpose, and of a talent already demonstrated, Flannery went through a master's program in writing at Iowa, where she wrote the stories that were later reworked into *Wise Blood*. She struck out for New York, the time-honored destination of fledgling writers. After a short time she moved to Connecticut to board with her friends Robert and Sally Fitzgerald, also literary people and devout Catholics.

On the train for Georgia around Christmastime, 1950, Flannery became seriously ill. At Emory Hospital in Atlanta, tests confirmed the worst: she had lupus. When this initial bout ended, she was too weak to climb stairs. She faced not only eventual death but, in the meantime, gradual disability caused both by the disease and by the ACTH (a form of cortisone) used to treat it. There was the prospect of increasing dependence; mobile life in a distant city seemed out of the question.

Andalusia Farm, home of Flannery O'Connor.

At Andalusia Farm, the descendants of Flannery's peacocks.

Meanwhile Regina had inherited from one of her brothers Andalusia Farm, 500 acres of pasture and woodland some five miles out of Milledgeville on the Eatonton highway. On a rise above a large pond and a stand of pine trees was the farmhouse, built when the rolling tract was part of a plantation; a tall white frame house with a reddish roof, black shutters, and a steep brick stair leading to its broad front porch. After Flannery got out of the hospital, she and Regina moved to the farm, where Flannery could have a bedroom-study on the ground floor.

"You run the farm," Flannery told her mother, "and I'll do the writing." Inexperienced, but resourceful and quick on the uptake, Regina, mansion-bred daughter of the mayor of Milledgeville, ran the farm. It was a dairy farm until, as Regina put it, "I saw the light." Life became a little easier when she changed over to cattle raising. Occasionally the sale of timber brought in some extra money.

In her bedroom to the left of the front entry, at a desk topped by two unpainted apple crates that served for shelves, Flannery wrote each morning until noon. Then she and Regina would drive into Milledgeville for lunch at the Sanford House, an elegant home-turned-restaurant with deservedly famous food and a framed copy of the South's edict of secession in its front hall. In the afternoon Flannery tended her geese, swans, and peacocks, chatted with visitors over Coca-Colas on the front porch, or painted. Several of her pictures—a self-portrait with a pheasant, a view of the barn, a study of flowers in a bowl, and others—still hang in the farmhouse.

A disciplined writer, Flannery sat at her desk for the allotted time each morning whether the work was going well or not, rewriting voluminously, refusing to take shortcuts in order to meet other people's timetables. In 1954 she published her first collection of stories, which took its title from one of her most famous pieces, "A Good Man Is Hard to Find." The following year her hipbones had so deteriorated, either from the disease or from the side effects of the drugs used to control it, that she had to use crutches from then on. While her disease added greatly to the stress of working, in Flannery O'Connor's case, as in the cases of other artists—Elizabeth Barrett Browning is the classic example—bad health was not utterly devoid of secondary gains. Flannery once asked a talented friend with several children if she wrote every day. The lady replied that she was sometimes prevented from writing by "domestic responsibilities." With characteristic honesty and lack of self-pity Flannery rejoined, "I'm fortunate that this disability relieves me of other duties."

Her fiction is full of mothers past middle age with adult children who, because of some defeat or deformity, are still at home after the age when they would ordinarily have left. In her stories Flannery could ring all the changes on the incompatibility, tension, and rage latent in such situations. But her penetration was too deep not to expose the final truth that even the most oppressive parent is not ultimately responsible for a child's failure to deal with what is his or hers to deal with: financial ineptitude, self-deceptive intellectual pretensions, a wooden leg.

Defeat, like violence, has a paradoxical meaning in her stories. It can make way for the workings of grace in the soul. To describe it in terms of the secular tradition, it can be the beginning of insight or vision, as in the Oedipus cycle, which Flannery read before completing *Wise Blood*. Whatever the horror of the violent event in her stories— as when little Norton hangs himself in "The Lame Shall Enter First"— it is a corrective for something even worse in the previous state of things. It restores the spiritual equilibrium. ". . . I have found," she once wrote, "that violence is strangely capable of returning my characters to reality and preparing them to accept their moments of grace. Their heads are so hard that almost nothing else will do the work. This idea, that reality is something to which we must be returned at considerable cost, is one which is seldom understood by the casual reader, but it is one which is implicit in the Christian view of the world."

What Flannery O'Connor might have used as material for her art if the lupus had not caused the trajectory of her life to double back on itself, it is impossible to say. As it was, her fiction is of a piece with the environment where, until her death at the age of thirty-nine, she and her mother nurtured each other with shared religious faith and an inimitable dry humor. The pastures, the red clay roads, the suns that dripped like blood behind the pine woods, the operation of farm machinery, the hiring and firing of help, the making of small business deals vital to the survival of people living on a scant margin, the alienation between Southern whites and blacks, the bond between Southern whites and blacks, the ignorance of the self-styled wise, the absurdity and the efficacy of backwoods revivalism—these were the stuff of her fiction. "An idiom characterizes a society," she once said, and she enriched the texture of her stories with dialect that could heighten the effects of warmth, bitterness, or comedy. If dialect could emphasize the poverty or ignorance of its speakers, it could also suggest spontaneity and naturalness as opposed to the stiffness of conventional speech and logic. In "The Displaced Person" Mrs. Shortley, who is semirespectable and semigrammatical, tries to explain to some hired hands what a displaced person is. Their matter-of-fact simplicity, fleshed out in a total lack of grammar, momentarily thwarts her attempt to inculcate prejudice.

> "It means they ain't where they were born at and there's nowhere for them to go—like if you was run out of here and wouldn't nobody have you."
> "It seem like they here, though," the old man said in a reflective voice. "If they here, they somewhere."
> "Sho is," the other agreed. "They here."

Flannery's last stories, which appeared in the collection titled *Everything That Rises Must Converge,* were literally written in the face of death. She had to have abdominal surgery in April, 1964, and the operation reactivated her lupus. In May and June she alternated between work on the book and sieges in the hospital. As it was becoming apparent that the lupus was out of control, she continued to labor at two new stories for the collection, "Parker's Back" and "Judgement Day." Death, or an insight so cataclysmic that it seems hardly less demanding than death, is in the climax of each story in this last group: Julian's mother's stroke in "Everything That Rises Must Converge"; the fatal struggle between little Mary Fortune Pitts and her grandfather in "A View of the Woods"; Mrs. Turpin's devastating realization, in "Revelation," that all our righteousnesses are as filthy rags, that she shares the squalid creaturehood of white trash and even her own hogs. To be facing death, Flannery once wrote, is to be "in the most significant position life offers the Christian." She mailed her last story to Robert Giroux, her editor and publisher, in July, 1964, and died August third.

20

Paul Laurence Dunbar:
A Singer in Dayton

Paul Laurence Dunbar in his study, "Loafin' Holt." Ohio Historical Society

It was in Dayton, Ohio, that Paul Laurence Dunbar was born in 1872 to a Civil War veteran and his wife, both of whom had begun life as slaves in Kentucky. It was to Dayton that Dunbar returned in 1903, his literary achievements and his grief over his ruined marriage alike interrupted by the onset of advanced tuberculosis. He spent his last days with his aged mother in the modest but gracefully designed brick house at 219 Summit Street that he had bought for her out of his earnings as an author and lecturer.

There was a certain historical logic to the fact that an outstanding black poet, journalist, and writer of fiction should have been born in Dayton. Abolitionism was a tradition in that city, which had been an important station on the Underground Railroad. In Dunbar's time some five thousand blacks in Dayton were struggling to earn a living and to make sense out of the new freedom that Northern whites were so willing to grant in the abstract, but so slow to underwrite with social acceptance or economic opportunity. Before he graduated from high school Dunbar had served as editor of a black newspaper, the *Tattler,* printed by Wilbur and Orville Wright. Dunbar tried to make the short-lived paper an influence for solidarity in the black community.

In a day when slavery, war, and economic insecurity made it extremely difficult for black families to keep from becoming fragmented, the Dunbars had roots in Dayton. Paul's mother, Matilda Dunbar, had a mother, a brother, and a sister there. Since she had two sons from a former marriage, Paul had two older half brothers, and he had cousins as well. Each in his own way, the Dunbars valued literacy. In his old age Paul's father, a plasterer, taught himself to read. His mother learned her letters by inducing children who passed her home to come in and teach her. As a little slave girl she had been allowed to listen when whites read poetry, and she retained a love of the songs and stories she had heard from blacks and whites in Kentucky. After her husband died in 1885, she had to support her boys by taking in washing. Even as she worked over her tub, she would pause to spell out one line at a time from the Bible or another book.

Paul wrote his first poem at the age of seven, and became obsessed with rhymes. A precocious child, he did well in school and met with support and encouragement from his teachers. When he entered high school, he was the only black student there. He was loaded with honors. He was elected a member, and later president, of the Philomathean Literary Society. He was editor of the school newspaper, and well known locally as a writer by the time he graduated.

Immediately after graduation in 1891 he found that the community which had been so generous to him in childhood held out no opportunities for him as an adult. Later he wrote a short story called "One

Man's Fortunes,'' about a black university graduate who returns to his formerly friendly hometown to look for work. When he applies to the clerical department of a factory, he is told to report to the head janitor. Dunbar became an elevator operator in the Callahan Building at four dollars a week, with no other prospect in sight.

In 1892 it happened that the Western Association of Writers, which usually held its annual meeting in Indiana, met in Dayton. One of Dunbar's teachers, a Mrs. Helen Truesdell, arranged to have him read before this group. In an article that was widely circulated, the poet James Newton Matthews, who attended the convention, described the "slender Negro lad, as black as the core of Cheops' pyramid,'' who "ascended the rostrum with the coolness and dignity of a cultured entertainer, and delivered a poem in a tone 'as musical as is Apollo's lute.' ''

Matthews's highly complimentary article brought Dunbar the favorable notice of James Whitcomb Riley, whom he greatly admired, and created a ready-made audience for his first book of poems, *Oak and Ivy*. By 1894 Dunbar had left the elevator behind and was in the way to become a celebrated writer. His second book, *Majors and Minors*, was glowingly reviewed by William Dean Howells in *Harper's*. With the publication in 1896 of *Lyrics of Lowly Life*, studded with such classics as "The Spellin' Bee,'' "A Ante-bellum Sermon,'' and "When Malindy Sings,'' and embellished with an introduction by Howells, Dunbar was famous.

Ecstatic over what Howells's praise had done for him, Dunbar realized only gradually that the eminent critic's accolade was a mixed blessing. Howells had spoken of the young poet's "brilliant and unique achievement'' and insisted, "I held that if his black poems had been written by a white man, I should not have found them less admirable.'' But he expressed a preference for Dunbar's dialect poems, which, as he said, embodied "a finely ironical perception of the negro and his limitations. . . .'' The net effect of this statement was unintentionally to belittle dialect and speakers of dialect, and to create for Dunbar a stereotyped success that, right up to the present, has thrown his fiction and powerful, elegant journalistic prose into obscurity.

Dunbar was a sophisticated, complicated man; the differences among his literary voices are sometimes startling. He was best known as the author of such lines as these from "The Real Question,'' a humorous poem about the silver versus gold controversy:

> Well, you folks kin keep on shoutin' wif you' gold er silvah cry,
> But I tell you people hams is sceerce an' fowls is roostin' high.
> An' hit ain't de so't o' money dat is pesterin' my min',
> But de question I want answehed's how to get at any kin'!

The home of Paul Laurence Dunbar at 219 North Summit Street, a landmark in Dayton since Dunbar's mother died in 1934.

But he was also an accomplished journalist, an articulate exponent of racial issues, and an advocate of the kind of solidarity among blacks that later surfaced as part of the concept of black power. For instance, in one of his essays he challenged a statement by a prominent white editor that criminality was on the rise among Negroes:

> Statistics may prove anything, but in this case especially they are inadequate. . . . No one has the right to base any conclusions about Negro criminality upon the number of prisoners in the jails and other places of restraint. Even in the North the prejudice against the Negro reverses the precedents of law, and every one accused is looked upon as guilty until he is proven innocent. In the South it is worse. . . . A fight upon the street, picking up coal, with the accusation of throwing it off the cars, brawling generally, what with white boys would be called children's fights land the black boy in jail, and so the percentage of criminals increase, and the Northern friend of the Negro holds up his hands in dismay at the awful things he sees before him.

Regardless of its long-range effects on Dunbar's literary identity, the success of his early lyrics brought relief from hardship and, for the moment, turned his life into a veritable Cinderella's ball. He lectured in England and was warmly received; he courted and married Alice Ruth Moore of New Orleans, an exquisitely beautiful young woman who was herself a gifted writer. Spurred on by the recognition he had received and by his desire to provide for Alice and his mother, he stepped up his literary output. Between 1898 and 1900 he wrote two novels, two books of short stories, the lyrics for the hit musical *Clorindy,* and two volumes of poetry.

But in 1899, just as the income from his books and platform readings plus a clerkship in the Library of Congress had given him a solid financial underpinning, he contracted pneumonia. For the rest of his life, struggles to keep up his productivity alternated with bouts of severe illness. In 1902 he and Alice separated. The next year he returned to Dayton to live out his remaining three years, exhausted, incurably ill, and, as he described himself, "a broken-hearted man."

At home at 219 Summit Street, Dunbar spent a great deal of time in the second-floor study that he called his "Loafin' Holt." His desk is still in the study, as are his books, among which are volumes of Gibbon, Carlyle, Stevenson, Kipling, and such popular novelists of his day as Winston Churchill and Paul Leicester Ford. A pair of stirrups that he used when he rode horseback in Colorado to try to improve the state of his lungs remains in the study. His bedroom closet holds his suits, hats, and shoes; in another corner of the bedroom is a bicycle, a gift from his high school friend Orville Wright.

The small parlor downstairs in the front bay is furnished with Matilda Dunbar's sofa and chairs, upholstered in sea-green velvet. Her carpet and her flowered wallpaper, faded with age but otherwise hardly deteriorated, are still in the parlor, whose focal point is the ponderous Dunbar family Bible. Baby dresses that Matilda made by hand for Paul and photos of Paul, Matilda, and Alice round out the collection of mementos that spans the entire life of the man who was a friend of Frederick Douglass and W. E. B. Du Bois, and whose poetry linked the tradition that included James Whitcomb Riley and Eugene Field to younger poets who would eventually figure in the Harlem Renaissance, such as Countee Cullen and Langston Hughes.

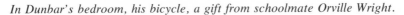

In Dunbar's bedroom, his bicycle, a gift from schoolmate Orville Wright.

21

The Riley Old Home, Greenfield, Indiana

James Whitcomb Riley, by John Singer Sargent. Riley was unhappy that the portrait showed his crippled hand. Indianapolis Museum of Art. Painted on commission from the Art Association.

On October 7, 1849, the very day that Poe died in Baltimore, James Whitcomb Riley, the Hoosier poet, was born. This was not the only ironic association between Riley and the author of "Annabel Lee." In his early twenties Riley, certain that his poetry had all the qualifications for magazine publication except a famous author, wrote a poem called "Leonainie" and passed it off as a work by Poe, discovered on the flyleaf of a dictionary in a Richmond inn. To Riley's surprise, the poem attracted national attention, and spawned more posthumous "discoveries." When Riley explained the hoax, public opinion was hard on him, though he was guilty of nothing except proving that the only part of a poem many "critics" could read was the signature. But after two years of embarrassment he was offered a job on the *Indianapolis Journal*. From then on he became increasingly successful.

The author of "The Raggedy Man," "When the Frost Is on the Punkin'," and "Squire Hawkins' Story" had what tradition sanctions as the proper background for a folk poet. He was born in a log cabin when Greenfield was a village with three or four hundred inhabitants. Soon after his birth his father, Reuben A. Riley, an able lawyer and an extraordinarily skilled carpenter, built his family the modest but comfortable frame house that still stands at 250 West Main Street in Greenfield. Over steaming kettles of boiling water in the backyard he bent walnut timbers to form the curving staircase and railing that lead from the front hall to the second floor. The mantels, doors, and woodwork, all of walnut, are also his handiwork.

Today the house is filled with Riley furniture, supplemented by pieces that belonged to contemporaries of the Rileys. A well-rounded display of basic household items from the mid-nineteenth century— rope beds, kitchen utensils, linsey-woolsey coverlets—is embellished with objects that illustrate the tastes and even the whims of the period. In front of the fireplace in the parlor stands a charming tilt-top table, with a painting of a spired village set in a laquered papier-mâché frame inlaid with mother-of-pearl, that was Mrs. Riley's. On the mantel above is a "chainey dog," a popular mid-Victorian ornament. There are several specimens of Reuben Riley's craftsmanship: a cradle, a washstand, and a jewelry box, romantically decorated, which he made for his wife. Her Howe sewing machine, on display in the guest room, was the first sewing machine in Hancock County. On the walls are a variety of shadow-box pictures made by the ladies of the Riley family from yarn and dried flowers, from flower petals dipped in wax, from human hair. A press in the master bedroom holds christening dresses and school clothes that were passed down from child to child.

Among the Riley family photographs beside the stairs is a picture of Mary Alice Smith, who came to live with the Rileys when she was

The home of James Whitcomb Riley at 250 West Main, Greenfield, Indiana. The log cabin in which Riley was born became the kitchen of this house.

In the living room at Riley Old Home, the black walnut woodwork crafted by Riley's father, his mother's whatnot and English tilt-top table.

In Indianapolis, Riley's Lockerbie Street house.

fourteen because her parents were dead. While she "washed the cups an' saucers up" to earn her board, she told the children stories of

> . . . the Gobble-uns 'at gits you
>   Ef you
>   Don't
>   Watch
>   Out!

Years later Riley wrote a poem about her, and "Little Orphant Allie," renamed by an editor "Little Orphant Annie," became a permanent addition to American literature. In honor of the little boy who was stolen by the "Gobble-uns" in the poem, a small pair of pants and an old-fashioned "roundabout," a child's shirt with a full, gathered bodice under its yoke, hang on a door in the "rafter room," where the Riley boys slept.

James Whitcomb Riley's roots in this house were extraordinarily deep. During the Civil War his father left his successful law practice to serve as a captain of Union cavalry and was injured in a shell explosion. As a result he was unable to practice law with his accustomed vigor after the war, and the family lost the house that he had timbered and pegged with his own hands. Mrs. Riley was profoundly upset. Before she died in 1870, young Jim promised her that someday he would buy the homestead back.

In 1894 Riley, by then a wealthy and famous poet and platform reader, repurchased the house his father had built. He was then living for most of each year with Major and Mrs. Charles Holstein in their home on Lockerbie Street in Indianapolis. Riley's Lockerbie Street residence, a warmly elegant brick house with ivy-covered walls and festive-looking oak doors with frosted glass panes, is a well-known center of interest in Indianapolis today. The street itself, just two blocks long, is the center of a small historic district called Lockerbie Square. Riley lived on Lockerbie Street for the rest of his life, except for the time he spent traveling and visiting friends, like Joel Chandler Harris in Atlanta. But he spent his summers at the Greenfield home, browsing around the "old swimmin' hole" a mile away and other haunts described in "A Country Pathway" and "Out to Old Aunt Mary's." Prominent in a circle of Indiana writers that included Booth Tarkington, George Ade, and Meredith Nicholson, Riley was a Hoosier to the end of his days. He died in 1916, while the American reading public was still feeling the impact of Edgar Lee Masters's *Spoon River Anthology,* published the year before. Masters made a village setting the forum for a new kind of voice, full of questionings and ironies that were unknown to Riley's generation.

22 Eugene Field House, St. Louis

Field at the Chicago Daily News *office.* Kraft Photo Collection

St. Louis, in the "gaslight" days around the turn of the century, was a center of culture, with elegant residences, a busy social season, and an outstanding educational institution, Washington University, founded by T. S. Eliot's grandfather. The city had a tradition of competitive journalism, given impetus by the career of Joseph Pulitzer. It had an innovative magazine, *Reedy's Mirror,* in which Edgar Lee Masters first published the poems of *Spoon River Anthology.* The *Mirror* also published the early work of Carl Sandburg, Edna St. Vincent Millay, and Sara Teasdale. Teasdale and T. S. Eliot were born in St. Louis in the 1880s, and their family homes still stand in the city. At a later period Tennessee Williams lived in St. Louis, and the apartment that was the setting for the events he dramatized in *The Glass Menagerie* exists today. But the most prominent of the literary landmarks in St. Louis is the birthplace of Eugene Field at 634 South Broadway. This three-story brick town house, built in 1845, five years before Field was born, is the oldest surviving residence in the mid-city area. Like the Whitman home in Camden it is a lonely indicator of change, holding its own amid expressway interchanges and urban sprawl.

Eugene Field is best remembered today for his children's poems, such as "Wynken, Blynken, and Nod," "The Sugarplum Tree," and "The Duel" ("The Gingham Dog and the Calico Cat"). Almost anyone fifty or over can quote the opening lines of his "Little Boy Blue":

> The little toy dog is covered with dust,
> But sturdy and staunch he stands . . .

This poem about the death of a little boy is similar to a number of pieces by Field's friend James Whitcomb Riley, but Field's writing, fed by his interest in Old English and Latin literature, was more refined.

Though born in St. Louis, Field had roots in the East as well. His father, Roswell Martin Field, was a native of Vermont and, incidentally, a relative of Marshall Field. Roswell impulsively married a young woman he hardly knew, who soon afterward left him and married an old fiancé without the formality of a divorce. The state of Vermont refused to prosecute her for bigamy, and Roswell was so outraged that he took himself off to St. Louis and proceeded to become a prominent attorney. It was he who, acting on behalf of the former slave, initiated the Dred Scott case in 1848. His portrait hangs in the Field House, as does a portrait of his second wife, also a New Englander, who died when Eugene was six. After their mother's death, Eugene and his brother Roswell went to Amherst, Massachusetts, to be brought up by their father's niece, Mary Field French. The house where Eugene Field

The Eugene Field House at 634 South Broadway, St. Louis: holding its own amid expressway interchanges and urban sprawl.

lived from age six to fifteen still stands in Amherst near the Jones Library, funds for which were donated to the town by Field's cousin by marriage, Samuel Minot Jones.

Field attended three colleges without graduating from any, and when he inherited money after his father's death, he larked off to Europe and spent all the cash not held in trust. Meanwhile, working as a journalist in St. Joseph, Missouri, he had fallen in love with fourteen-year-old Julia Comstock, seven years his junior. They courted so assiduously that her parents, with some misgivings, allowed Julia to marry Field at sixteen. For all his early love of being fancy-free, Field evidently found much happiness in his marriage, and in his eight children.

On the *Denver Tribune* in the early '80s, Field gained a reputation for wit and inventiveness and became notorious as a practical joker. On the day before Oscar Wilde was to arrive in town for a platform engagement, Field dressed in a suit similar to those worn by the famous aesthete and had himself driven all over Denver with a lily in his hand. Wilde arrived the next day to find accounts of his appearance on the city streets the day before in all the papers. Though puzzled, he never lost his aplomb, and when he learned the truth remarked, "A splendid advertisement for my lecture!"

In 1883 Field was hired by the *Chicago Daily News,* to write, as he put it, "anything I pleased." With the move to Chicago he established himself as a leader in an up-and-coming journalistic and literary community that included Finley Peter Dunne ("Mr. Dooley"), George Ade, Hamlin Garland, and later, shortly after Field's time, Theodore Dreiser and Carl Sandburg. He became the first great personal by-line columnist, dealing out humor, verse, satire, and commentary from the department called "Sharps and Flats" that was his kingdom until he died in 1895. He reviewed real and imaginary books. He wrote verses and attributed them, without permission, to William Dean Howells, Helena Modjeska, and other famous cronies of his. He satirized the railroads for giving passes to newspapers in exchange for favorable publicity. He did a bit of investigative reporting to prove that ex-President Hayes, a self-proclaimed teetotaler while in the White House, was getting part of his income from saloon property in Omaha. He presided over the cultural development of Chicago with such zeal that Eastern newspapers began calling the city "Colonel Eugene Field's town." He lambasted such New England luminaries as James Russell Lowell and Charles Dudley Warner for falling back on warmed-over material when they lectured in Chicago, and gave Easterners to understand that there were critics worthy of the name in "Porkopolis." Field was repeatedly offered jobs with the *New York Sun,* but he refused to leave Chicago.

For all his fame, Field never made money, and didn't even have a home of his own until the last year of his life, when he moved to "Sabine Farm," on the north side of Chicago near Lake Michigan. Just as he and Julia had fitted up the house with spaces for the books and objects of real and imaginary *vertu* that he loved to collect, he died. Subsequently the house burned down along with most of its contents, including a valuable collection of toys. The antique toys in the Field House in St. Louis are not Field's, but were donated in memory of those he had collected. The parlor and dining room of the house are furnished with opulent eighteenth-century pieces, the property of Field's parents. The south room on the third floor holds a few furnishings from Sabine Farm. Dresses, a nightgown, and a bathing suit worn by Julia Field are displayed there, along with a dressing gown, medicine kits, a collar box, and collars that belonged to her husband. Eugene and Julia Field's Denver home was maintained as a memorial for some years by one of the city's most famous residents, Mrs. J. J. ("Unsinkable Molly") Brown. The little house now stands in Washington Park, Denver, to which it was moved from its former location on West Colfax Avenue opposite the U.S. Mint. Field is buried in the cemetery of the Church of the Holy Comforter in Kenilworth, a small community outside Chicago.

23 🏠

George Washington Cable
in New Orleans and Northampton

"Raised cottage" built for George Washington Cable and his family in the Garden District, 1313 Eight Street, New Orleans.

In the mid-1880s George Washington Cable's tales of New Orleans rivaled the works of Mark Twain in popularity with American audiences. Cable's stories of a New Orleans that had already passed into legend by the time of the Civil War are still the classics of their type. They captured, even as it was disappearing, the seasoned mixture that was the old city: the markets and cafés bustling with French, Spanish, Cajuns, and Americans; the imposing plantations along the river; the shuttered houses in which, behind the bars of wrought-iron balconies, beautiful half-caste women lived out tragic destinies.

Cable himself did not have deep roots in Louisiana's past, though he was born in New Orleans in 1844, in a house on Annunciation Square that no longer exists. He came of Virginia and New England stock; his grandparents on his father's side had owned slaves and freed them. Like his parents, Cable was a staunch Presbyterian, and extraordinarily devout and conscientious all his life, though not humorless about it. His friend Mark Twain once wrote to William Dean Howells, *"You know that when it comes down to moral honesty, limpid innocence, and utterly blemishless piety, the apostles were mere policemen to Cable."*

In Cable's reminiscences about his early life, New Orleans emerges as a child's paradise of gardens, marketplaces, and riverside wharves. He recalled going with his father to market in the morning before breakfast: "There is always a delightful uproar in these places in the hour of dawn; a bewildering chatter of all the world talking at once, mostly in German and French: a calling, a hallooing, a pounding of cleavers, a smell of raw meat, of parsley and potatoes, of fish, onions, pineapples, garlics, oranges, shrimp and crabs. . . ." And he added, "Children love New Orleans! I have seen a great many large cities but I cannot think I have ever seen one so green with trees or so full of songbirds and flowers."

His world shattered in 1859, when two cargo ships in which his father had invested heavily burned in the harbor of New Orleans. Within months his father died, and young Cable had to quit school and help support the family. In 1862, working as a counting room clerk in a store on Canal Street, he witnessed the fall of New Orleans to Union forces. He saw the city's cotton taken to the wharves and set on fire; its flames could be seen as far as thirty miles. He saw the masts of the Yankee fleet coming up the river and heard the weeping and crying as the streets filled with people evacuating their homes.

Forced to leave the city temporarily, Cable enlisted in the Confederate cavalry and served until the war was over. When he returned to New Orleans, the spectacle of the South trying to work its painful way through the problems of the Reconstruction forced him to reflect on

"Tarryawhile," home of George Washington Cable, at 23 Dryads Green, Northampton, Massachusetts.

George Washington Cable (right) with sidekick Mark Twain on the lecture circuit in 1884. Kraft Photo Collection

the issue of racial equality as the war itself had not. He worked for a time as a reporter on the *Picayune,* then became a bookkeeper for a firm of cotton shippers. In his spare time he combed the municipal archives for nuggets of story material embedded in old newspapers and historical documents. In 1873 he published the first of his stories of old New Orleans, "'Sieur George," in *Scribner's Monthly,* and on its heels came "Belles Demoiselles Plantation" and "'Tite Poulette."

The following year Cable, by then married and the father of four, built a house at 1313 Eighth Street, in the Garden District. To this house, surrounded by orange and fig trees, came Lafcadio Hearn, Oscar Wilde, Mark Twain, and Joel Chandler Harris, whose house, the Wren's Nest, is still a landmark in Atlanta. Cable was living in the Eighth Street house when yellow fever struck his family in 1878, killing his four-year-old son and nearly killing two of his daughters.

With his romantic stories and his accomplished renditions of Creole folk songs, Cable was an extremely popular platform performer, and made a famous tour with Mark Twain in 1884–1885. Cable had it written into their contract that there would be no traveling on Sunday; his partner snorted a little, but honored the agreement. In 1892–1893 Cable toured with Eugene Field, then at his peak of fame as the laureate of Chicago, his insignia a crown of frankfurters.

In 1885 Cable moved to Northampton, Massachusetts. The move may have been caused partly by his increasingly liberal views on race relations, which kept him from being perfectly comfortable in New Orleans. On the other hand, he and his family always maintained that they had moved because his wife's health demanded a more bracing climate, and because many of his literary friendships, such as the one with Mark Twain, had solidified in the North. In 1892 he built a Dutch colonial house on a street off Paradise Road, not far from Smith College. Since he was the very first settler on the new street, he named it "Dryads Green" after Dryad Street in New Orleans, and planted a row of oaks along it. His house, "Tarryawhile," still stands at 23 Dryads Green, now privately owned. At the time Cable owned most of what is now the block on which his house stands, and since his houseguests were usually invited to plant a tree on his property, the present neighborhood is studded with trees planted by celebrities of the late nineteenth and early twentieth centuries: Sir James M. Barrie, Henry Van Dyke, Minnie Maddern Fiske, Alice Freeman Palmer (a maple planted by Sir Arthur Conan Doyle died during its second winter). Cable was a leader in the founding of the People's Institute in Northampton, an organization devoted to assisting working people who wanted to educate themselves. He is buried, with his wife and mother, in Bridge Street Cemetery in Northampton.

24 🏠

Edgar Lee Masters and the Spoon River Country

Edgar Lee Masters at twelve with his grandmother, the "Lucinda Matlock"
of Spoon River Anthology. *Courtesy of Mrs. Ellen C. Masters*

When Chicago was a feisty young postwar town, when downstate Illinois was still haunted by the memory of a Lincoln that not all men had loved, a boy who would draw on the elements of Greek tragedy to challenge the sentimental view of small-town life was growing up in Petersburg. Edgar Lee Masters was the son of a lawyer who had weathered shaky professional beginnings to become a state's attorney, and who was at one time a close colleague of Lincoln's old partner, William A. Herndon. As a boy Masters often watched the two on the green in front of the courthouse, "where Herndon talked of Lincoln and told stories grave and obscene, while my father laughed."

Masters's mother was an intelligent, high-strung woman with no flair for homemaking. Evidently neither she nor her husband was gifted in the management of money or of children. By Masters's own account his boyhood home was a place where meals were indifferent, heat scarce, and hired help incompetent. When he was six and ill with pneu-

The home of Edgar Lee Masters, a leader of the literary revolt against the village, at the corner of Eighth and Jackson streets, Petersburg, Illinois.

monia he was left alone all one evening, and an uncle found him choking with croup. The family moved from one rented house to another until Masters's grandfather, Davis Masters, known locally as Squire Masters, bought them a small house on Braham Hill. Today the house stands at Eighth and Jackson streets, three blocks west of its original site. In his autobiography Masters wrote, "Altogether I was not happy in this house that Grandfather gave us, though we lived here in plenty. From the farm Grandfather sent us loads of potatoes and turnips, of apples, of fuel wood, of everything."

As often as he could, young Masters broke away for visits to his grandfather's farm, located some five miles north of town near a bend in the Sangamon River. Everywhere on the farm, in the barn with the cows and horses, in the workshop, in the smokehouse, and most of all in the kitchen, where his grandfather and the hired man swapped stories while his grandmother cooked abundant meals, Masters felt a security and delight that he very seldom experienced in his own home. Transcendence and harmony—feeling tones that are conspicuously absent in his descriptions of life in the Braham Hill house—infuse his voice as he speaks of his pioneer grandparents. His grandmother, Lucinda Masters, was the "Lucinda Matlock" of *Spoon River Anthology,* the woman who farmed the prairie and raised twelve children, "shouting to the wooded hills, singing to the green valleys." The exuberant spirit of her life is captured in his verse:

> What is this I hear of sorrow and weariness,
> Anger, discontent and drooping hopes?
> Degenerate sons and daughters,
> Life is too strong for you—
> It takes life to love Life.

When Masters was eleven his family traveled across the Spoon River bottoms, a region of mud flats and cottonwood jungles that he described as "one of the most forbidding pieces of country that I know anything about," to settle in Lewistown, Illinois, the county seat of Fulton County. During his adolescence Masters continued to visit his grandparents on their farm, and he worked there every summer from the time he was fourteen until he was twenty. After attending Knox College for a year and reading law with his father in Lewistown, he left for Chicago, where he became a successful lawyer, practicing for a time in the same firm as Clarence Darrow. Along with Vachel Lindsay and Carl Sandburg, he became one of the leaders of the poetic renaissance spearheaded by *Poetry* magazine.

The Masters home in Petersburg, though not abundantly furnished today, contains souvenirs of many phases of Edgar Lee Masters's life. A cherry desk on which he did a good deal of writing while he was living at the Chelsea Hotel in New York sits in the front room. The room that is believed to have been the parlor during his family's occupancy is furnished with several pieces from his grandparents' home, including a highboy in which Squire Masters used to keep one of his grandchildren's favorite treats, peach leather. There is a marble-top table from the Masters house in Lewistown, a house that still survives with major alterations. There is a clock, originally the property of Masters's great-grandfather, which Masters kept in his Chicago home.

Off the front room, to the right of the front door, is a museum room that holds a desk from the office where Masters's father worked in partnership with Herndon. In the same room are photographs of people from Petersburg and Lewistown who were prototypes of characters in *Spoon River Anthology*. There is, for instance, a picture of Hannah Armstrong, the woman who went to Washington to see Lincoln in person and ask him to discharge one of her sons from the Union army after the other one had been killed. In his New Salem days Lincoln had boarded at her house, and wrestled with her husband, brawny Jack Armstrong. Hannah Armstrong was a friend of Masters's grandmother.

Some of the people portrayed in *Spoon River Anthology* are buried in the Oak Hill Cemetery in Lewistown, some in the Oakland Cemetery in Petersburg. The grave of Ann Rutledge, with the epitaph written by Masters for the *Spoon River Anthology* engraved on the stone, is a dramatic reminder that the first realistic study of village life in our literature came from a region already deeply imbued with a mythology. The fact that the mythology centered around Lincoln is of course important; Masters, like Sandburg and Lindsay, was interested in Lincoln all his life. But what is most important is simply that there was a local mythology that gave even ordinary gossip and reminiscence on the Sangamon an almost epic quality, and that it habituated one young listener to the way of seeing that is art.

25 🏠

Ellen Glasgow in Richmond

Ellen Glasgow in the 1920s: for the South, no more moonlight and magnolias. From *The Woman Within* by Ellen Glasgow, copyright 1954, by Harcourt Brace Jovanovich. Reproduced by permission of the publishers.

"If I were to walk out into the country and pick a scene for a book," Ellen Glasgow once wrote, "it would remain as flat and lifeless as cardboard; but the places I loved or hated between the ages of three and thirteen compose an inexhaustible landscape of memory." She was born in 1873 in Richmond, Virginia, where her father, a descendant of Scotch-Irish settlers in western Virginia and a stern Calvinist, was manager of the Tredegar Iron Works. Her mother was a gently bred Tidewater lady who drew enough strength from the pieties of her day to raise ten children amid the anxieties and deprivations of the Civil War and the Reconstruction.

Ellen, the eighth child, was frail and often sick. But she spent happy days with her mammy, exploring the mellow streets lined with tulip and magnolia trees, going to market, and playing on Church Hill. Besides their house at 101 Cary Street, where Ellen was born—a house that still stands, but with its facade altered beyond recognition—the Glasgows also owned a farm, which Ellen loved passionately. There she tended the verbena and heliotrope in her own little garden, or roamed with her pointer puppy over acres of scrub pine and broom sedge, the rampant shrub from which Virginia fields had to be perpetually reclaimed.

As Ellen neared her teens, the long-delayed reactions to years of hard work and stress closed in on her mother, whose life became a series of nervous collapses, each one depressing to the household and terrifying to Ellen. She developed what Ellen called "a horror" of the farm, and so it was sold. Ellen's father insisted that her pointer must also be given up. For years she had nightmares involving the dog and the mistreatment she feared he would suffer apart from her; this led to a lifelong obsession about the welfare of animals.

Meanwhile the family had moved to an imposing Greek revival house of gray stucco on the corner of Main and Foushee streets. Years later Ellen wrote in her memoir, *The Woman Within,*

> This is the square gray house where I have lived for the rest of my life, and where I have written all my books, with the exception of *Life and Gabriella.* The many tragedies of my life, and a fair measure at least of the happiness, have come to me in this house. The fibers of my personality are interwoven, I feel, with some indestructible element of the place; and this element is superior to time and chance, as well as to the material substance of brick and mortar.

The memory of loss was what Ellen brought to the house at 1 West Main, and more such memories were accumulated there as time went on. Her mother died when she was twenty. By the time she was forty-

This spacious Greek Revival town house at 1 West Main in Richmond was Ellen Glasgow's home from 1887 until her death in 1945.

three she had seen her father, her brother Frank, and Cary, the sister with whom she was closest, carried out of it to their graves. But in that house she had the happiness of entertaining cherished friends, among them Alfred Harcourt, Irita Van Doren, for over thirty years literary editor of the *New York Herald Tribune,* James Branch Cabell, and Marjorie Kinnan Rawlings. There she became intimate with Henry W. Anderson, the "Harold S." of her memoir, who was her fiancé for a short time and her friend for some twenty years. There, too, she turned herself into a literary artist, working in her spacious study on the second floor, with its English wallpaper depicting Mediterranean houses with red tile roofs, and its crowded bookshelves. She was so fond of the wallpaper that she stipulated in her will that it should be preserved, and this proviso was observed by the Association for the Preservation of Virginia Antiquities, which purchased the house two years after she died in 1945. The house now serves as humanities center for the Richmond public school system, to which it is leased by the APVA.

Even as Ellen Glasgow's early life had to be fought for against recurring illnesses, and her enjoyment of social contacts had to be maintained in the face of the deafness that threatened it from middle life on, so her literary career was begun against resistance. Visiting New York at twenty-two, she lunched with an editor from Macmillan who told her, with the kindest intentions, that she should stop writing and have babies, that the greatest woman was the one who had the finest babies. She was unimpressed.

> That might be true. I did not stop to dispute it. However, it was true also that I wanted to write books, and not ever had I felt the faintest wish to have babies. Other women might have all they wanted, and I shouldn't object. But I was not made that way, and I did not see why I should pretend to be what I wasn't, or to feel what I couldn't.

Having decided to become a writer, she had to buck the appetite of the public, including the Southern public, for sentimental literature, and particularly for romantic or cause-serving stories about the South. An elderly townswoman once came to 1 West Main to plead, "If only I had your gifts, I should devote them to proving to the world that the Confederacy was right." But while Ellen loved the "imperishable charm" of the South, she "revolted from its stranglehold on the intellect."

She decided that what Southern literature needed was "blood and irony," and she set out to be, and became, the first major Southern realist. In what is probably her most important novel, *Barren Ground,* she was by conscious intention not only a realist but a feminist. As she wrote in *A Certain Measure,* she saw in *Barren Ground* "a complete reversal of a classic situation. For once, in Southern fiction, the betrayed woman would become the victor instead of the victim." The setting of the novel was the rural Virginia that she knew from her childhood days on the farm, with the sullen broom sedge as a symbol of the waste and inertia that has to be fought continually by those who would live well. Her heroine, Dorinda Oakley, survives a tragic love affair to turn two starving plantations into thriving farms. In tribute to Dorinda her creator said, "She exists wherever a human being has learned to live without joy, wherever the spirit of fortitude has triumphed over the sense of futility."

26

F. Scott Fitzgerald in St. Paul: On the Threshold of the Jazz Age

Summit Terrace, 599 Summit Avenue, St. Paul, where F. Scott Fitzgerald wrote This Side of Paradise.

F. Scott Fitzgerald, chronicler of the life of the "beautiful and damned" in New York and on the Riviera, was born in 1896 in an apartment house in St. Paul, Minnesota. Now a condominium, the three-story brick building with white woodwork trimming its balconies still stands at 481 Laurel Avenue, not far from Summit Terrace, where Fitzgerald's parents moved later and stayed for the rest of their lives.

Fitzgerald's mother's people were Irish, "potato-famine Irish," as he put it, but more prosperous by his time than the genteel Marylanders of his father's family, who were distant relatives of Francis Scott Key. In 1933 Fitzgerald wrote to John O'Hara, *"The black Irish half of the family had the money and looked down upon the Maryland side of the family who had, and really had, that certain series of reticences and obligations that go under the poor old shattered word 'breeding' (modern form 'inhibitions'). So being born in that atmosphere of crack, wisecrack and countercrack I developed a two-cylinder inferiority complex . . . I spent my youth in alternately crawling in front of kitchen maids and insulting the great."* From 1898 to 1908 the Fitzgeralds lived in Buffalo and Syracuse, where young Scott's father, Edward Fitzgerald, was sent by his employer, Procter and Gamble. Afterward they moved back to St. Paul and lived at several addresses on Laurel, Holly, and Summit avenues, settling finally at 599 Summit, in the row of turreted brownstones that is Summit Terrace. During this time Scott attended St. Paul Academy, Newman School in Lakewood, New Jersey, and Princeton.

In 1919 Fitzgerald, recently discharged from the army, was in a black depression because his job as an ad copywriter in New York wasn't bringing in enough money to convince his fiancée, Zelda Sayre, that the two of them had a future together. Seventeen years later he recalled,

> I retired, not on my profits, but on my liabilities, which included debts, despair, and a broken engagement and crept home to St. Paul to "finish a novel."
> That novel, begun in a training camp late in the war, was my ace in the hole. I had put it aside when I got a job in New York, but I was as constantly aware of it as of the shoe with cardboard in the sole, during all one desolate spring. It was like the fox and goose and the bag of beans. If I stopped working to finish the novel, I lost the girl.

Working in his third-floor front bedroom at 599 Summit Avenue, Fitzgerald completed *This Side of Paradise*. After the story had been mailed away to prospective publishers, he took a job repairing the roofs of railroad cars at the Northern Pacific shops in St. Paul. Then

Scribner's accepted the book. Fitzgerald remembered, ". . . that day I quit work and ran along the streets, stopping automobiles to tell friends and acquaintances about it. . . ."

This Side of Paradise is the story of the coming of age of a young man in the period immediately following the war. In his searchings, his ways of dealing with love, religion, aesthetics, money, its hero closely resembles Fitzgerald. Later known as "the Bible of Flaming Youth," *This Side of Paradise* reached the market in 1920, along with another novel that commented on the flamboyance of the postwar years—in this case indirectly, by contrast with an older period that its author, Edith Wharton, called *The Age of Innocence*. Within a couple of years Fitzgerald and Mrs. Wharton were correspondents; she sent him one of the most illuminating critical appreciations of *The Great Gatsby* that he ever received. The year 1920 saw the publication of yet a third major

Scott, Zelda, and Scottie Fitzgerald in Paris, 1925. National Archives

American novel with an overtone of social history, Sinclair Lewis's *Main Street*. Fitzgerald wrote Lewis an enthusiastic letter, congratulating him *"as a writer and a Minnesotan."*

A month after *This Side of Paradise* came out, Fitzgerald and Zelda were married. Following a short, hectic life in New York, they spent a year, from the fall of 1921 to the fall of 1922, in St. Paul. Their daughter Scottie was born there while Fitzgerald was putting the finishing touches on *The Beautiful and Damned*. After that novel was published early in 1922, he worked on *Tales of the Jazz Age,* which was published just before he and Zelda moved back to New York again.

St. Paul figures as a setting in Fitzgerald's work, though unobtrusively. The city "beyond Chicago," one of the two twin cities near bluffs over the Mississippi, which is the home of Basil Duke Lee in most of the "Basil and Josephine" stories, is clearly St. Paul. In *The Great Gatsby* the Midwestern background of the characters, particularly of Nick Carraway, is played off against the affluent Long Island setting where the story unfolds. The Midwest represents "the fundamental human decencies," the straight grain of experience, as opposed to the "distorted quality" of life in the East. In the end Carraway, who is partially identifiable with Fitzgerald, reminisces:

> One of my most vivid memories is of coming back West from prep school and later from college at Christmas time. Those who went farther than Chicago would gather in the old dim Union Station at six o'clock of a December evening, with a few Chicago friends, already caught up into their own holiday gayeties, to bid them goodbye. I remember the fur coats of the girls returning from Miss This-or-That's and the chatter of frozen breath . . . and the long green tickets clasped tight in our gloved hands. And last the murky yellow cars of the Chicago, Milwaukee and St. Paul railroad looking cheerful as Christmas itself on the tracks beside the gate.
>
> When we pulled out into the winter night and the real snow, our snow, began to stretch out beside us and twinkle against the windows, and the dim lights of small Wisconsin stations moved by, a sharp wild brace came suddenly into the air. . . .
>
> That's my Middle West—not the wheat or the prairies or the lost Swede towns, but the thrilling returning trains of my youth, and the street lamps and sleigh bells in the frosty dark, and the shadows of holly wreaths thrown by lighted windows on the snow. I am part of that, a little solemn with the feel of those long winters, a little complacent from growing up in the Carraway house in a city where dwellings are still called through decades by a family's name.

27 🏠

Jack London and Wolf House

The ruins of Wolf House. Arson was suspected, but never proved.

In 1876, when Jack London was born there, San Francisco still had the rawness of a frontier settlement compounded by the roughness of a port city. London's early status in that boisterous town of hard fists and soft money was so low, he said later, that he had no "outlook," only an "uplook." He was the illegitimate son of Flora Wellman, a young woman from a wealthy Ohio family who made her living in San Francisco as a piano teacher, and an erratic traveling astrologer. He got his name from John London, a somewhat inept and unlucky but decent man who married his mother a few years later.

At fourteen London escaped from a confining job in a cannery where he was working for ten cents an hour by borrowing money from a woman who had wet-nursed him as a baby, buying a boat, and poaching oysters from private beds in the estuary at Oakland. At fifteen he was known locally as the "Prince of the Oyster Pirates." As the title suggested, he showed more than enough talent at his profession to keep the soup bubbling at home and have money left over to drink at Heinold's First and Last Chance Saloon. He wrote later, "I was a capitalist. I owned a boat and a complete oyster-pirating outfit. I had begun to exploit my fellow-creatures. I had a crew of one man. As captain and owner I took two-thirds of the spoils, and gave the crew one-third, though the crew worked just as hard as I did and risked just as much his life and liberty." Evidently there was no love lost between London and most of his acquaintances of this period; he was under no illusions about the kind of comradeship that generally exists among men who

Heinold's First and Last Chance Saloon, Oakland, Jack London's hangout in his oyster pirate days.

Reassembled in the House of Happy Walls, Jack London's writing desk (left), business desk, and mementos of his days as Alaskan prospector and captain of the Snark.

run in packs for survival. But Johnny Heinold was a friend, and even more important than his occasional loans to London was the fact that his generosity seems to have kept alive a spark of faith in human nature for London in his salad days. Heinold's First and Last Chance, its floor tilted by the earthquake of '06, still stands in Jack London Square near the bay in Oakland.

In 1897 London went to Alaska. He found no gold but survived a winter trip through the Chilkat Pass. Before that he had been unable to get a start in writing, but his Klondike stories were an immediate hit. He scored a lasting success in 1903 with *The Call of the Wild,* which was not only an extremely popular adventure story but a classic of naturalism, showing as it does how a domesticated dog reverts to primitive patterns in order to survive in the Alaskan wilderness.

A veteran of economic struggles since his childhood, Jack London had become an active socialist by the time he was twenty. But a stubborn strain of individualism in his philosophy gave rise to an inconsistency in his practice that loomed larger as he became successful and, consequently, wealthy, with a full sense of his rights to the money that he had, as he saw it, earned. Unlike the common instance of the young leftist rebel who becomes a conservative when he gets a little property, London's case in the end was tragic. His socialism was hardly more than an intellectualization superimposed on deeper feelings that alternated between grandiosity and anger. His early struggles had been too hard—not for his phenomenal energy and adaptiveness, but for his self-image and his trust of any environment except one controlled entirely by himself. Meanwhile his life of action continued. He built an oceangoing boat, the *Snark,* and from 1907 to 1909 sailed the Pacific with his second wife, Charmian Kittredge.

In 1905 London had taken the first step toward creating a private Utopia by purchasing 129 acres in the Valley of the Moon, near Glen Ellen, California. "Beauty Ranch" eventually expanded to 1,500 acres, and by 1910 London and his wife had designed the house of their dreams. On a crest of Sonoma Mountain, with a staggering view of the surrounding ranges slashed by deep gorges, they began the construction of a massive house with walls of volcanic rock and gigantic redwood logs for timbers. Over three years London poured some $70,000 into the house, sometimes forcing himself to write in order to meet his expenses.

By late summer, 1913, "Wolf House" was well on the way to completion. But on the night of August 22 the Londons, sleeping in a cottage on the ranch, were awakened by voices. Smoke and flames could be seen coming from the direction of Wolf House. They drove the half mile to the site—slowly, for London said, "What's the use of hurry? If that is the Big House burning, no one can stop it now." It was the truth. The red tile roof had already collapsed, and the first home not rented or makeshift that Jack London would have had was in ruins.

London was never the same man after this loss; his health declined and he died just three years later, at the age of forty, of an overdose of drugs. Beauty Ranch is now Jack London State Park. Charmian remained on the ranch after her husband died, and built a large house of native stone on another beautiful crest a little less than a mile away from Wolf House. In this building, "The House of Happy Walls," are gathered objects the Londons collected on their voyage to the islands of the Pacific, the bell, chronometer, and barometer from the *Snark,* London's brass bed, his Oregon myrtle business desk, his dictaphone, and other small souvenirs of his work and travels. A winding trail leads from the House of Happy Walls to Wolf House, with its fractured pillars of purplish stone rising from among redwood and live oak trees. London is buried just a few yards off the trail between the two houses. His grave is marked by a boulder that was too large to be set into the walls of Wolf House.

28

O. Henry in Austin:
Cops, Robbers, and the
Rolling Stone

The O. Henry Museum at 409 East Fifth Street, Austin, the setting for the brief happy home life of the Porters.

"Fiction is tame as compared with the romance of my own life," said O. Henry, just before he died at the age of forty-seven. Certainly the life of William Sydney Porter had all the earmarks of an O. Henry story: the real and specious climaxes, the hoaxes, the twists, the ironies. In 1896, for instance, we see Porter on a banana boat bound for Honduras, fleeing charges of embezzling from the First National Bank of Austin, Texas. Back home in Austin his wife Athol cares for their small daughter and battles the fevers of tuberculosis. Like Della in "The Gift of the Magi," Athol struggles against a temperature pushing 105 to knit a point lace handkerchief, which she sells for twenty dollars to be able to send her husband a package during his first Christmas away from home. Soon her mother writes Porter that Athol is dying. Will he leave his Central American retreat and risk conviction by coming home?

"Always do the right thing," said Mark Twain. "This will gratify some people and astonish the rest." Porter went back to Austin to be with Athol and their child, and was apprehended. In 1897 Athol died. The next year Porter was tried for embezzlement and sentenced to five years in the Ohio State Penitentiary, which at that time took small consignments of federal prisoners. He actually served only three years of his sentence, and was spared the worst of prison life by being given a

William Sydney Porter "behind bars" in a teller's cage at First National Bank, Austin. Austin-Travis County Collection, Austin Public Library

Ohio State Penitentiary, where Porter was jailed for embezzling from the First National Bank of Austin. Ohio Historical Society

job as a prison pharmacist. In the penitentiary he began to write and publish short stories under the name O. Henry. The *nom de plume* is thought to have come from a ballad, "Root, Hog, or Die," which he knew from his days as a ranch hand in Texas:

> Along came my true lover about twelve o'clock,
> Saying, Henry, O, Henry, what sentence have you got?

From 1893 to 1895 Porter, Athol, and their daughter Margaret had lived in a frame cottage at 308 East Fourth Street in Austin, now moved to 409 East Fifth Street. Porter was then working as a teller at the First National Bank. By 1894 he was publishing a tabloid newspaper, the *Rolling Stone,* in Austin and later in San Antonio as well. It contained short stories and cartoons by Porter, local news items, and fillers that were humorous after the fashion of newspaper humor in those days. If his career hadn't been forcibly diverted by the embezzlement charge, he might have spent years writing such tidbits as

> Lives of great men all remind us
>   We can try our hand at rhyme,
> But we carry off behind us
>   Footprints of an editor's No.11 shoe
> Nearly every time.

The *Rolling Stone* attracted attention in Texas, and even drew encouragement from the famous humorist Bill Nye, but it never became a paying concern. In 1895 Porter shut it down and, partly due to his experience on the *Rolling Stone,* became a columnist for the *Houston Daily Post.* As the embezzlement charges closed in on him, he continued to write, selling a story to a newspaper syndicate in New York on the eve of his trial.

Porter, under his alias, emerged from prison as a fiction writer of note and, due to his reluctance to talk about his past misfortunes, as a somewhat mysterious figure. When he was invited to go to New York as a regular contributor to *Ainslee's,* he left his daughter with Athol's mother and stepfather, Mr. and Mrs. Roach, who had stood by him during his wife's illness and his own trial. For years Margaret hardly knew her father except through letters; she led a brief, lonely life and died of tuberculosis at thirty-eight.

O. Henry is justly criticized for the repetitiveness and superficiality of much of his work, but his position in literary history is strategic. He was the first popular chronicler of a New York comprising not only the privileged "four hundred" who dominated the works of Edith Wharton and Henry James, but the city's entire, struggling "four million": the Irish, Italians, Jews; the underpaid shopgirls, the impecunious young artists of the Village, the vagrants who spent the summers on park benches and the winters in the big hotel where meals were on the house. His story, "A Retrieved Reformation," based on a character he knew in prison, was made into a Broadway show, *Alias Jimmy Valentine.* The show became the prototype of the "crook play," the ancestor of such hits as *Guys and Dolls.*

O. Henry's Austin home is of interest partly because it is often forgotten that the author of *The Four Million* and *The Voice of the City* came to New York by way of the Southwest. He was born near Greensboro, North Carolina, and is buried in Asheville, in the same cemetery as Thomas Wolfe. His Austin cottage contains mementos of the family life that ended so sadly in 1897–1898. On display in one of the bedrooms is a quaint walnut bedroom set that belonged to the Roaches, and doll furniture that Porter made for his daughter. The house contains several photos of the Porters and Roaches, and of sites well known to them but no longer extant, such as the old First National Bank. Visitors may see facsimiles of several issues of the *Rolling Stone,* originals of which are preserved at the University of Texas at Austin. Also on view at the house is a symbol of O. Henry's later success—a facsimile of the *New York World* for Sunday, December 10, 1905 (the original, too fragile to be exhibited, is preserved at the Austin Public Library). That issue of the *World,* the Christmas edition, has "The Gift of the Magi" on its colorful front cover.

29 🏠

Owen Wister and the Wild West

Owen Wister and a cavalry horse. Kraft Photo Collection

The flick of cards and chips, low, casual talk, the clinking of glasses—and at a corner table a surly cowpuncher mutters, "It's your bet, you son of a bitch." The tall, dark man across from him lays his gun on the table. The saloon goes deadly quiet. Suddenly American literature gains a new kind of folk hero as the black-haired man drawls, "When you call me that, *smile.*"

The Virginian, the first and still the best cowboy novel, was the prototype of all our Westerns—books, comics, movies, and television shows, including the long, popular series based on the novel and starring James Drury. Before the heyday of television the book was made into movies four times; a stage version ran for ten years. Published in 1902, it has all the familiar ingredients of the cowboy story, climaxed by the final High Noon-style shootout between the Virginian and his enemy Trampas (a lying polecat). But *The Virginian* is no more like an ordinary mass-market horse opera than *Tom Sawyer* is like the Katzenjammer Kids. With its rich depiction of Wyoming and the cattle industry in the 1880s, and its witty, sensitive portrayal of its hero, *The Virginian* ranks with the best of our regional literature.

The author of *The Virginian* was a Philadelphian, a Harvard graduate, and the grandson of the famous English actress, Fanny Kemble. At ten Owen Wister spoke and wrote good French; at twenty-two, on a visit to Bayreuth, he played one of his own piano compositions for Franz Liszt, who commended his talent. In 1885, when he was twenty-five, he became ill and vaguely restless. He was treated by S. Weir Mitchell, the physician whom, incidentally, Edith Wharton consulted about the nervous collapses she experienced in her thirties. Mitchell, who wisely advised Wharton to write, wisely advised Wister to seek health and wholeness in the West.

In those days many young fellows used the West as a safari ground, very much as wealthy Americans used Africa in the twentieth century. Wister planned to build himself up by riding, camping, fishing, and hunting big game—deer, elk, antelope, mountain sheep. That summer he visited a ranch owned by friends of his family near Medicine Bow, Wyoming, and discovered the wilderness of the Yellowstone, the Tetons, and the desert between Cheyenne and Rawlins. He saw antelope grazing on sagebrush flats that stretched away to indigo mountains topped with perpetual snow. No longer just a tourist, Wister knew he had found a home.

For fifteen years, from 1885 to 1900, Wister spent a part of each year—sometimes as much as six months—in the West. He had wanted to become a composer but had become a lawyer instead, and his visits west gave him breathing room after winters of stifling routine.

In 1891 he wrote to his mother, *"Nothing can make me forget the homesickness I feel for it* [Wyoming] *every day when I am in the East."*

Wister visited British Columbia, Washington, Texas, Arizona, and other parts of the West, but usually spent as much time as possible in Wyoming, camping or staying at ranches and military posts. He traveled by rail, by stage, on horseback, and on foot, and met soldiers, cowboys, Indians, prospectors. Once he stayed on a ranch owned by a man who abused his horses. On a ride with Wister one day the man flew into a rage and gouged a horse's eye out. Wister made him the prototype of the vicious Balaam in the story "Balaam and Pedro," which later became an episode in *The Virginian*. Wister traveled around Arizona and absorbed the lore of the Earp-Clanton feuds. He actually met Wyatt Earp briefly on a ranch near Fort Grant. At Yellowstone in 1893 he met Frederic Remington, whose illustrations of Wister's Western stories later became classics no less than the stories themselves.

In 1911, some ten years after he had written *The Virginian*, Wister took his wife and four of their children to see Wyoming. They stayed

The Owen Wister cabin in its original setting near Jackson Hole, Wyoming. The cabin is now at Medicine Bow. National Park Service photo

at a dude ranch near Jackson Hole, in the Snake River country north-west of Medicine Bow. They fished, explored, watched an old wrangler at the ranch do fancy roping, and rode, rode, rode. "Fording Snake River, loping through the sage brush with no trail, we went into the foothills as far as our laboring horses could climb," recalled the author's daughter, Fanny Kemble Wister. "We were not too young to be stunned with admiration by the Tetons, and we loved the acres of wild flowers growing up their slopes—the tremulous Harebell blue and frag-ile, the Indian Paintbrush bright red, and the pale, elegant Columbine."

By the next summer Wister had bought 160 acres near Jackson Hole. The family returned in joyful anticipation of building a cabin and staying on their own ranch. As Fanny Kemble Wister remembered, "We could not drive fast enough to get to it. When we came to the stone marking the boundary between Idaho and Wyoming, we yelled with joy." The family and a manservant brought from home built a two-story cabin near the dude ranch where they had stayed the year before. They moved into the dwelling before it was finished, and stayed until snow fell in October. Then, Fanny wrote, "with hideous reluc-tance, we had to start East."

They couldn't have known that it was to be their last summer on the ranch. The next year Mrs. Wister died in childbirth, and from then on her lonely husband threw himself into war work and visits to Eu-rope. The Wister cabin stood at Jackson Hole until the National Park Service at Moose, fearful that the shifting Snake River would demolish it, disassembled the cabin and gave it to the town of Medicine Bow. It now stands in Medicine Bow next to the railroad station, across High-way 30 from the historic Virginian Hotel, built in 1911 and named in honor of Wister and his book.

Among other landmarks connected with *The Virginian* was the Goose Egg Ranch House near Casper, built in 1881–1882 at the conflu-ence of the Platte River and Poison Spider Creek. In the novel that ranch house was the scene of a barbecue and dance during which the Virginian switched all the sleeping babies into the wrong clothes, so that the guests took their long journeys home only to find themselves with the wrong children. Unfortunately the famous stone house, a monument to the early days of the cattle industry in the area, was demolished in 1951.

Except for the addition of fences, cattle gaps, and paved highway, Medicine Bow and its immediate surroundings still fit the general de-scription given in the opening pages of *The Virginian*, where Wister enumerates the town's twenty-nine buildings. That part of Wyoming is still undergoing "development"—a euphemism for the removal of some of the state's resources by interests outside the state. Over half the present population of Medicine Bow live in mobile homes; many are employed by a national oil company that is mining coal and uranium in the area. The town hopes to make the Wister cabin part of a historic complex that will provide its residents with a cultural focus.

Though the Wisters spent only a short time in the cabin, its presence in Medicine Bow anchors Wister and his memory to the place where he spent the time that he valued most. Fanny Kemble Wister remarked, in the preface she wrote for her father's Western journals, "Thinking back forty years to our summers in Wyoming, I see that going West in 1885 made my father. Taking us to undomesticated Jackson Hole linked us to his youth, making us in spirit next of kin to the country of his choice."

30

Robinson Jeffers and Tor House

Tor House, home of Robinson Jeffers, above the sea at Carmel, California.

The United States might have lost a major poet if the outbreak of war in 1914 had not prevented Robinson Jeffers and the woman who had divorced her husband in order to marry him from moving to England. As it was, Robinson and Una Jeffers, both California residents before their marriage, settled in Carmel. In those days Carmel was a village with about three hundred fifty people, not yet the famous retreat for artists that it became a short time later. The uninhabited cliffs above the rocky beaches reminded Una of Dartmoor—treeless moorlands, covered in springtime with lupine and poppies, like the Salinas Valley a few miles away. Here, Jeffers wrote later, "I could see people living—amid magnificent unspoiled scenery—essentially as they did in the Idyls or the Sagas, or in Homer's Ithaca. Here was life purged of its ephemeral accretions. Men were riding after cattle, or plowing the headland, hovered by white sea-gulls, as they have done for thousands of years, and will for thousands of years to come."

Tor House, the Jefferses' family home, was built on a cliff at Mission Point in 1919. Jeffers helped as local stonemasons set granite boulders from the beach below into place for the walls. Later he himself built a garage and a tower a few yards south of the house, trundling the heavy rocks up the cliff in a wheelbarrow. The tower, begun around 1924, took several years to finish. Both Una and her husband had Yeats in mind when they built it. Jeffers wrote a friend, *"We call it the Hawk's Tower for the sake of a sparrow-hawk that used to perch daily on my scaffolding, so we have hawk gargoyles and a key-stone with a hawk carved on it."* A marble stone in the parapet is inscribed, "R.J. suis manibus me turrem falconis fecit" ("with his hands he made for me the tower of the hawk"). As time went on Jeffers added a dining room to the house, and a wall between the house and the tower. He was assisted with the later additions by his son Donnan, who eventually settled at Tor House with his wife and children.

Jeffers's California landscape gave him images: the rainwashed skies, an occasional boat in the distance, the water curling around rocks near the shore where sea lions played, the majestic revolutions of gulls and hawks, gnarled cypress trees, towering redwoods. In the Preface to his *Selected Poetry* he shared with his public the origin of "Roan Stallion," a poem that shows how human beings will murder the magnificence of nature in order to carry on degenerate relationships and pursue ends that aren't worth pursuing:

> *Roan Stallion* originated from an abandoned cabin that we discovered in a roadless hollow of the hills. When later we asked about its history no one was able to tell us anything except that the place had been abandoned ever since its owner was killed by a stallion.

. . . I was quarrying granite under the sea-cliff to build our house with, and slacking on the job sat down on a wet rock to look at the sunset and think about my next poem. The stallion and the desolate cabin came to mind; then immediately, for persons of the drama, came the Indian woman and her white husband, real persons whom I had often seen driving through our village in a ramshackle buggy. The episode of the woman swimming her horse through a storm-swollen ford at night came also; it was part of her actual history. . . . So that when I stood up and began to handle stones again, the poem had already made itself in my mind.

The elegant loneliness of Jeffers's cliffs is now almost impossible to recreate even in the imagination, crowded as that part of Carmel is today by beautiful but densely set homes. Tor House, now the property of Mr. and Mrs. Donnan Jeffers, is furnished largely as it was in the poet's later life. The house, with all its additions, is built of stones, some brought from England and Ireland, with great redwood timbers visible on the inside. The dining room, with the benches and table that Robinson and Una had made by a carpenter in Old English style, has something of the atmosphere of a miniature mead hall, or refectory. The room also houses a bronze bust of Jeffers by Jo Davidson, who created the distinguished sculpture of Gertrude Stein at the National Portrait Gallery.

Between the dining room and the living room a tiny book-lined nook serves as library; the diminutive room was the kitchen when the house was in its first phase. In the living room the rugged look of the

From the ocean side, Tor House and (right) Hawk Tower.

The dining room at Tor House. Jeffers added this and other rooms to the original structure after he built Hawk Tower.

ceiling is softened by warm tones from old Oriental rugs, a few antique furnishings rich in character, and rosy upholstery in the deep window seats. Before the large bay window stands Una's grand piano; through the window one sees a superb view of the Pacific. In another part of the room stands one of the melodeons on which Una enjoyed playing Irish folk songs. Off the living room is the bedroom that Jeffers was thinking of when he wrote,

> I chose the bed downstairs by the sea window for a good deathbed
> When we built the house. . . .

As it happened, Jeffers did die at Tor House, in his sleep, in 1962, while he was sharing his home with Donnan, his wife Lee, and their four children.

Jeffers did not ordinarily do his writing in Hawk Tower, but in the attic of Tor House. Today, however, his desk and his heavy chair, made of timbers from an old mission near Carmel, may be seen on the ground floor of the tower. Built into the walls of the tower are stones from the Great Wall of China, lava from Hawaii, and a porthole from the ship on which Napoleon escaped from Elba. The tower is a symbol of universality, perspective, and permanence, or such permanence as

the changing nature of things affords. Jeffers, who in his imagination identified the task of the stonemason with that of the poet, wrote in "To the Stone-Cutters,"

> For man will be blotted out, the blithe earth die, the brave sun
> Die blind and blacken to the heart:
> Yet stones have stood for a hundred years, and pained thoughts found
> The honey of peace in old poems.

Though such prophecies in his poetry are often read as vituperations against the human race, Jeffers was by no means eager for the final cataclysm. No one ever more thoroughly detested clutter—the clutter of clamoring egos, cheap sentiments, trashy objects. It was not misanthropy, only a desire for clean, noble silences—for contact with the natural universe of which he believed man to be a part—that led him to live in partial seclusion. He was abetted by a wife who loved the Pacific landscape, and ideas and poetry, with a passion like his own. Their mutual commitment to the way of life they built together, to their children, and to the setting of it all, was exceptional. When they had been married for twenty-five years Jeffers wrote to Una, ". . . *I should love to know you and the boys for hundreds of years to come, and the beauty of things.*"

Directory of Authors' Homes

The following is a list of the houses that are the focal points of the thirty chapters in this book. Given here are the names of the houses; their addresses; brief, general directions as to how to reach them; and the names of the organizations that administer them, except in cases where the organization and the house itself are virtually one and the same. Before going to a private home you should phone or write to arrange your visit, and it is urged that any arrangement to view private homes be made with all courtesy and discretion.

SHERWOOD ANDERSON

Private home, formerly the residence of Sherwood Anderson
129 Spring Avenue
Clyde, Ohio 43410
Clyde is about 40 miles southeast of Toledo, at the intersection of U.S. 20 and Ohio 101. From U.S. 20 take Main Street south, turn right on West Cherry, left on Spring Avenue.

GEORGE WASHINGTON CABLE

Private home, formerly a residence of George Washington Cable
1313 Eighth Street
New Orleans, Louisiana 70115
From St. Charles Avenue take Seventh Street south to Chestnut, go 1 block west to Eighth, then right one-half block.

Private home, formerly "Tarryawhile," a residence of George Washington Cable
23 Dryads Green
Northampton, Massachusetts 01060
From I-91 or U.S. 5-Massachusetts 10, take Massachusetts 9 west past Smith College, turn left on Harrison, go 1 block to Dryads Green (the house is located at the intersection).

WILLA CATHER

Willa Cather Childhood Home
Third and Cedar streets
Red Cloud, Nebraska 68970
Red Cloud is near the southern boundary of Nebraska, some 110 miles south-west of Lincoln. Begin at the Willa Cather Pioneer Memorial Museum, at the intersection of U.S. 136 and U.S. 281; contact Willa Cather Pioneer Memorial, Red Cloud, Nebraska 68970, (402)746-2653.

EMILY DICKINSON

Emily Dickinson House
Faculty residence, Amherst College
280 Main Street
Amherst, Massachusetts 01002
(413)542-2321 (Office of the Secretary, Amherst College)
Amherst is on Massachusetts 9, about 7 miles northeast of Northampton in western Massachusetts. In Amherst, take Pleasant Street to Main.

PAUL LAURENCE DUNBAR

Paul Laurence Dunbar House
219 North Summit Street
Dayton, Ohio 45417
(513)224-7061
From I-75, take U.S. 35 west, turn left at Third Street, right at Summit; contact Ohio Historical Society, Ohio Historical Center, Columbus, Ohio 43211.

RALPH WALDO EMERSON

Ralph Waldo Emerson House
28 Cambridge Turnpike
Concord, Massachusetts 01742
(617)369-2236
Concord is in the Boston area, northwest of Lexington. Take Massachusetts 2 or 2A to Concord; the house is just east of the center of town on Cambridge Turnpike. Contact Ralph Waldo Emerson Memorial Association, 28 Cambridge Turnpike, Concord, Massachusetts 01742.

WILLIAM FAULKNER

Rowan Oak
Old Taylor Road
Oxford, Mississippi 38677
(601)234-3284
Oxford is in northeastern Mississippi at the intersection of Mississippi 6 and 7.

From the State Highway 6 Bypass, take South Second Street to Old Taylor Road; contact the University of Mississippi, Oxford, Mississippi 38677,(601)232-5944.

EUGENE FIELD

Eugene Field House and Toy Museum
634 South Broadway (3 blocks south of Busch Stadium)
St. Louis, Missouri 63102
(314)421-4689
From I-40 east, take Broadway exit. From I-40 west, I-70, I-55, or I-44, take Market Street-Civic Center exit; go 2 blocks west to Broadway, turn left (south), and go 6 blocks. Contact Landmarks Association of St. Louis, Inc., 611 Olive Street, Room 2187, St. Louis, Missouri 63101.

F. SCOTT FITZGERALD

Private home, formerly the residence of F. Scott Fitzgerald
599 Summit Avenue (Summit Terrace)
St. Paul, Minnesota 55102
From I-94 take Dale Street (Route 53) south; the house is near the intersection of Dale and Summit.

ELLEN GLASGOW

Ellen Glasgow House
Humanities Center, Richmond Public School System
1 West Main (corner of Foushee and Main streets)
Richmond, Virginia 23219
(804)780-5062
From the convergence of major routes in Richmond, take Main (one-way west) or Cary (one-way east) to Foushee (6 blocks east of Belvidere); from Cary, turn left on Foushee to Main. Contact Association for the Preservation of Virginia Antiquities, 2705 Park Avenue, Richmond, Virginia 23220.

NATHANIEL HAWTHORNE

The Old Manse
Monument Street near North Bridge
Concord, Massachusetts 01742
(617)369-3909
Concord is in the Boston area, northwest of Lexington. From Massachusetts 2 or 2A follow the signs posted on the highway to Concord Center and Monument Street; contact the Trustees of Reservations, 224 Adams Street, Milton, Massachusetts 02186.

ERNEST HEMINGWAY

Ernest Hemingway Home and Museum
907 Whitehead Street
Key West, Florida 33040
Take U.S. 1 to Whitehead, turn right to the corner of Whitehead and Olivia;
contact Bernice Dickson, owner, (305)296-5811 or (305)294-1575.

O. HENRY

O. Henry Museum
409 East Fifth
Austin, Texas 78701
(512)472-1903
From I-35, take Sixth Street exit; take Sixth west 2 blocks to Neches, then
Neches south 1 block to Fifth (house is across intersection). Contact City of
Austin Parks and Recreation Department.

ROBINSON JEFFERS

Tor House
26304 Ocean View Avenue
Carmel, California 93921
Carmel is on California 1, on the Pacific coast at the southern end of Monterey
Bay. At the end of Ocean Avenue, turn left on Scenic Road, then left on Stuart
Way to Ocean View.

SINCLAIR LEWIS

Sinclair Lewis Boyhood Home
812 West Sinclair Lewis Avenue
Sauk Centre, Minnesota 56378
Sauk Centre is about 95 miles northwest of Minneapolis, just north of I-94.
From I-94, take U.S. 71 (Main Street) to Sinclair Lewis Avenue; contact Sin-
clair Lewis Foundation, Sinclair Lewis Interpretive Center, I-94 at U.S. 71,
Sauk Centre, Minnesota 56378, (612)352-6892.

JACK LONDON

Wolf House
Jack London State Park
London Ranch Road
Glen Ellen, California 95442
(707)938-5216
Glen Ellen is some 40 miles north of San Francisco, on California 12. The sign for
the turnoff to the house is on California 12, 8 miles north of Sonoma; contact Cal-
ifornia Department of Parks and Recreation, Sonoma, California 95476.

EDGAR LEE MASTERS

Edgar Lee Masters Memorial Museum
Eighth and Jackson streets
Petersburg, Illinois 62675
Petersburg is on Illinois 97, about 17 miles northwest of Springfield. From the business district, take Douglas west to Eighth, turn left to Jackson.

H. L. MENCKEN

H. L. Mencken House
Dormitory, University of Maryland
1524 Hollins Street
Baltimore, Maryland 21223
From the convergence of U.S. 1 and U.S. 40 take U.S. 1 south to Hollins Street and turn east; contact the University of Maryland School of Social Work, 525 West Redwood, Baltimore, Maryland 21201, (301)528-7794.

FLANNERY O'CONNOR

Andalusia Farm, private property, formerly the residence of Flannery O'Connor
Milledgeville, Georgia 31061
Milledgeville is about 26 miles northeast of Macon, at the intersection of U.S. 441 and Georgia 49; Andalusia Farm is 5 miles north of Milledgeville on U.S. 441.

EDGAR ALLAN POE

Edgar Allan Poe Cottage
Poe Park, Grand Concourse at Kingsbridge Road
Bronx, New York 10467
Grand Concourse is accessible from I-87, I-95 (Cross Bronx Expressway), or Bronx River Parkway. Take Grand Concourse to Kingsbridge Road at East 194th Street. Contact Bronx County Historical Society, 3266 Bainbridge Avenue, Bronx, New York 10467, (212)881-8900.

MARJORIE KINNAN RAWLINGS

Marjorie Kinnan Rawlings State Historic Site
Route 3, Box 92
Hawthorne, Florida 32640
(904)466-3672
Hawthorne is on U.S. 301, some 15 miles southeast of Gainesville. Rawlings's home is on State Road 325; contact Florida Department of Natural Resources, 202 Blount Street, Tallahassee, Florida 32304.

JAMES WHITCOMB RILEY

Riley Old Home
250 West Main Street
Greenfield, Indiana 46140
(317)462-5462
Greenfield is just east of Indianapolis on U.S. 40, which goes directly to the Riley home; contact Riley Old Home Society or City of Greenfield.

CARL SANDBURG

Carl Sandburg Birthplace
331 East Third Street
Galesburg, Illinois 61401
(309)342-2361
Galesburg is on I-74, about 38 miles northwest of Peoria. From the major approaches to Galesburg, signs will direct you. Contact Illinois State Historical Library, Old State Capitol, Springfield, Illinois 62706.

JOHN STEINBECK

The Steinbeck House
132 Central Avenue (corner of Central and Church Street)
Salinas, California 93901
Salinas is on U.S. 101, about 25 miles southeast of Santa Cruz. From U.S. 101, take North Main, right at Market, left at Church to Central; from California 68, take South Main, left at Alisal, right at Church to Central. Contact the Valley Guild, 132 Central Avenue, Salinas, California 93901, (408)424-2735.

MARK TWAIN

Mark Twain Memorial
351 Farmington Avenue
Hartford, Connecticut 06105
(203)525-9317
From I-84 take Exit 46 to Sisson Avenue, turn right on Farmington.

EDITH WHARTON

The Mount
Located on a private way off Plunkett Road
Lenox, Massachusetts 01240
Lenox is near the western boundary of Massachusetts, some 5 miles south of Pittsfield. Take U.S. 7 to the turnoff marked Center at Foxhollow; contact the Center at Foxhollow, Lenox, Massachusetts 01240, (413)637-2000.

WALT WHITMAN

Walt Whitman House
330 Mickle Street
Camden, New Jersey 08102
(609)964-5383
In Camden, take Broadway to Mickle Street, turn west (signs will direct you); contact Walt Whitman Association or New Jersey Department of Environmental Protection, Trenton, New Jersey, (609)292-2023.

LAURA INGALLS WILDER

Laura Ingalls Wilder-Rose Wilder Lane Home and Museum
Mansfield, Missouri 65704
(417)924-3626
Mansfield is on U.S. 60 about 37 miles east of Springfield; the Wilder home is 1 mile east of Mansfield on Business Route 60.

OWEN WISTER

Owen Wister Cabin
On U.S. 30-287 across from Virginian Hotel
Medicine Bow, Wyoming 82329
Medicine Bow is some 50 miles northwest of Laramie, on U.S. 30-287; contact Virginian Hotel, (307)379-2377.

THOMAS WOLFE

Thomas Wolfe Memorial
48 Spruce Street
Asheville, North Carolina 28807
(704)253-8304
Asheville is just north of I-40, about 90 miles northwest of Charlotte. Near the convergence of U.S. 70 and U.S. 25, watch for a large sign; contact North Carolina Department of Cultural Resources, 109 East Jones Street, Raleigh, North Carolina 27611.

Notes on Sources

Chapter 1. H. L. Mencken and the Hollins Street House

Page 15, lines 11–14: From H. L. Mencken, "Notes on Journalism," *Chicago Tribune,* September 19, 1926. Quoted in *Menckeniana,* a publication of the Pratt Free Library, Baltimore, Fall, 1975.

Pages 15–17: Mencken's reminiscences about his childhood are taken from H. L. Mencken, *Happy Days: 1880–1892* (New York: Alfred A. Knopf, 1940).

Page 19, lines 1–5: From H. L. Mencken, *A Little Book in C Major* (New York: John Lane, 1916). Reprinted in H. L. Mencken, *The Young Mencken: The Best of His Work,* ed. Carl Bode (New York: Dial Press, 1973).

Page 19, lines 6–7: H. L. Mencken in the *Smart Set,* December, 1919.

Page 19, lines 8–15: From "The National Letters," in H. L. Mencken, *Prejudices: Second Series* (New York: Alfred A. Knopf, 1920).

Page 19, lines 19–20: Mrs. Wharton's remark to Sara Norton is quoted in R. W. B. Lewis, *Edith Warton: A Biography* (New York: Harper and Row, 1975), p. 43.

Pages 19–22: All remaining Mencken quotations are from *The Letters of H. L. Mencken,* ed. Guy J. Forgue (New York: Alfred A. Knopf, 1961), with "A Personal Note" by Hamilton Owens. Mencken's remark about Sara's prognosis (page 9, lines 21–25) is quoted by Owens.

Chapter 2. Hawthorne and the Old Manse

Except where designated otherwise, all quotations from Hawthorne are from "The Old Manse," in *Mosses from an Old Manse,* Riverside Edition (Boston: Houghton Mifflin, 1883).

Page 24, line 41 ("No castles, no cathedrals, and no kings"): From Emerson's poem, "America, My Country."

Page 25, lines 16–17; page 28, line 37 to page 30, line 5; page 30, lines 10–11: All citations to Hawthorne's notebook are to Nathaniel Hawthorne, *The American Notebooks,* ed. Randall Stewart (New Haven: Yale University Press, 1932).

Page 27, lines 10–13; page 30, line 20 ("borrowed qualities"); page 30, lines 26–30; page 31, lines 15–22: Quoted in Julian Hawthorne, *Nathaniel Hawthorne and His Wife: A Biography* (Boston: Houghton Mifflin, 1884).

Page 27, lines 13–15; page 30, line 37, to page 31, line 5: From Rose Hawthorne Lathrop, *Memories of Hawthorne* (Boston: Houghton Mifflin, 1897).

Page 30, lines 26–30: Ralph Waldo Emerson, *The Heart of Emerson's Journals,* ed. Bliss Perry (Boston: Houghton Mifflin, 1926), p. 182 (September, 1842).

Chapter 3.   Carl Sandburg and the Railroad Town

Except for selections from Sandburg's poetry, all quotations in this chapter are from Carl Sandburg, *Always the Young Strangers* (New York: Harcourt, Brace, 1953).

Page 36, lines 28–31: "Threes," from *Smoke and Steel* (New York: Harcourt, Brace, 1920).

Page 37, lines 30–35: "Illinois Farmer," from *Cornhuskers* (New York: Henry Holt, 1918).

Page 40, lines 31–40: From "The Man in the Street is Fed" and "The People Will Live On," in *The People, Yes* (New York: Harcourt, Brace, 1936).

Chapter 4.   Emily Dickinson and the Homestead

All quotations not otherwise designated are from *The Letters of Emily Dickinson,* ed. Thomas H. Johnson (Cambridge, Massachusetts: Belknap Press of Harvard University Press, 1958).

Page 50, lines 16–19: Martha Dickinson Bianchi, *Emily Dickinson Face to Face* (Boston: Houghton Mifflin, 1932), p. 7.

Pages 50, 51: The poems are from *The Poems of Emily Dickinson,* ed. Thomas H. Johnson (Cambridge, Massachusetts: Belknap Press of Harvard University Press, 1955).

Page 52, lines 33–34 ("our friend who has just now put on Immortality"): From Clara Newman Turner, "My Personal Acquaintance with Emily Dickinson," in the Emily Dickinson Collection at the Jones Library, Amherst, and reprinted in Richard B. Sewall, *The Life of Emily Dickinson* (New York: Farrar, Straus and Giroux, 1974).

Chapter 5.   Hemingway and the Island in the Sun

Page 54, lines 38–40; page 55, lines 22–23; page 57, lines 13–21; page 58, lines 8–34; page 60, lines 1–12: In these passages I am indebted to Carlos Baker, *Ernest Hemingway: A Life Story* (New York: Scribner's, 1969).

Page 57, lines 21–27: From a letter to Ivan Kashkeen, reprinted in *Soviet Literature* 11 (1962).

Page 58, lines 32–34: Ernest Hemingway, "Who Murdered the Vets?" in *New Masses* 16 (September 17, 1935).

Page 59, lines 4–15, 21–31; page 60, lines 33–39: For details about Hemingway's fight with Wallace Stevens, his first meeting with Martha Gellhorn, and the disposal of his belongings after his departure from Key West, I am indebted to James McLendon, *Papa: Hemingway in Key West* (Miami: E. A. Seeman, 1972).

Chapter 6.   Thomas Wolfe, the Angel, and the Boardinghouse

Page 64, lines 9–10; page 67, lines 7–11; page 69, line 36, to page 70, line 2; page 70, lines 5–8; page 71, lines 12–16; page 73, lines 8–13: From Mabel Wolfe Wheaton, *Thomas Wolfe and His Family* (New York: Doubleday, 1961).

All other quotations in this chapter are from Thomas Wolfe, *Look Homeward, Angel* (New York: Scribner's, 1929).

Chapter 7.   Marjorie Kinnan Rawlings: A Newcomer at Cross Creek

Biographical information about Marjorie Kinnan Rawlings before she became established at Cross Creek, about the writing of *The Sojourner,* and about her death, is taken from Gordon Bigelow, *Frontier Eden: The Literary Career of Marjorie Kinnan Rawlings* (Gainesville: University of Florida Press, 1966).

With the exception of the brief quotations from her testimony at her libel trial (page 82, lines 27–34), which are taken from local newspapers, all other citations not attributed in the text are to Majorie Kinnan Rawlings, *Cross Creek* (New York: Scribner's, 1942).

Chapter 8.   John Steinbeck: Salinas and the Long Valley

For concrete details about Steinbeck's boyhood in Salinas, his relationship with his sister Mary, his interest in biology, and his activities with the B.A.S.S.F.E.A.J., I am indebted to Nelson Valjean, *John Steinbeck: The Errant Knight* (San Francisco: Chronicle Books, 1975). The anecdote about the falling cross is from information on file at the Steinbeck house.

Page 86, lines 29–31, 37–38; page 87, lines 29–31 ("in spite of mother and hell"); page 92, lines 29–31: From John Steinbeck, *Journal of a Novel: The East of Eden Letters* (New York: Viking Press, 1969).

Page 87, line 5 ("a passionate sewer-on of buttons"); page 87, line 35, to page 88, line 1; page 88, lines 32–33; page 92, line 34, to page 93, line 4; page 93, lines 10–11 ("no world beyond the mountains"): From John Steinbeck, *Travels With Charley* (New York: Viking Press, 1962).

Page 87: The anecdote about Olive's airplane ride is from John Steinbeck, *East of Eden* (New York: Viking Press, 1952).

Page 91, lines 11–12: In Willa Cather, *My Ántonia* (Boston: Houghton Mifflin, 1918).

Pages 91–92: Quotations in the account of Steinbeck's investigations of the migrant camps are from John Steinbeck, *Steinbeck: A Life in Letters,* ed. Elaine Steinbeck and Robert Wallsten (New York: Viking Press, 1975).

Chapter 9.   Willa Cather, The Prairie, and Red Cloud

For all concrete information about Willa Cather's childhood in Webster County, her relationships with the Miners, Anna Pavelka, Lyra Garber, Professor Schindelmeisser, and other local people who figured in her novels, and her dealings with Hollywood, I am indebted to Mildred R. Bennett, *The World of Willa Cather* (Lincoln: University of Nebraska Press, 1961).

Page 95, lines 29–36: From Willa Cather, *O Pioneers!* (Boston: Houghton Mifflin, 1913).

Page 95, line 38, to page 96, line 5; page 104, lines 11–16: From Willa Cather, *My Ántonia* (Boston: Houghton Mifflin, 1918).

Page 96, lines 25–26 ("were kind neighbors"): From Willa Cather, "Nebraska: The End of the First Cycle," *Nation* 117 (September 5, 1923).

Page 98, line 41, to page 99, line 3: Willa Cather, in an interview with Eleanor Hinman in the *Lincoln* (Nebraska) *Sunday Star,* November 6, 1921.

Page 100, lines 16–20: Willa Cather, in an interview with Flora Merrill in the *New York World,* April 19, 1925.

Page 103, line 16, to page 104, line 3: Willa Cather, in an interview published in the *Omaha Bee,* October 29, 1921. Reprinted courtesy of the *Omaha World-Herald.*

Page 104, lines 26–30: From H. L. Mencken, "The Novel," in *Prejudices: Third Series* (New York: Alfred A. Knopf, 1922).

Chapter 10. Mark Twain: A Connecticut Yankee at Home

Page 106: Quotations from Mark Twain's letters to the *Alta California* are reproduced from photostat copies in Volume II of *Mark Twain Memorabilia* (Willard S. Morse Collection) in the archives of the Connecticut State Library, Hartford.

Page 109, lines 6–8: This quotation, my information about Mark Twain's finances, and the pointers for those about to enter Heaven (page 114) are from Albert Bigelow Paine, *Mark Twain: A Biography* (New York: Harper and Brothers, 1912).

Page 109, line 9, to page 110, line 6: From Mary Lawton, *A Lifetime with Mark Twain: The Memories of Katy Leary, for thirty years his Faithful and Devoted Servant* (New York: Harcourt, Brace, 1925).

Page 110, lines 15–17: From William Dean Howells, *My Mark Twain* (New York: Harper and Brothers, 1910).

Page 110, lines 31–39; page 114, lines 6–17: From *The Autobiography of Mark Twain,* ed. Charles Neider (New York: Harper and Brothers, 1959).

Page 111, lines 17–21: From *Mark Twain's Letters,* ed. Albert Bigelow Paine (New York: Harper and Brothers, 1917), Vol. I, p. 220.

Page 112, lines 22–26: Both quotations are from Mark Twain, *Following the Equator* (1901).

Page 113, lines 40–41 ("I am notorious, but you are great"): From Clara Clemens Gabrilowitsch, *My Father Mark Twain* (New York: Harper and Brothers, 1931).

Pages 114–115: For information about the restoration of the Mark Twain home, see Wilson Faude, "Mark Twain's Connecticut Home," *Historic Preservation* 26 (April-June, 1974).

Chapter 11. Emerson in Concord

Biographical information is taken from Edward Waldo Emerson, *Emerson in Concord: A Memoir* (Boston: Houghton Mifflin, 1889), and information on file at the Emerson House.

Citations to Emerson's journals are to *The Heart of Emerson's Journals,* ed. Bliss Perry (Boston: Houghton Mifflin, 1926). References to essays by Emerson are to "The American Scholar," "Self-Reliance," and "Fate." Thoreau's remark, quoted in the first paragraph, is from his "Civil Disobedience."

Page 118, lines 25–26 ("my boy is gone"): From a letter written by Emerson January 28, 1842, now the property of the Ralph Waldo Emerson Memorial Association, Concord.

Page 121, lines 4–5: From James Russell Lowell, "Emerson the Lecturer," first published in the *Atlantic Monthly* in 1861.

Page 122, lines 18–19: From *The Correspondence of Thomas Carlyle and Ralph Waldo Emerson,* ed. Charles Eliot Norton (Boston: Houghton Mifflin, 1883), Vol. II, pp. 236–237.

Chapter 12.   Edgar Allan Poe: Empty Shrines on the Eastern Seaboard

My chief source of biographical information, including Mrs. Gove's descriptions of the Fordham cottage and the last stages of Virginia's illness, is Arthur Hobson Quinn, *Edgar Allan Poe: A Critical Biography* (New York: D. Appleton, 1941). For information about the Gimbel collection in Philadelphia and about the remaining mementos of Poe's early life I am indebted to the Philadelphia Free Library and the Poe Museum, Richmond. Citations to Poe's letters are to *The Letters of Edgar Allan Poe,* ed. John Ward Ostrom (Cambridge, Massachusetts: Harvard University Press, 1948). The remarks by Whitman are from Horace Traubel, *With Walt Whitman in Camden, March 28–July 14, 1888* (New York: Mitchell Kennerley, 1915).

Chapter 13.   Edith Wharton "At Home": The Mount in Lenox, Massachusetts

Page 134, lines 18–19: From Percy Lubbock, *Portrait of Edith Wharton* (New York: D. Appleton-Century, 1947), p. 25. All other quotations are from Edith Wharton, *A Backward Glance* (New York: Scribner's, 1934).

Chapter 14.   William Faulkner and Rowan Oak

Page 140, lines 1–12: Biographical sketch submitted by Faulkner to *Forum Magazine* early in 1930. This, and all quotations from Faulkner's letters, are from *Selected Letters of William Faulkner,* ed. Joseph Blotner (New York: Random House, 1977). For all biographical information I am indebted to Joseph Blotner, *Faulkner: A Biography* (New York: Random House, 1974), supplemented by information from Professor James Webb of the University of Mississippi.

Chapter 15.   Sinclair Lewis: No Castles on Main Street

Page 146, lines 7–14; page 146, line 32, to page 147, line 2; page 147, lines 5–13; page 148, line 8, to page 149, line 16: For information adapted in these passages I am indebted to Mark Schorer, *Sinclair Lewis: An American Life* (New York: McGraw Hill, 1961).

Page 146, line 18 ("more than was the village custom"): From Sinclair Lewis, "Breaking into Print," *Colophon* 2 (Winter, 1937). Reprinted in Sinclair Lewis, *The Man From Main Street: Selected Essays and Other Writings, 1904–1950,* ed. Harry E. Maule and Melville H. Cane (New York: Random House, 1953).

Page 147, lines 2–4: Quoted in Dorothy Thompson, "The Boy and Man from Sauk Centre, *Atlantic* 206 (November, 1960).

Page 147, lines 15–43: From Sinclair Lewis, "Harry, the Demon Reporter," in "I'm an Old Newspaperman Myself," *Cosmopolitan,* April and May, 1947. Reprinted in *The Man From Main Street.*

Page 149, lines 10–13: From Sinclair Lewis, Introduction to *Main Street,* Limited Editions Club (1937). Reprinted in *The Man From Main Street.*

Page 151, lines 18–21: Quoted in Charles Breasted, "The 'Sauk-centricities' of Sinclair Lewis," *Saturday Review* 36 (August 14, 1954).

Chapter 16. Laura Ingalls Wilder: The House at the End of the Road

Page 153, lines 13–17: The fact that the Garland and Ingalls families both lived in Burr Oak is pointed out by Donald Zochert in *Laura: The Life of Laura Ingalls Wilder* (Chicago: Henry Regnery, 1976).

Information about the Wilders' journey from De Smet to Missouri, with Laura's comments, is taken from *On the Way Home* (New York: Harper and Row, 1962), a transcription of the diary Laura kept on the trip, with an introduction by her daughter, Rose Wilder Lane.

Chapter 17. Walt Whitman and the Mickle Street House

Page 161, lines 21–39: Walt Whitman, "Autiobiographia: Some Personal and Old Age Jottings," in Edmund Clarence Stedman, *Selections from Whitman: Poetry and Prose,* ed. Arthur Stedman (Philadelphia: David McKay, 1892).

Page 163, lines 6–9: The visitor was Colonel James M. Scovel, quoted in William Sloane Kennedy, *Reminiscences of Walt Whitman* (London: Alexander Gardner, 1896), p. 12.

Page 163, line 37, to page 164, line 2: From Horace Traubel, *With Walt Whitman in Camden, March 28–July 14, 1888* (New York: Mitchell Kennerley, 1915).

Page 164, lines 14–16: From *The Letters of Carl Sandburg,* ed. Herbert Mitgang (New York: Harcourt, Brace, and World, 1968).

Chapter 18. Sherwood Anderson's Vanishing Winesburg

In addition to the sources listed below, I am indebted to the Clyde Public Library and to Mr. Thaddeus Hurd, son of Sherwood Anderson's boyhood friend Herman Hurd, for biographical information.

Page 166, lines 9–14; page 167, lines 3–4 ("as a bird flies out of a bush"): From Sherwood Anderson, *A Story-Teller's Story,* ed. Ray Lewis White (Cleveland: Case Western Reserve, 1969).

Page 166, lines 17–23: From Sherwood Anderson, *Tar: A Midwestern Childhood,* ed. Ray Lewis White (Cleveland: Case Western Reserve, 1969).

Page 166, lines 28–29: From *Letters of Sherwood Anderson,* ed. Howard Mumford Jones and Walter Rideout (Boston: Little Brown, 1953).

Page 167, line 23, to page 168, line 15: From *Sherwood Anderson's Memoirs* (New York: Harcourt, Brace, 1942).

Page 170, lines 23–24: From John Steinbeck, *Journal of a Novel: The East of Eden Letters* (New York: Viking Press, 1969).

Chapter 19.   Flannery O'Connor: Redemption in Slash Pine Country

For biographical information I am indebted to Robert Stuart Fitzgerald's Introduction to Flannery O'Connor, *Everything That Rises Must Converge* (New York: Farrar, Straus and Giroux, 1965), and to Louise Hardeman Abbot, "Remembering Flannery O'Connor," *Southern Literary Journal* 2 (Spring, 1970).

Page 175, lines 31–37; page 176, lines 38–39: From "On Her Own Work," in Flannery O'Connor, *Mystery and Manners,* ed. Sally and Robert Fitzgerald (New York: Farrar, Straus and Giroux, 1969).

Page 176, line 8 ("An idiom characterizes a society"): From Flannery O'Connor, "The Regional Writer," in *Mystery and Manners.*

Chapter 20.   Paul Laurence Dunbar: A Singer in Dayton

Page 179, lines 10–13: Matthews's description of Dunbar, first printed as a letter to the *Indianapolis Journal,* is reprinted in the General Introduction to *The Paul Laurence Dunbar Reader,* ed. Jay Martin and Gossie H. Hudson (New York: Dodd, Mead, 1975).

Page 180, lines 6–11: From Paul Laurence Dunbar, "Is Higher Education for the Negro Hopeless?", *Philadelphia Times,* June 10, 1900. Reprinted in *The Paul Laurence Dunbar Reader.*

Chapter 21.   The Riley Old Home, Greenfield, Indiana

For biographical information on Riley, and for information about the contents of the Riley Old Home, I am indebted to the Riley Old Home Society.

Chapter 22.   Eugene Field House, St. Louis

Biographical information is taken from Slason Thompson, *Eugene Field: A Study in Heredity and Contradictions* (New York: Scribner's, 1901).

Chapter 23.   George Washington Cable in New Orleans and Northampton

Biographical information is taken from Lucy Leffingwell Cable Bikle, *George W. Cable: His Life and Letters* (New York: Scribner's, 1928).

Page 192, lines 16–19: From *The Mark Twain-Howells Letters,* ed. Henry Nash Smith and William M. Gibson (Cambridge, Massachusetts: Belknap Press of Harvard University Press, 1960), p. 419.

Page 192, lines 20–30: From George W. Cable, "New Orleans," *St. Nicholas,* December, 1893. Quoted in Bikle.

Chapter 24.   Edgar Lee Masters and the Spoon River Country

Page 196, lines 9–10: From Edgar Lee Masters, *The Sangamon* (New York: Farrar and Rinehart, 1942), p. 73.

Except for the lines from "Lucinda Matlock" in *Spoon River Anthology,* all other citations in this chapter are to Edgar Lee Masters, *Across Spoon River: An Autobiography* (New York: Farrar, Straus and Giroux, 1969).

Chapter 25.   Ellen Glasgow in Richmond

Page 200, lines 1–4; page 202, lines 12–14; page 202, lines 29–31: From Ellen Glasgow, *A Certain Measure: An Interpretation of Prose Fiction* (New York: Harcourt, Brace, 1943).

Page 202, lines 4–8: From Ellen Glasgow, *The Woman Within* (New York: Harcourt, Brace, 1954).

Chapter 26.   F. Scott Fitzgerald in St. Paul: On the Threshold of the Jazz Age

Page 204, lines 10–17: From *The Letters of F. Scott Fitzgerald,* ed. Andrew Turnbull (New York: Scribner's, 1963).

Page 204, line 25, to page 205, line 3: From F. Scott Fitzgerald, "Early Success," in *The Crack-up,"* ed. Edmund Wilson (New York: New Directions, 1945).

Page 206, lines 21–41: From F. Scott Fitzgerald, *The Great Gatsby* (New York: Scribner's, 1925).

Chapter 27.   Jack London and Wolf House

Page 208, lines 17–22: From Jack London, *What Life Means to Me,* in *Cosmopolitan,* March, 1906.

Page 210, lines 24–25: Quoted in Charmian London, *The Book of Jack London* (New York: Century, 1921).

Chapter 28.   O. Henry in Austin: Cops, Robbers, and the *Rolling Stone*

Most of the biographical information in this chapter was supplied by the O. Henry Home and Museum. The bit of light verse on page 213, lines 16–20, is from a facsimile of the *Rolling Stone,* January 26, 1895, supplied by the museum.

Chapter 29.   Owen Wister and the Wild West

All citations in this chapter are to *Owen Wister Out West: His Journals and Letters,* ed. Fanny Kemble Wister (Chicago: University of Chicago Press, 1958).

Chapter 30.   Robinson Jeffers and Tor House

Page 221, lines 10–15; page 223, lines 8–9; page 224, lines 4–7: From *The Selected Poetry of Robinson Jeffers* (New York: Random House, 1937). The description of the headlands around Carmel is from the Preface.

Page 221, lines 22–25; page 224, lines 18–20: From *The Selected Letters of Robinson Jeffers, 1897–1962,* ed. Ann N. Ridgeway (Baltimore: Johns Hopkins Press, 1968).